BLACK TROOPS

WHITE COMMANDERS

AND FREEDMEN

DURING THE

CIVIL WAR

Howard C. Westwood

With a Foreword by
JOHN Y. SIMON

Carbondale
and
Edwardsville

SOUTHERN ILLINOIS UNIVERSITY PRESS

Library of Congress Cataloging-in-Publication Data
Westwood, Howard C., 1909–
    Black troops, white commanders, and freedmen
during the Civil War / Howard C. Westwood : with a
foreword by John Y. Simon.
        p.   cm.
    Includes bibliographical references and index.
    1. United States—History—Civil War, 1861–
1865—Participation, Afro-American. 2. United
States—History—Civil War, 1861–1865—Afro-
Americans. 3. Afro-Americans—History—To
1863. I. Title.
E540.N3W47   1992
973.7′415—dc20   91-577
    ISBN 0-8093-1751-6   CIP

The paper used in this publication meets the minimum re-
quirements of American National Standard for Information
Sciences–Permanence of Paper for Printed Library Materi-
als, ANSI Z239.48-1984. ⊚

Contents

Foreword

"**I** HAVE no purpose, directly or indirectly, to interfere with the institution of slavery in the States where it exists," said President Abraham Lincoln in his first inaugural address. "I have no lawful right to do so, and I have no inclination to do so." Yet war came, with all its unanticipated consequences. Two years later, Lincoln wrote to Andrew Johnson, then military governor of Tennessee, about the "great *available* and yet *unavailed* of, force for restoring the Union. The bare sight of fifty thousand armed, and drilled black soldiers on the banks of the Mississippi, would end the rebellion at once." Lincoln believed that persuading a prominent Democrat and slaveholder like Johnson to recruit would increase the political and psychological effect of such an army, but Johnson did not even reply. Revolutions beget counterrevolutionaries.

Howard C. Westwood's interest in various aspects of military emancipation led to the series of essays collected in this book, probing significant and dramatic episodes of the Civil War. Arming blacks carried political and social implications extending beyond wartime service. This major and irreversible consequence of the conflict forced commanders in the field as well as legislators and administrators in Washington to reappraise traditional thought and practice. Some rode, others resisted, the revolutionary tide. Consequently, on the battle lines as well as at Washington, inconsistency pervaded the treatment of black soldiers.

Initial hesitation and ambiguity in federal policy toward black participation in the war led David Hunter and Benjamin F. Butler to preempt Washington officials. Acutely sensitive to the separation of civil and military functions, Ulysses S. Grant followed Lincoln's policy with a model mixture of restraint in murky areas, vigor where clarity existed. William T. Sherman characteristically followed an idiosyncratic course.

Before the Civil War, professional officers constituted a highly conservative segment of American society; war forced upon some an unprecedented revolutionary role.

Caught amid governmental inconsistencies and military anomalies, blacks themselves participated in reformulating positions in wartime and staking claims that they might press afterward. Whether or not to accept inequity in pay raised powerful issues of black identity, since discrimination in pay foreshadowed discrimination in citizenship. Appointing white officers for black troops, which softened initial white objections to black enlistment, became standard. Under this practice, however, black noncommissioned officers like Sgt. William Walker, Third South Carolina Colored Infantry, assumed leadership disproportionate to rank.

Black soldiers reversed potential manpower resources of the Confederacy and furnished approximately 10 percent of the army that won the war. The changing status of blacks led to wrenching problems for Confederate captors of black troops, illustrated in the case of prisoners in South Carolina, and to legal consequences of emancipation that ensnared the Reverend Fountain Brown in Arkansas. The tumultuous innovation of black military service in the Civil War represents an ideal opportunity to assess both the reactions of white political leaders and officers to social revolution and also the response of blacks so suddenly freed and armed. Westwood's essays assembled in this book, which pursue vital historical issues in scholarly depth, reflect a personal interest kindled many years ago.

Born less than forty-five years after the Civil War ended, Westwood retains memories of the half dozen veterans who lived in his boyhood hometown, Tecumseh, Nebraska, who so proudly led Memorial Day and Fourth of July parades. During visits to his grandparents in Troy, Missouri, he met a black veteran whose cabin wall displayed an enormous battle painting. Westwood attended Swarthmore College, then Columbia Law School, where he was selected by United States Supreme Court Justice Harlan F. Stone as his clerk for the 1933–34 term. Almost inevitably this prestigious post led to an offer from a major Washington law firm, Covington & Burling, with the invitation extended by Dean Acheson. Westwood's association with the firm continues to the present, and he has written as well as lived its history.

Within two years, the young lawyer took on a major assignment for the Air Transport Association, representing all scheduled airlines, which no longer received government subsidies, had limited safety regulations, and were threatened by antitrust prosecution if they attempted to avoid wasteful competition. In response, Westwood helped to put together and to steer through Congress legislation enacted as the Civil Aeronautics Act of 1938, which gave him a leading role in airline law for years afterward, interrupted only by his enlistment as a private in the Marines during World War II. Service as a drill instructor at Parris Island left lasting echoes in his style and language.

Westwood returned to the law, assumed a major part in the steel seizure case of 1952, and won a four-year battle to extradite former president Pérez Jiménez to Venezuela. At the same time, he took an increasing interest in legal aid in Washington and in the National Legal Aid and Defender Association, which led to his crucial role in the passage of the act creating the National Legal Services Corporation. Indignation about racial segregation, reinforced by impressions gained as a volunteer instructor at Howard University Law School, led him to fight for integration of the Bar Association of the District of Columbia, his own law firm, and at least one prestigious social club.

For recreation, Westwood had often read about the Civil War and in 1955 joined the Civil War Round Table of the District of Columbia, where eventually he delivered a paper annually. In 1974 he reached the conventional retirement age of sixty-five, decided that his most rewarding years in law lay behind, and began to pursue his Civil War interests in greater depth and with publishable results. A passion for accuracy of detail led him to dogged pursuit of original documents in the National Archives too often neglected by other scholars and to the creation of the important articles collected in this book. These articles, which deepen an understanding of the significance of blacks in the Civil War, also serve to introduce their indomitable author.

John Y. Simon

Acknowledgments

THE AUTHOR is most indebted and deeply grateful to Dr. Elaine Everly and to Mr. Michael Musick of the National Archives for their generous and most perceptive guidance to his research in the preparation of the articles that make up the chapters in this book. He is thankful, too, to the late Dr. Sara Jackson, then of the National Historical Publications and Records Commission, for her thoughtful encouragement of his efforts. He is grateful also to others, too numerous to list, for their great help in research on many particular points. And he is most appreciative to the several journals in which the articles originally appeared for their permission to reprint them.

1

Lincoln's Position
on Black Enlistments

WHAT part was played by Abraham Lincoln in making soldiers of black men?

There always had been blacks in the United States Navy. But the army long had been pure white, and so it was at the Civil War's beginning, not because Congress had required it but because the Executive had chosen to keep it so. Yet by the war's end a substantial share of the army had become black. A review of President Lincoln's role in that change reveals the difficulty in making for the blacks a new place in our society.

In 1860 the total black population in the free states was only about two hundred thousand, somewhat less even than the free blacks in the slave states. Thus the free states' potential for black soldiers was not enough to warrant raising a troublesome issue. But in the slave states there were some four million slaves. The able-bodied men among such a number were a potential significant indeed, were they to be available.

The question of the army's resorting to the black potential was delicate. There was strong antiblack prejudice among most people in the free states, and in the loyal slave states the idea of arming the black man was anathema. Among many there was fear that any such arming might lead, somehow, to savage slave uprisings with massacre of defenseless white civilians. The war was almost half over before the government began serious steps to make the black a soldier. Even then it was well over another year before he was clearly on the way to becoming a soldier full-scale.

The war was not far along when the president focused on a question

Originally published in *Lincoln Herald* 86, no. 2 (Summer 1984):101–12. Reprinted by permission of *Lincoln Herald*.

of arming blacks. One of the first problems studied by Union planners was how to effect the proclaimed blockade of the Confederacy. To do so it was essential that blockaders have bases along the South Atlantic coast. In the course of the summer of 1861 organization of a navy-army expedition to establish such bases had begun. As planned, there was no provision to do more than seize a couple of good anchorages and protecting perimeters. So there would no be great land force in the expedition; it would be less than fifteen thousand.[1]

Yet, once established, to maintain the position securely and efficiently for extensive naval activity further manpower could be used to aid in fortifying, constructing facilities, and operating. It would be in an area of dense slavery, and it was assumed that blacks would be found to work with the troops. Accordingly instructions for the army commander, as drafted in the War Department, provided in sweeping terms for making use of slaves found available. In October the draft was submitted to the president. Carefully he inserted a phrase excluding from any such use "a general arming" of the blacks.[2]

With that limitation what became the Port Royal, South Carolina, expedition of November 1861 was carried out. And the army commander, Brig. Gen. Thomas W. Sherman, observed the limitation faithfully. Although scant resistance by the Confederates and precipitate flight by white residents from a large section of the coast between Charleston and Savannah handed to the Union much more than the intended perimeter, with consequent demands on Sherman quite beyond what had been anticipated, Sherman avoided not only a "general arming" but any arming at all of the many thousands of slaves coming under his dominion.[3]

Even as General Sherman was establishing the position in South Carolina, the president took another action, before the year's end, of more general import than the instruction to Sherman. The secretary of war, Simon Cameron, submitted a draft of his annual report that included a passage asserting that "it is the right, and may become the duty of the Government to arm and equip" slaves, "and employ their services against the rebels, under proper military regulation, discipline, and command." The president deleted that passage. But Cameron already had made his draft available to the press. So, as 1861 ended, the president's refusal to recognize even "the right" to arm slaves became widely known.[4]

In the meantime, voices in the North favoring slave emancipation as a war aim, though a small minority, had been growing increasingly strident and often included in their advocacy taking blacks into the army. Yet even in the first weeks of 1862 any possible gain from arming blacks remained of little practical moment. There had not been severe drains on white manpower, nor had Union forces much penetrated the great black regions of the states in rebellion. The Union held only fringes of Virginia, the Port Royal coastal area, and bits elsewhere, with invasion of Tennessee but beginning. At that time, moreover, the general public in the North probably thought the rebellion soon would collapse without occasion for extensive conquest.

Between that time and late July 1862 the war changed. The Union mounted a large offensive in Virginia, but met with most disillusioning repulse. A navy-army expedition up the Mississippi from its mouth succeeded in an army's occupation of the New Orleans area, but efforts onward failed. In South Carolina, where Maj. Gen. David Hunter had superseded General Sherman at the end of March, a move toward Charleston was frustrated. In Tennessee, though there had been Union success that even had reached into Mississippi, a seeming impasse was in effect. That there would be a short war was proved an illusion, and many thousands more men were demanded for the Union's armies.

Furthermore, notably in Tennessee and Louisiana, the Union forces found themselves, almost suddenly, with crowds of footloose blacks on their hands. While, in South Carolina, such a problem had appeared the previous November, it had been limited and stable; but out west it was growing. With realization that the war would go on and on, what to do about the black man loomed as a critical issue. No longer, in the North, was emancipation sentiment confined to a few radicals. And with increasing masses of black men available the question of how best to use those men in the armed services so as to ease demands on white manpower was becoming very immediate in many a Northern household and factory, whatever concern it might evoke in the loyal slave states.

As a result Congress enacted two important statutes on July 17 at the very end of its session. One, the Second Confiscation Act, provided for emancipation of slaves of masters who persisted in rebellion, and in very general terms authorized the president to employ blacks in the war effort and "organize and use them in such manner as he may judge best."[5] The other, the Militia Act—an inappropriate title, for it was a set of miscellaneous military provisions—included an authorization to the president to receive blacks "into the service of the United States" for labor or "any military or naval service," with emancipation of any slaves so employed, and their families, were their masters rebels.[6] But, as we have noted, the president already had full power to make use of blacks, and the military services had been doing so all along as laborers for both the army and the navy and as regular crew members for the navy. On a critical view, it might have been wondered what, apart from the emancipation provisions, the legislation accomplished.

Nonetheless the actions of Congress did seem to signal mounting favor for some sort of arming of blacks. Within a few days the president's response to that signal was called for. The issue was posed by General Hunter from down in South Carolina.

When Hunter had taken over from Sherman he had a dream of conquest going far beyond the capacity of the white army available to him. While somewhat reinforced since its landing, that army never exceeded about eighteen thousand.[7] To make reality of Hunter's dream he would have to make soldiers of slaves. In May 1862 he set about doing so, with a decree of emancipation of slaves in his military department and with black enlistment.[8] He sought no approval from Washington; he did not even bother to report either action to the high command. But the president, on hearing of the emancipation decree, promptly announced that, if it had been made, it was void.[9] As to enlisting black soldiers, however, the President took no action. Word of it of course seeped northward. One can only guess, but it may be that the president figured that Hunter's black enlistment soon would end because, without approval from Washington, he would be unable to pay the men.

Moreover it already had been decided, in late April, to take a special step for governing affairs in South Carolina. General Sherman's quartermaster, Capt. Rufus Saxton, had returned to Washington with Sherman and in reporting on the blacks around Port Royal had made a good impression with his perception of their needs and abilities. So Saxton was promoted to brigadier general and ordered back to South Carolina as military governor, though in general subject to the army commander. His arrival in Port Royal did not occur until late June because the president and secretary of war—by then Edwin Stanton— had diverted him to defend Harpers Ferry from Stonewall Jackson. His successful performance there added to the esteem he had won.[10] While Kentucky congressmen were outraged at Hunter's black enlistment,[11] the president may have felt that he need not react immediately because, in due time, he would get from Saxton sensible guidance on black affairs in South Carolina.

But before Saxton could get oriented in his new job, the question of arming South Carolina blacks came to the president in circumstances demanding his answer. As June ended and July began, the Seven Days Battles created a crisis leading to a hurried call on Hunter for reinforcements for the Union's Virginia forces. With his army being depleted, Hunter finally sent an urgent request to Washington that he be permitted to enlist blacks.[12] Hunter's request was received at about the time the July 17 statutes were adopted, so, with them fresh on the books, the secretary of war on July 21 presented the request at a cabinet meeting. Cabinet members favored approval, but the president "expressed himself as averse to arming negroes" and the question was postponed until the next day's cabinet meeting. On the next day "the question of arming slaves was . . . brought up. . . . The President was unwilling to adopt this measure. . . ." But he did announce his intention to issue an emancipation proclamation to cover all slaves in areas still in rebellion on the next January first. In the discussion the president gave the impression that, while arming blacks "like other soldiers" would be undesirable, "he was not unwilling that Commanders should, at their discretion, arm, for purely defensive purposes, slaves coming within their lines."[13]

Since Hunter wanted to arm blacks "like other soldiers," his request would not be granted. In any case he was making the question academic for, before the end of July, he sent off an applicaton for leave that, in due course, would be granted.[14] Further, without awaiting response to his plea to arm blacks, he disbanded the unit that he had "enlisted." Indeed, unpaid, many, if not most, of the men already had deserted.[15] Seemingly the question of black enlistment in South Carolina had been disappearing even as the president was facing up to it.

But in late August a related question was presented by the highly regarded General Saxton, in a letter to the secretary of war brought by Rev. Mansfield French. French was a leader in a project to build a self-supporting black civilian community in the Port Royal area, sponsored by the Treasury Department. He was accompanied by Robert Smalls, a black man who, in May, had become a national hero. As head of a Confederate slave crew, he had abducted the dispatch boat of the Charleston commander when the crew's white officers were ashore for a night, and delivered her to Union blockaders. So heroic was the feat that Congress, before May ended, had enacted a special statute providing a "prize" award to Smalls and his fellow slaves. Thus French gained stature by having Smalls with him; he was received by the secretaries of war, navy, and treasury. Indeed Smalls held the secretary of the treasury's interest for "nearly an hour with his story."

Saxton's letter asked that he be allowed to arm black laborers in the civilian community to protect it from Confederate raids. Doubtless very deliberately, he did not refer to them as proposed "soldiers." Thus he did not sound like the aggressive Hunter. His restraint worked. On August 25, 1862, the day Saxton's letter was delivered, the secretary of war replied, in a letter taken back by French and Smalls, authorizing Saxton to enlist in the military service, under white officers, up to five thousand blacks, as well as to organize black laborers. Thus, for the first time during the war, Union black soldiers were approved.[16]

While there is no direct evidence that the president knew of his secretary of war's action, it was consistent with the president's views expressed at the July cabinet meeting, for the secretary's letter said that the black soldiery was authorized "in order to guard the plantations and settlements . . . and protect the inhabitants thereof. . . ." In any case, in view of the attention given French and Smalls by official Washington, the president must have known what was going on; and surely it is most unlikely that, so soon after the president's refusal of General Hunter's aspiration, the action on Saxton's request would have been taken without the president's knowledge.

So it was that in the fall—Saxton took a trip north during September—the organizing of the black First South Carolina Volunteers began.[17] By that time the president had issued the Preliminary Emancipation Proclamation. In it was not a word about a black soldiery, so the bar against black soldiers continued.[18] But the South Carolina situation, as put by General Saxton, fitted the breach in that bar that the president had suggested at the July cabinet meeting: a local commander's discretion to arm slaves "for purely defensive purposes." That the breach was no wider is indicated by the war department's refusal, in August and September, to approve Sen. James Lane's recruiting of any but white soldiers in Kansas.[19] Indeed, in early August, when a delegation had come to the president with a proposal to recruit blacks in Indiana, he had declined, lest, he said, it would mean loss for the Union of a far greater number of white manned bayonets from the loyal border slave states, and in late September he refused a black regiment offered by the governor of Rhode Island.[20]

While these questions were being dealt with in Washington, a variant was arising in Louisiana. The Union army commander there, Maj. Gen. Benjamin F. Butler, had had his hands full ever since his occupation of New Orleans on May 1, 1862. His army was only about the size of the one General Sherman had landed at Port Royal. Though at Port Royal there had been some reinforcement, for Butler not a man more would be sent, and by late July he feared, with apparent reason, a determined effort by the Confederates to put an end to his conquest.[21] One of his principal subordinates, Brig. Gen. John W. Phelps, was an ardent abolitionist and wanted to organize black soldiers, including slaves—indeed had begun doing so. Butler refused approval, insisting that only the president could authorize the arming of blacks. In protest, Phelps submitted his resignation. Butler forwarded the whole matter to Washington where Phelps' resignation was promptly accepted.[22] But even as that was happening Butler had begun appraising a free black resource in Louisiana: free blacks who had been taken into the militia by the Confederate state government soon after the war began. On Butler's coming, though the other Confederate forces had fled the New Orleans area, the black militiamen had stayed and now proved quite willing to enlist in Butler's army. So, just after mid-August, Butler began such enlistment, subject to the approval of the president, and on August 27 wrote Washington of his action, requesting approval. He pointed out that there could be no objection even by the Confederates since he was but following Confederate footsteps.[23]

It is not known exactly when Butler's request reached Washington—it had to be ocean borne—or what notice it had on receipt. But, without hearing from Washington, Butler proceeded with enlistment of two black regiments and, by November, was starting on a third.[24] At that time he wrote Washington again, saying that absent contrary word he had assumed approval of his action but would prefer explicit approval. To that he did receive a response. It reached him but a short time before he was relieved of his Louisiana command by Maj. Gen. Nathaniel P. Banks in mid-December. The response informed Butler that the secretary of war had stated that the matter was left to the discretion of the local commander.[25]

Butler's recruiting had gone beyond the free blacks who had been eligible for the Confederate militia. He had regarded as free, and so proper for his enlistment, slaves of masters claiming British or French citizenship; such slaves were free, Butler reasoned, because British and French law prohibited slavery. And, in time, he treated as free the slaves of masters who had refused loyalty to the Union; they were free, he insisted, by virtue of the Second Confiscation Act, and so he could enlist them.[26]

There was nothing secret about Butler's action from August on. It is inconceivable that it was not known by the president, though it may be that some of the subtleties of Butler's reasoning as to who was "free," and so subject to his enlistment, may not have been fully understood. It may be also that Butler's August 27 request for approval did not receive much attention; it reached Washington after the shock of Second Manassas and on the eve of Antietam, when the secretary of war and the president were preoccupied. But even if that request suffered bureaucratic burial, there was no overlooking of Butler's course in the news reaching Washington in following weeks from the press and otherwise.

When Butler began his black enlistment it might well have been regarded as designed merely for "defense," for, unquestionably, at the time, he thought a Confederate offensive against him was brewing. In that sense, then, his action might have been deemed, in Washington, as not unlike General Saxton's provision for "defense" of his Port Royal community. But threat of attack on Butler soon faded, and in a very short time he was organizing his own aggressive move into the plantation area west of New Orleans that began in late October, and his blacks played a part in that move.[27]

Nor, indeed, was General Saxton limiting his blacks strictly to "defense." As part of their training during the fall he had some units raiding Confederate territory and proudly reported to the secretary of war a good performance.[28]

In short, during the fall of 1862, neither in Louisiana nor in South Carolina were the newly armed blacks being confined to a purely defensive role, such as the president, at the July cabinet meeting, had suggested he was willing to tolerate. Again, while there is no direct evidence of the president's knowledge of what was happening in those areas, it is hard to believe that he was uninformed. And on January 1, 1863, he took action that went well beyond his July suggestion.

That action was a provision in the Final Emancipation Proclamation that had not been included in the preliminary proclamation. After defining areas that the president regarded as still in rebellion, and decreeing freedom for all slaves in those areas, even though owned by loyal masters, he provided that those freedmen "will be received into the armed services of the United States to garrison forts, positions, stations, and other places and to man vessels of all sorts in said service."[29] This was very different from the president's July suggestion. "Vessels of all sorts" included river and ocean vessels much used in attack. Garrisoning various places could include garrisoning incident to offensives. And whereas the July suggestion contemplated no more than giving a local commander discretion in the indicated use of fugitive slaves coming to him, the president now was prescribing an affirmative program to take the freed slaves into the armed services, to be implemented by all the army and navy.

However, the proclamation said nothing of blacks, North or South, who previously had been free men. And what of slaves in the Confederate areas that the proclamation defined as not still in rebellion: parts of Union-occupied Virginia, the New Orleans area, and all of Tennessee? Moreover, what of the blacks in the loyal slave states? Suffice it to say that the president and his government were very soon accepting black men into the armed services regardless of their status or home territory. The president himself took a significant step within a few days after the proclamation; on his initiative a Union officer was authorized to go to Louisiana to organize a brigade of blacks whether found within or beyond the New Orleans area.[30] From then on black recruiting was authorized quite beyond the emancipated slaves, and in the course of the spring the war department itself embarked on a nationwide black recruiting program (restrained only in the loyal slave states) conducted in the Mississippi Valley by the adjutant general and elsewhere by a new bureau, the Bureau of Colored Troops.[31]

It is notable that, at the time the adjutant general was about to go to the valley to begin his work, the president wrote Andrew Johnson, military governor of Tennessee, strongly approving what he had heard was Johnson's thought of raising a black military force, though Tennessee had been excluded from the proclamation. The president waxed enthusiastic, saying, "The bare sight of 50,000 armed and drilled black soldiers upon the banks of the Mississippi would end the rebellion at once."[32] Though he never announced it formally, on New Year's Day 1863 the president had dissolved all of the bar against black soldiers.

There remained, however, the question whether the black soldier would be confined to garrison duty as stated in the proclamation. The president's specifying that duty for the emancipated slave seems to have been very deliberate. On Christmas Eve the Confederate president had issued a proclamation, doubtless prompted by the Union's black enlistment in South Carolina and Louisiana, ordering that captured armed slaves and their officers should be turned over to state authorities "to be dealt with according to the laws of said states."[33] That meant that such captives could be treated as engaged in, or aiding, slave insurrection, a capital crime in every such state. On January 10 the president sent for his secretaries of war and navy to consult on "the employment of the contrabands, and as the Rebels threatened to kill all caught with arms in their hands, to employ them where they would not be liable to be captured. On the ships he thought they were well cared for, and suggested to [the secretary of war] that they could perform garrison duty at Memphis, Columbus, and other places and let the soldiers go on more active service."[34]

Four days later the president wrote the general commanding at Fort Monroe and Yorktown, Virginia, asking whether it would not be feasible for him to garrison with black troops, thereby releasing whites for duty elsewhere.[35]

Nonetheless it became evident very soon that confinement of blacks to garrison duty was never required and never seriously intended by the president himself. Even South Carolina black soldiers, in March 1863, were sent off in the front line of an attack that captured Jacksonville, Florida; and the president wrote General Hunter—who had been returned to the command of that area—that he was "glad to see the accounts," with no intimation that there was a violation of any required confinement to garrisoning.[36] During that year there were other notable instances where local commanders had black units engaged in the firing line of an attack.[37] But that was by no means so of all commanders. As late as May 1864, in the first stage of the great Union offensive in Virginia, Lt. Gen. Ulysses S. Grant had blacks in the Army of the Potomac assigned to duty in the rear, especially guarding the trains.[38] Not until the siege of Petersburg began were black soldiers in Virginia on front-line duty to a significant extent.[39] And in the Mississippi Valley even in mid-June 1864 black troops were so disproportionately employed in "labor and fatigue duties" at forts and posts that the adjutant general found it necessary to issue an order that there be required of them only "their fair share of the fatigue duty with the white troops."[40] While the president continued to be involved personally in black recruitment, notably in working around difficult recruiting problems in the border slave states,[41] he left it to the military command, from the beginning, to determine how to use the blacks, at most making an occasional suggestion.

Yet the president's concern about Confederate treatment of captive blacks proved warranted. The Confederate Congress in May 1863 superseded the presidential proclamation with a provision that all captured black soldiers, slave or free, would be turned over to state authorities. Though it was not provided that captured officers of black units would be turned over to the states, they were made subject to prosecution before military courts, with a possible death penalty.[42] Moreover, to an extent still uncertain, there were times when some captives from black units were summarily murdered. Generally, however, the Confederate treatment fell short of executions, "legal" or otherwise. In the main that treatment became a withholding of the captives from prisoner exchange, at least in the case of the enlisted men, with instances of enslaving the blacks or putting them at labor not permissible for regular prisoners.[43]

Nonetheless the president did not revive his thought of confining the army's black units to garrison duty. His reaction, on July 30, 1863, was an order for retaliation by the Union for Confederate treatment of captives that violated the rules of war.[44] But that order proved to be little more than a threat; the president shrank from the danger that retaliation would lead to retaliation. The Union authorities, however, did make the Confederate treatment of black captives a principal cause for suspending the prisoner exchange cartel, a problem that persisted without solution to the war's end.

Even as the Confederates were discriminating against black Union soldiers, the Union's own Executive was doing so too, albeit in a different way. That was in the black soldier's pay.

The secretary of war's August 25, 1862, authorization to General Saxton to enlist black soldiers provided that they were to be paid the same as whites. For a private that was, per month, $13 plus clothing or a $3.50 clothing allowance, with more for higher ranks. Black soldiers in South Carolina were paid at those rates until the following summer. But in June 1863 the secretary of war announced that the War Department solicitor had determined that black soldiers, whatever their rank, could be paid only $10 a month, of which $3 could be in clothing, so blacks would be paid only at that rate.[45] The Militia Act of July 17, 1862, to which we have referred, prescribed that rate of pay for blacks employed under that statute.

The only pertinent ruling of the War Department's solicitor thus far found said no more than that blacks employed pursuant to the Militia Act were to be paid at that rate; it did not say what the secretary of war attributed to the solicitor—that all black soldiers were necessarily in the service pursuant to that statute.[46] As we have seen, there was abundant other authority for enlisting blacks.[47] Moreover, when the Militia Act was being considered in the senate (there was no significant debate in the House), a Senator questioned its need since under preexisting law there was nothing to prevent the president from enlisting black soldiers, and a leading proponent replied that the measure did not deal with proposed black soldiers but was meant only for taking blacks "in a special mode . . . to do the labor of our Army."[48] Indeed, although the Militia Act by its express terms applied to the navy quite as fully as to the army, the navy continued to pay its black crewmen at the regular rates, never treating that act as a limitation.[49] And the reasoning of opinions rendered by the attorney general later, in 1864, is flatly inconsistent with the view that the executive's power to take blacks into the armed services derived only (if at all) from the 1862 Militia Act.[50]

It is scarcely credible, then, that the secretary of war, an eminent lawyer, believed that black soldiers could be enlisted only under that Militia Act, subject to its pay discrimination, and that his equal pay directive to General Saxton in August 1862 had been illegal. Rather it is all but certain that when it was decided to begin full black soldier recruitment nationwide, with anti-black prejudice still extensive though declining, it was decided also that the touchy issue of black equality should be ducked by the Executive and shifted to Congress. We may be sure that in determining a question so political the president himself was involved.

That that is what happened is strongly hinted in what the president said to the eminent black leader, Frederick Douglass, on August 10, 1863. Douglass had been engaged in black recruitment, and on that day met with the president for the first time. A principal purpose was to protest the newly adopted pay discrimination. The president replied "that the wisdom of making colored men soldiers was still doubted; that their enlistment was a serious offense to popular prejudice; . . .

that the fact that they were not to receive the same pay as white soldiers, seemed a necessary concession to smooth the way to their employment at all as soldiers; but that ultimately they would receive the same."[51] On that day Douglass also met with the secretary of war for the same purpose. On the pay discrimination issue the secretary "went into an interesting history of the whole subject of the employment of colored troops, briefly mentioning some of the difficulties and prejudices to be surmounted, gave a history of the bill drawn up by himself giving equal pay . . . to colored troops as to whites and spoke with much apparent regret that his bill thou' passed in the house had been defeated in the senate on what he considered quite an insufficient reason alleging that the President already possessed necessary powers to employ colored troops. . . . [He] was in favor of giving the same pay to black as to white soldiers."[52]

What had happened in Congress earlier in 1863 is significant and is rather different from the secretary's "history" imparted to Douglass. Early in the short session of the 37th Congress the House Military Affairs Committee had the black troop issue before it, but by late January had taken no action. On January 12 Thaddeus Stevens, chairman of the House Ways and Means Committee, had introduced a bill dealing with the issue. Then on January 27, he submitted a substitute. It was generally understood that the substitute was drafted by the secretary of war. It authorized the president to enroll volunteering blacks, slave or free, in the "land and naval service" at pay "not to exceed that of other volunteers." On the next day, January 28, a motion to refer the bill to the Military Affairs Committee was overwhelmingly defeated. Then, after stalling tactics by opponents of the measure that prolonged the session until 5:35 in the morning of the next day, it was understood that the bill would be taken up on reconvening later that day with no committee reference.[53] Debate raged each day through Saturday, January 31, and on the following Monday, February 2, after still more debate, the bill was adopted by vote of 83 to 54.[54]

Stevens told the House that the War Department desired the legislation because of fear that the 1862 Militia Act did not put the black "upon the same footing" as the white soldier, making it doubtful that, if such a black were captured by the enemy, the department could maintain that he was entitled to treatment as a regular prisoner of war.[55] But to marshal support Stevens repeatedly amended his measure in significant respects, including, on the pay issue, provision that black "privates or laborers . . . in the military or naval service" could be paid no more "than ten dollars per month, with the usual allowance of clothing and rations." For blacks of other ranks the bill's provision that pay was "not to exceed that of other volunteers" was retained.[56]

In the Senate the House measure went to the Committee on Military Affairs and Militia, chaired by Henry Wilson of Massachusetts. On February 13 the committee reported it, recommending that "it ought not to pass." On the floor Wilson explained that "the authority intended to be given by it is sufficiently granted" by the 1862 Militia Act.[57] On February 26 Wilson introduced a proposed amendment to the House measure to substitute a provision that men "received into the service" under the 1862 Militia Act "shall be mustered in, organized, armed, and equipped as other troops . . . and governed by the rules and Articles of War, and by such other rules and regulations . . . as may be prescribed."[58] But Congress' short session ended on March 3 with no further action.

The Executive's decision to go to Congress on the issue of black equality, and the event, thus made it virtually impossible, politically, to escape the $10 less $3 mandate of the 1862 Militia Act. The navy went on ignoring it, but the navy's public impact was limited and there was nothing new about its black element. But the army, suddenly to be thrown open to scores of thousands just emerging from the narrow confines of field-hand slavery, was a very different case. Even Congressman Stevens, the Executive's agent in the House, had had to propose for black privates a $10 pay limit. The "popular prejudice" to which the president referred in his talk with Douglass could not be ignored.

In the summer of 1863 the greatest black potential for the Union armies seemed to be in the Mississippi Valley where in July General Grant had won the river with his Vicksburg victory. On the day before his talk with Douglass the president had written Grant about that potential. Thousands of black troops, said the president, should be organized along the Mississippi, "relieving all white troops to serve elsewhere."[59] While the president did not explain his suggestion, it seems evident that he surmised that this would give the blacks a chance to prove themselves, with the impact of white troops' prejudice minimized. A white soldier, however at first he might scorn black riflemen, might be delighted to have them mastering miasmic watery lands while he and his white fellows moved on to more attractive duty.

So, with blacks given a fair opportunity to perform, the president doubtless felt confident that, as he told Douglass, the pay inequality "ultimately" would be corrected.

The president's confidence was not ill-founded. While there never was segregation to the extent the president suggested to Grant, so that black troops never had such an exclusive domain as the president seemed to propose, there were notable instances, during 1863, of blacks' involvement in battle, and they performed well. Indeed, they had done so even before the president wrote Grant. On the assembling of a new Congress in December the president was able, in his annual message, to assert, as to blacks, that "it is difficult to say they are not as good soldiers as any." And he asked congressmen's "careful attention" to the annual report of the secretary of war.[60] That report urged equal pay to the black soldier.[61] That prejudice against the black soldier had declined dramatically was well illustrated in a song at a banquet in January 1864 given by the officers of the New York Irish Brigade. The Irish had been strongly prejudiced, but eloquently the song proclaimed their readiness to have "Sambo" share "the right to be kilt," even to enjoy "the largest half" of that privilege.[62]

In early February 1864, Senator Wilson and his committee, who had put a stop to the 1863 legislative effort, proposed pay equality for the black soldier, and "ultimately," in June, just as the president had said, Congress adopted it, retroactive to January 1. (That the navy had been correct in its view all along was implicitly affirmed, for the legislation referred only to "soldiers" and the "military service.")[63]

What then was the part played by Abraham Lincoln in making soldiers of black men?[64]

He certainly was no leader in this regard at the outset. Rather, he responded to growing pressure, and cautiously. While he took a notable initiative in the Final Emancipation Proclamation, it was weeks more before it became clear not only that the bar was dissolved but that his own administration was aggressively embarked on black soldier recruitment. Even then he allowed the issue of pay equality for the soldier to be shifted to Congress. It remained for the blacks themselves to demonstrate their worth. Only then did the president step forward to urge recognition that they were "as good soldiers as any."

In the Union's black soldiery, our society took a first long step toward making blacks not only free but equal. It has taken more than a century before genuine equality finally may be realized. However hesitant

President Lincoln may have been in initiating and then pursuing that first step, it now seems in relation to our society's slow pace since to have been swift.[65]

Notes

1. Reports of the Blockade Board of July 5 and 13, 1861, U.S. War Dept., *The War of the Rebellion: A Compilation of the Official Records of the Union and Confederate Armies*, 70 vols. in 128 pts. (Washington, 1880–1901; rpt. National Historical Society, Gettysburg, 1972), ser. 1, vol. 53, pt. 2:64–73 (hereafter cited as *ORA*; all citations will be to ser. 1 unless otherwise shown); order of asst. sec. war to Gen. Thomas W. Sherman, Aug. 1, 1861, *ORA*, 6:168; testimony of Gen. Sherman about the Port Royal expedition to Joint Committee on the Conduct of the War (JCCW) Apr. 15, 1862, *Report of JCCW*, H. of Rep., 37th Cong., 3d Sess. (1863), 3:291–94 (hereafter cited as *JCCW*); Rowena Reed, *Combined Operations in the Civil War* (Annapolis, Naval Institute Press, 1978), pp. 8–10.

2. Order of acting sec. war to Gen. Sherman, Oct. 14, 1861, *ORA*, 6:176–77; A. Howard Meneely, "The War Department 1861" (Ph.D. diss., Columbia Univ., New York, 1928), pp. 341–43.

3. Capt. Rufus Saxton, Gen. Sherman's quartermaster, also testified about the Port Royal expedition to the JCCW on Apr. 15, 1862. Asked whether it would "have been safe to have trusted arms in the hands of the colored men there," he answered in the affirmative, saying that "most undoubtedly" they could be used "against the rebels," *JCCW*, 3:330.

4. Benjamin P. Thomas and Harold M. Hyman, *Stanton: The Life and Times of Lincoln's Secretary of War* (Alfred A. Knopf, New York, 1962), pp. 133–34; Erwin Stanley Bradley, *Simon Cameron, Lincoln's Secretary of War* (Univ. of Pennsylvania Press, Philadelphia, 1966), pp. 202–4.

5. 12 *U.S. Stat.* 592.

6. 12 *U.S. Stat.* 599.

7. Gen. Hunter to sec. war, Mar. 27 and Apr. 3, 1862, *ORA*, 6:254, 263–64; return for June 1862, Dept. of South, *ORA*, 14:362.

8. General order by command of Gen. Hunter, May 9, 1862, *ORA*, 14:341; Gen. Benham to Mr. de la Croix, approved by Gen. Hunter, May 7, 1862, and Gen. Hunter to Gen. Stevens, May 8, 1862, *ORA*, ser. 3, 2:29–30.

9. Proclamation of May 19, 1862, *ORA*, ser. 3, 2:42–43.

10. Sec. war to Gen. Saxton, Apr. 29, 1862, and to Gen. Hunter with enclosures, June 16, 1862, *ORA*, ser. 3, 2:27, 152–53; orders by Gen. Saxton at Harpers Ferry, May 26 to June 2, 1862, Dept. of South—Special Orders, etc., of Gen. Saxton, May 1862–Dec. 1863, RG 393, Nat. Arch.; Gen. Saxton to sec. war, June 30, 1862, reporting arrival at Port Royal on June 27, Letters Rec'd by Adj. Gen. Office, No. 1063S, RG 94, Nat. Arch., M 619, Roll 140. Saxton's testimony to the JCCW, referred to above, shows his grasp of affairs at Port Royal. Saxton received a personal letter of thanks from the secretary of war, dated June 17, 1862, for his performance at Harpers Ferry. In 1893 he was awarded the Medal of Honor for that performance. His Medal of Honor file tells of his meeting with the president

and secretary of war in May 1862 when he was hurriedly sent to deal with the Harpers Ferry emergency. The letter of thanks and the Medal of Honor file are in Saxton's personnel file, Letters Rec'd by Appointment, Commission and Personal Branch of the Adj. Gen. Office, File No. 1302, ACP 1879, RG 94, Nat. Arch.

11. Reaction among Kentuckians is illustrated by remarks on the floor of the House, *Cong. Globe*, 37th Cong., 2d Sess., pt. 4: 3121–25.

12. Gen. Hunter to sec. war, July 11 and 12, 1862, *ORA*, 14:363, 364.

13. David Donald, ed., *Inside Lincoln's Cabinet: The Civil War Diaries of Salmon P. Chase* (Longmans, Green & Co., New York, 1954), pp. 96, 99–100. In Roy P. Basler, Marion Dolores Pratt, and Lloyd A. Dunlap, eds., *Collected Works of Abraham Lincoln*, 8 vols. (Rutgers Univ. Press, New Brunswick, 1953–55), 5:338, there is an undated Lincoln memorandum indicating no objection to recruiting free negroes, slaves of disloyal owners, and, on masters' consent, slaves of loyal masters. Basler guessed that the memorandum was written on July 22, 1862, the date of the cabinet meeting. It is clear that the guess is incorrect. Doubtless it was written in connection with drafting a general order issued more than a year later in connection with recruiting blacks in the loyal slave states; the *ORA* so place it, *ORA*, ser. 3, 3:855–56, 860–61.

14. Notation of letter from Gen. Hunter to Army Hdqrs. applying for leave, July 30, 1862, Register of Letters Rec'd by Hdqrs. of the Army, no. 114, RG 108, Nat. Arch.; leave granted, Aug. 22, 1862, *ORA*, 14:376.

15. Gen. Hunter to sec. war, reporting disbanding, Aug. 10, 1862, *ORA*, ser. 3, 2:346. There is much evidence of the blacks' discontent and desertion in contemporary diaries, letters, and news items; and see Thomas Wentworth Higginson, *Army Life in a Black Regiment* (1870; rpt. Michigan State Univ. Press, East Lansing, 1960), pp. 272–74.

16. Rev. French to Mr. Whipple, Aug. 23 and 28, 1862, The Amistad Research Center, New Orleans; Okon Edet Uya, *From Slavery to Public Service: Robert Smalls, 1839–1915* (Oxford Univ. Press, New York, 1971), pp. 12–16; the award statute, 12 *U.S. Stat.* 904; Gen. Saxton to sec. war, Aug. 16, 1862, and sec. war to Gen. Saxton, Aug. 25, 1862, *ORA*, 14:374–76, 377–78. Uya says, p. 19, that on their trip to Washington Rev. French and Smalls saw the president, citing Dorothy Sterling, *Captain of the "Planter": The Story of Robert Smalls* (Doubleday & Co., Garden City, 1958), pp. 103–5. Sterling's excellent book is unannotated. On inquiry, she replied on Feb. 20, 1984, that she relied on Smalls' own reminiscences. It is notable, however, that Rev. French's letter to Mr. Whipple of Aug. 28, written on the day he expected to leave Washington with Smalls to deliver the secretary of war's letter to Gen. Saxton, says nothing of seeing the president though it tells of meeting with the several secretaries.

17. *New York Times*, Sept. 10, 1862; Gen. Saxton to sec. war, Oct. 13 and 29, 1862, *ORA*, ser. 3, 2:663, 695.

18. James D. Richardson, comp., *A Compilation of the Messages and Papers of the Presidents, 1789–1897*, 10 vols. (Published by the Authority of Congress, Washington, 1896–99), 6:96–98.

19. Sec. war to James H. Lane, Aug. 23 and Sept. 23, 1862, *ORA*, ser. 3, 2:445, 582.

20. New York *Tribune*, Aug. 5, 1862; Lincoln to Gov. Sprague, Sept. 20, 1862, Basler, *Collected Works*, 5:431. Also on Aug. 6, 1862, word was sent to the

governor of Wisconsin that "the President declines to receive Indians or negroes as troops," *ORA*, ser. 3, 2:314. See also Asst. Adj. Gen. Buckingham to governor of Wisconsin, Aug. 6, 1862, *ORA*, ser. 3, 2:314.

21. Gen. Butler, testimony to JCCW, Feb. 2, 1863, *JCCW*, 3:353–54, 356–57; Gen. Butler to his wife, July 30, 1862, *Private and Official Correspondence of Gen. Benjamin F. Butler During the Period of the Civil War*, 5 vols. (The Plimpton Press, Norwood, Mass. 1917), 2:124; Gen. Halleck to Gen. Butler, Aug. 7, 1862, *ORA*, 15:544; Gen. Butler to sec. war, Aug. 14 and 16, 1862, and to Gen. Halleck, Aug. 27, 1862, *ORA*, 15:548–49, 552–53, 555–57.

22. Principal items in the communications to and from Gen. Phelps and Gen. Butler's submission to sec. war are at *ORA*, 15:534–36, 542–43. That the resignation was accepted promptly appears in C. Roselius to Gen. Butler, Aug. 20, 1862, *Butler Correspondence*, 2:207.

23. Gen. Butler to sec. war, Aug. 14, 1862, and to Gen. Halleck, Aug. 27, 1862, *ORA*, 15:548–49, 555–57.

24. Gen. Butler testimony to JCCW, *JCCW*, 3:357–58.

25. Gen. Butler to Gen. Halleck, Nov. 6, 1862, and Gen. Halleck to Gen. Butler, Nov. 20, 1862, *ORA*, 15:162, 601.

26. Gen. Butler testimony to JCCW, *JCCW*, 3:357–58.

27. Gen. Butler to Gen. Halleck, Oct. 24 and Nov. 2, 1862, and Gen. Strong, by order of Butler, to Gen. Weitzel, Nov. 2, 1862, *ORA*, 15:158–63.

28. Gen. Saxton to sec. war, Nov. 12 and 25, 1862, *ORA*, 14:189–93. It should be observed that the secretary of war's letter to Saxton of Aug. 25 had contained a paragraph, separate from the paragraph authorizing enlistment of blacks, that authorized Saxton "by every means in your power to withdraw from the enemy their laboring force and population, and to spare no effort consistent with civilized warfare to weaken, harass, and annoy them, and to establish the authority of the Government of the United States within your department." Literally read, this provision would seem to authorize full-scale offensive action by Saxton throughout the department, which embraced South Carolina, Georgia, and Florida, and use of the prospective black troops in such action. Such a reading seems unreasonable since Saxton was the mere governor, subject to the army department command. A more reasonable reading is that it was a bit of rhetoric, intended to encourage Saxton and the military at Port Royal to maintain open avenues for fugitive blacks from beyond Union lines.

29. Richardson, *Messages and Papers of the Presidents*, 6:157–59.

30. Dudley Taylor Cornish, *The Sable Arm: Negro Troops in the Union Army, 1861–1865* (1956; rpt. W. W. Norton & Co., New York, 1966), pp. 100–101.

31. Cornish, *Sable Arm*, pp. 99, 103–6, 110–11, 129–31.

32. *ORA*, ser. 3, 3:103.

33. James D. Richardson, comp., *A Compilation of the Messages and Papers of the Confederacy, Including the Diplomatic Correspondence, 1861–1865*, 2 vols. (United States Publishing Co., Nashville, 1905), 1:269–74 at 274.

34. Howard K. Beale, ed., *Diary of Gideon Welles*, 3 vols. (W. W. Norton & Co., New York, 1960), 1:218.

35. Basler, *Collected Works*, 6:56.

36. *ORA*, 14:435–36.

37. Cornish, *Sable Arm*, pp. 132–56, tells in detail of 1863 engagements. One, Milliken's Bend, was a case of defending against an attack.

38. Illustrative orders by or at the direction of Gen. Grant, John Y. Simon, ed., *The Papers of Ulysses S. Grant* (Southern Illinois Univ. Press, Carbondale, Ill., 1967–), 10:403–4, 467–68, 473–74.

39. Cornish, *Sable Arm*, pp. 271–83.

40. *ORA*, ser. 3, 4:431.

41. Benjamin Quarles, *Lincoln and the Negro* (Oxford Univ. Press, New York, 1962), pp. 160–67.

42. *ORA*, ser. 2, 5:940–41.

43. Confederate treatment of captured blacks is a long, involved story. A significant example is the course pursued at Charleston. Howard C. Westwood, "Captive Black Union Soldiers in Charleston—What to Do?" *Civil War History* 28, no. 1 (Mar. 1982):28–44 (reprinted herein as chapter 6).

44. Richardson, *Messages and Papers of the Presidents*, 6:177.

45. Sec. war to Gov. Tod, June 27, 1863, *ORA*, ser. 3, 3:420.

46. Quotation of the solicitor's opinion of April 25, 1863, *ORA*, ser. 3, 5:632–33. Well after the war, the gentleman who had been the solicitor wrote an extensive treatise on war powers. In it he included a lengthy and labored argument that the Militia Act, with its pay limitation, applied to all black soldiers and that the secretary had erroneously allowed equal pay in his August 1862 letter to General Saxton. William Whiting, *War Powers under the Constitution of the United States* (Lee and Shepard, Boston, 1871), pp. 479–511. In the course of this argument he said that in the legislative history of the Second Confiscation Act there had been a rejection of an amendment to authorize black troops. He was mistaken. The amendment in question had been proposed to a quite different measure and it raised different issues, being a proposal to allow volunteering of both whites and blacks in the rebel states, with provision for compensation to any loyal owner of a volunteering slave and his family, *Cong. Globe*, 37th Cong. 2d Sess., 2323, 2361–62.

47. We have noted that the president had full preexisting authority to enlist blacks in the armed services, and such authority had been long exercised in enlisting black sailors; also the Second Confiscation Act, which we have quoted, provided the president with sweeping authority with no pay limitation.

48. *Cong. Globe*, 37th Cong. 2d Sess., 3250–51. The minimal consideration in the House appears at 3397–98.

49. Navy enlistment even of "contrabands" was allowed at a rating up to "landsman," paying more than $10, and promotion to higher ranks at "the corresponding pay." Secretary of navy's circular, Dec. 18, 1862, *Official Records of the Union and Confederate Navies in the War of the Rebellion*, 27 vols. (Washington, 1894–1927), ser. 1, 5:201; 23:638. On the Mississippi the navy provided for promotion of "contrabands" to any rank short of petty officer. General order of Admiral Porter of July 26, 1863, *Official Records of the Union and Confederate Navies*, ser. 1, 25:327–28.

50. Opinions of Apr. 23 and July 14, 1864, *ORA*, ser. 3, 4:270–74, 490–93. The July opinion reasoned that the Militia Act dealt with employment of blacks only otherwise than as soldiers, and that the Executive was empowered to enlist black

soldiers under the general military legislation, which included no color limitation. This view was strongly reiterated by another attorney general in an opinion of Oct. 17, 1865, 11 *Ops. Atty. Gen.* 365.

51. Frederick Douglass, *Life and Times of Frederick Douglass* (Park Publishing Co., Hartford, 1881), pp. 350–53.

52. Letter from Douglass to Maj. Geo. L. Stearns, Aug. 12, 1863, filed in the "Douglas" sequence in Union Provost Marshal's File of One-Name Papers Relating to Citizens, RG 109, Nat. Arch., M 345, Roll 76. I am indebted to Prof. John Y. Simon, editor of *The Papers of Ulysses S. Grant*, for inviting this letter to my attention. It referred to Douglass' visit as on "Monday," which would have been Aug. 10. The letter states that he saw the secretary of war before seeing the president; his 1881 book says he saw the president first.

53. *Cong. Globe*, 37th Cong., 3d Sess., 282, 557, 570–83, 598, 600.

54. *Cong. Globe*, 37th Cong., 3d Sess., 598–607, 626–37, 649–64, 680–90.

55. *Cong. Globe*, 37th Cong., 3d Sess., 598–99.

56. The bill as first proposed, presumably as drafted by the secretary of war, is printed at *Cong. Globe*, 37th Cong., 3d Sess., 557. Amending by Stevens, as he maneuvered with the opposition, appears at 598, 602, 649, 688–89; as it finally was submitted to the House vote it is at 689. All along the bill had dealt with certain issues in addition to the matter of pay.

57. *Cong. Globe*, 37th Cong., 3d Sess., 695, 923–24; *Journal of the Senate*, 37th Cong., 3d Sess., 249.

58. *Cong. Globe*, 37th Cong. 3d Sess., 1307. The printed Wilson substitute for H.R. 675 is in the file of printed bills for the 37th Congress in the Law Library, Lib. of Cong.

59. *ORA*, 24, pt. 3:584.

60. Richardson, *Messages and Papers of the Presidents*, 6:179–91 at 184, 188–89.

61. *ORA*, ser. 3, 3:1132.

62. Cornish, *Sable Arm*, 229–31; Francis T. Miller, ed., *The Photographic History of the Civil War*, 10 vols. (1911; rpt., Thomas Yoseloff, New York, 1957), 9:176, 178.

63. 13 *U.S. Stat.* 129–30. The Militia Act, as we have seen, had referred to "military or naval service" and the 1863 Stevens bill had referred to "land and naval" and to "military or naval service." The 1864 legislation also provided that, if the attorney general ruled that blacks who had been free at the war's beginning had been entitled to equal pay from the time of enlistment, back pay should go to them to correct inequality even prior to January 1. The attorney general did so rule in his opinion of July 14, 1864, cited above.

64. We have not addressed the question of the race of officers of black units. Even by the end of the war there was but a handful of black officers, for the War Department approved them most grudgingly. There is little indication of the president's direct involvement in the question, but obviously he acquiesced in the department's policy. The officer question is extensively dealt with in Cornish, *Sable Arm*, 201–28.

65. John T. Hubbell, "Abraham Lincoln and the Recruitment of Black Soldiers," *Papers of the Abraham Lincoln Association* 2 (1980):6–21, is a perceptive exposition of the president's pace.

2

Grant's Role in Beginning Black Soldiery

$\mathbf{A}$s THE sun rose on the year 1863 Ulysses S. Grant had failed dismally in a move toward Vicksburg. Washington was so unsure of him that Secretary of War Edwin M. Stanton sent an agent, Charles A. Dana, to keep an eye on him. But when the sun set on that year there was pending in Congress a measure, soon to be adopted, that everyone knew would result in Grant's promotion to supreme command of all the Union armies.

During 1863 another man rose from a dubious state to a firm role in the Union's armies: the black man. Typically an illiterate slave just freed by the Final Emancipation Proclamation, now he was thrust suddenly into a critical place in society. The part played by Grant, during his own transition, in that black man's elevation merits notice.

Less than a year before the war, Grant had been residing in Missouri, a slave state. His wife Julia, daughter of a Missouri slaveholder, owned four slaves. Grant himself had owned a slave, whom he manumitted shortly before the war.[1] But he was neither proslavery nor antislavery; to him, it seems, the existence of slavery was simply a fact of life.

Even when war came, Grant maintained that slavery was not the issue. Indeed the war was a full year along before he concluded that it would not be swiftly ended with the old Union restored. That conclusion was impelled, apparently, by his experiences in the Battle of Shiloh in early April 1862, which resulted in fearful, unprecedented casualties for both sides, the first truly great battle of the war. Even

Originally published in *Illinois Historical Journal* 79, no. 3 (Autumn 1986):197–212. Reprinted by permission of *Illinois Historical Journal*.

after Shiloh—as late as mid-June—he wrote his wife that the war would be ended at once if only the Southern people could express themselves "untramelled" by their leaders. Secession feeling was maintained, he said, "by crying out Abolitionest against us." He stated further that such charges were "unfortunately sustained by the acts of a very few among us." He blamed "instances of negro stealing," particularly when the white owners were persons who might be otherwise "inclined to Union sentiments."[2]

Back in November 1861, before the war was much under way, when operations in the West were confined to the loyal slave states of Missouri and Kentucky, Grant's department commander, Maj. Gen. Henry W. Halleck, addressed the question of fugitive slaves. Halleck's General Order No. 3 warned: "[I]mportant information respecting the numbers and condition of our forces is conveyed to the enemy by means of fugitive slaves who are admitted within our lines." For remedy he directed that "no such persons be hereafter permitted to enter the lines of any camp or of any forces on the march, and that any now within such lines be immediately excluded therefrom." Halleck was quick to explain that the order did not apply to blacks "employed by proper authority in the camps," nor was it to prevent "all proper offices of humanity" to fugitive slaves, including giving food and clothing or offering other aid in order "to prevent suffering."[3]

On its face, Order No. 3 had the limited purpose of preventing leaks of information to the enemy, but within two months Grant gave it a broader purpose. In late December he wrote a post commander in Kentucky, "I do not want the Army used as negro ca[t]chers, but still less do I want to see it used as a cloak to cover their escape." With that reasoning he allowed a Unionist slaveowner to enter the post in search of his slaves. Within a few days Grant received a report from another post commander in Missouri who had prevented a prosecessionist slaveowner from recovering a fugitive "boy" and had instead kept the slave himself in useful employment. Grant notified the commander that he concurred on the grounds that the military should not help a supporter of rebellion.[4] In short, Grant seemed to be making of Order No. 3 not a mere prevention of information leaks but a measure by which the military could help the loyal and punish the disloyal.

On February 3, 1862, Grant began an invasion of seceded land with his move on Fort Henry, Tennessee, to be followed by Donelson and then his drive southward, culminating in early April with the Shiloh battle in Tennessee near the Mississippi state line. During that move, he no longer allowed citizens to come within his lines in search of slaves, yet he was determined to prevent alienating people who were not wedded to secession. He did his best to prevent "stealing" of blacks or any tolerance of their presence within his lines except for duly authorized employment. Weeks later, when Congress adopted an article of war prohibiting the military from "returning fugitives from service or labor who may have escaped," Grant suggested that slaves "carried off" from a loyalist by an army officer should not merely be turned out of camp but actually returned; presumably he reasoned that a "stolen" slave was not "escaped."[5]

Just after Shiloh, Halleck shunted Grant aside for a time. But in mid-July, with Halleck called to Washington to become general-in-chief, Grant was elevated to department commander. By then the army had penetrated northern Mississippi. On August 3 he wrote his father that he had but one desire, "to put down the rebellion. I have no hobby of my own with regard to the negro, either to effect his freedom or to continue his bondage." One of his first general orders, on August 11, amounted to a strong reiteration of Order No. 3, adding, "Officers and Soldiers are positively prohibited from enticing Slaves to leave their masters."[6]

Yet, once deep in black country, he began to comprehend that the war was taking on a new dimension. On August 19 he wrote his sister Mary that the slaves were "beginning to have ideas of their own and every time an expedition goes out more or less of them follow in the wake of the army and come into camp. I am using them as teamsters, Hospital attendants, company cooks &c. thus saving soldiers to carry the musket. I dont know what is to become of these poor people." Nevertheless, he concluded that his action had the effect of "weakning" the enemy. In short, however he might curb the "stealing" of slaves, the slaves themselves were creating a social upheaval that would harm the Southern cause. Indeed, in less than another month one of Grant's generals reported "a perfect stampede of contrabands" coming from the land beyond.[7]

Among those masses of fugitives, of course, were many who could not be employed in military work, notably women and children. For some time Grant attempted, *ad hoc*, to ease their plight. Then, in mid-November as he was starting an inland drive aimed at Vicksburg, he took a most important step. With "Negroes coming in by wagon loads," as he reported to Halleck, he decided that sheer charity was not good. Save for the merest children and the infirm, blacks who could not be employed by the military would be put to work "picking, ginning and baling all cotton now out standing in Fields." To take on responsibility for the fugitives' care and to see that they were engaged as fully as possible in productive labor on abandoned plantations, he appointed a chaplain of an Ohio regiment, John Eaton.[8] At first Eaton's responsibility was confined to the army's advance area, but in mid-December Grant enlarged it, naming the chaplain general superintendent of contrabands for the entire department.[9]

Grant explained to Eaton at the outset that the purpose was to transform the fugitives from a burden into an asset. When it had been made clear, he said, that the black man could work well as an independent being, rather than under slavery's lash, "it would be very easy to put a musket in his hands and make a soldier of him."[10] Grant was thinking ahead, for at that time the War Department had done little—and that most ambiguous—to allow a black soldiery.

Washington had approved black soldiers in only two instances. The first, where enlistment began in October 1862, was in a small Union foothold on the South Carolina coast that also embraced a portion of the Georgia coast and a port in northeast Florida. The other was in the Union enclave at and around New Orleans, where in late August Maj. Gen. Benjamin F. Butler began organizing black regiments, but Washington's approval was not given until late November.[11]

In the Final Emancipation Proclamation of New Year's Day, 1863, the president included an important new provision—that "such persons" emancipated by the proclamation would be "received into the armed service of the United States to garrison forts, positions, stations, and other places and to man vessels of all sorts in said service."[12] The proclamation, of course, did not apply to the nonseceded slave states. Also, it excluded important seceded areas, including Tennessee, a great portion of which was not Union occupied. Nor did the proclamation mention previously free blacks, North or South. Thus, literally, the proclamation's provision for receiving blacks into the military service fell far short of general approval of black enlistment. Moreover, since the proclamation did not apply to Kentucky and Tennessee, it did not reach what at that time was most of Grant's department. It is notable, too, that, as far as the army was concerned, it approved only garrison duty by the emancipated slaves. There is no record of Grant's reaction to the black soldier provision in the proclamation. One may speculate that he was preoccupied with the great puzzle of how to get at Vicksburg.

His inland drive, after proceeding auspiciously, suddenly had to be reversed because of enemy raids on his supply line and the base he had established at Holly Springs. He drew back, leaving only a part of the northern tier of Mississippi counties in Union hands. What he had intended as a coordinated move down the Mississippi River—commanded by his chief lieutenant, Maj. Gen. William Tecumseh Sherman—met with repulse. Nonetheless, by the end of January, Grant himself had gone down the river to establish his headquarters at Milliken's Bend, on the Louisiana side of the Mississippi somewhat above Vicksburg, determined that, somehow, he would finally get at and capture the critical enemy stronghold.

The black problem in Louisiana was rather different from what he previously had had to deal with. He had great need for manpower in watery country, and he was eager to have the help of able-bodied black laborers. But, under pressure as he was, the responsibility of caring for fugitive blacks was not welcome. Grant was not planning to settle down; as soon as he found a way, he intended to move on Vicksburg with every available soldier. Yet many planters were fleeing, taking with them able-bodied slaves but leaving behind "the old and very young" whom Grant could not ignore.[13]

He began at once to increase the use of blacks for military work. In time he prescribed that three hundred black laborers would be added to each division's pioneer corps. As to other blacks, Special Field Order No. 2, issued on February 12, warned: "The enticing of negroes to leave their homes to come within the lines of the army is positively forbidden." While blacks already within the lines would not be turned out, in the future no one—white or black—could enter or leave without duly issued authority.[14]

But that order fell far short of solving the black problem. Within four days after it was issued, Grant wrote Washington that, if it was intended to have plantations cultivated by blacks "coming into the Federal lines," he suggested Lake Providence on the Louisiana side of the river as most suitable for a colony. "The plantations are in a high state of cultivation," he noted, "well improved as to quarters, and the place easily protected."[15] There seems no indication that Washington responded to the suggestion, but in time great numbers of blacks were put to work on the abandoned plantations not only in the Lake Providence area but elsewhere near the west bank above Vicksburg.

In the meantime the seeming limitation on eligibility of blacks as soldiers was beginning to erode. Before January had passed, Gov. William Sprague of Rhode Island was authorized to organize a black regiment; so, too, was Gov. John Albion Andrew of Massachusetts, and in time recruits for that regiment would be sought throughout the North. In that same month Col. Daniel Ullmann of New York was commissioned a brigadier general and instructed to get ready to organize a black brigade in Louisiana, apparently without regard to slave status.[16] Those units would be officered by whites. In a few weeks more it became apparent that the War Department had decided that any able black man could become a soldier. On March 24, 1863, the secretary of war informed Adj. Gen. Lorenzo Thomas, then in Washington, that he was to go at once to "the west" with sweeping instructions. He was to see to it that "contrabands" would receive humane treatment and be enabled "to support themselves." More than that he was to have black soldiers organized "to the utmost extent." For their officers he was to select "willing" whites not only from existing officers but from any in the ranks, even privates. The next day, Thomas began the mission that would be his principal duty for the rest of the war.[17]

The geographic and status limitations of the Emancipation Proclamation were not applied to Thomas' activity. He began his work in Cairo, Illinois, on March 29, spent the day of April 2 at Columbus, Kentucky, and was in Memphis on April 4. While it may be that he engaged in no specific authorization of black soldiers until he reached Memphis, there he definitely began it.[18]

Then, after a fruitful stop at Helena, Arkansas, Thomas reached Lake Providence on April 8. There at last Grant's mid-February recommendation as to Lake Providence, if it had not been acted on before, was implicitly approved. Thomas, with his sweeping authority, provided for putting blacks to work on abandoned cotton plantations and decreed, "Protection will be afforded to the contrabands engaged in picking, when it can be done without injury to the service, until the organization of negro regiments, when that duty will be performed by them." Thus, early in the Union's program for black soldiers a very constructive role was foretold for those in Grant's theatre: the easing for white soldiers, sorely needed for critical combat, of the full burden of protecting thousands of black refugees engaged in learning a new life of self-support. In a few days more, on April 11, Thomas reached Grant at his Milliken's Bend headquarters.[19]

A few days before Thomas' arrival, Grant had received a personal letter from Halleck, saying: "It is the policy of the government to withdraw from the enemy as much productive labor as possible. . . . Every slave withdrawn from the enemy, is equivalent to a white man put *hors de combat*. Again, it is the policy of the government to use the negroes of the South so far as practicable, as a military force for the defence of forts, depots, &c."[20]

That policy was timely, for Grant had recently received a report from a division commander at Greenville on the riverbank in central Mississippi about a sortie against the enemy and the "great many negroes" who had followed him back. The commander asked, "What shall be done with these poor creatures." Grant replied on April 11, just after Thomas had come to him. The reply reveals that his adaptations of old Order No. 3, even with all the strain on his resources, were no more. He declared:

Rebellion has assumed that shape now that it can only terminate by the complete subjugation of the South. . . . [I]t is our duty therefore to use every means to weaken the enemy by destroying their means of cultivating their field, and in every other way possible. All the negroes you have you will provide for where they are issuing their necessary rations, until other disposition is made of them. You will also encourage all negroes, particularly middle aged males to come within our lines.

General Thomas, he added, had "authority to make ample provision for the negro." On April 19 Grant wrote Halleck: "At least three of my Army Corps Commanders take hold of the new policy of arming the negroes and using them against the rebels with a will. . . . You may rely on my carrying out any policy ordered by proper authority to the best of my ability."[21]

Thomas first appointed three commissioners to take immediate charge of having fugitive blacks work on plantations along the west bank between Milliken's Bend and Lake Providence, and the commissioners asked Grant to detail a white regiment for their protection until black regiments could take over the task. On April 18 Grant granted that request. With Grant's support, Thomas worked fast, meeting what seemd to him enthusiastic response, authorizing black regiments, assigning their officers (almost always involving promotions), and empowering recruiters, as well as furthering arrangement for cultivating the plantations. Initially not only the officers but also the first sergeants were white; later he was to find that black first sergeants were preferable.[22] As early as April 13 he commissioned Lt. Col. John P. Hawkins brigadier general to command the black units in the area. Though sorry to lose Hawkins' services in the Subsistence Department, Grant recommended him to Thomas, and he proved a fortunate choice.[23]

Then on April 23, Grant issued general orders, applicable throughout his department, for army protection of plantations on which fugitives worked. That came on the heels of general orders of the previous day, in which he directed that all his commanders "especially exert themselves . . . not only in organizing colored regiments and rendering them efficient, but also in removing prejudice against them." Grant was serious; on April 23 and again on April 27 he recommended dismissal from the service, rather than mere acceptance of resignations, of some officers who had tendered resignations because of "the Emancipation policy and the arming of the slaves."[24] Busy as Grant was during those last days of April in getting forces down the watery west bank for the crossing of the Mississippi below Vicksburg, he went out of his way to give support for Thomas' mission.

Apparently, Thomas could not resist the temptation to witness Grant's crossing of the river below Vicksburg at Bruinsburg, begun as April ended. Indeed, he himself promptly went over in the troops' wake. But he soon resumed his mission at Milliken's Bend, then traveled back to Lake Providence, and on to Memphis again. Late in May, however, his exertions brought on a fever. He went to Louisville to recuperate, but on June 15, at his doctor's insistence, he left for Washington and did not return to the Mississippi Valley until early August.[25]

Before his illness, Thomas had accomplished much, including even a side trip from Memphis to Corinth in extreme northeast Mississippi, where a substantial body of Grant's forces was centered.[26] He had authorized certain officers to form black regiments, but most of those new units did not fill up to their authorized numerical strength. Left behind him was great activity, but it needed shaping. And that Grant provided.

Grant's river crossing at Bruinsburg was followed by his brilliant campaign that had Confederate Lt. Gen. John Clifford Pemberton and his army closely besieged at Vicksburg, resulting in their surrender on

July 4. Despite Grant's need for troops during the siege, he did not neglect the plantations west of the river where Thomas' program to put blacks to work was barely under way. Knowing that the organizing and training of black troops was only beginning, Grant not only had left there six of his white regiments but sent back, from his besieging army, an additional brigade.[27]

The newly organized black units at Milliken's Bend along with white troops were attacked by a force of two or three thousand from the Confederate trans-Mississippi command on June 7. The attack was finally beaten off with gunboat help. A small affair in relation to other battling at that time, it was a landmark in the history of the Union's black soldiery. It was one of the two initial tests of black soldiers in a substantial battle, and they stood the test well. The first of the two had occurred a few days previous when black troops organized by Ben Butler were a relatively small part of a vain attack on Port Hudson, Louisiana, well to the south of Grant. At Milliken's, on the other hand, blacks were the principal troops engaged, and the battle was a Union victory. As Grant reported to Thomas, the blacks "had but little experience in the use of fire arms. Their conduct is said however to have been most gallant and I doubt not but with good officers they will make good troops."[28]

It is a fair guess that the Milliken's Bend affair contributed to a determination by Grant both to make black soldiers a truly significant part of his Mississippi Valley command and to sharpen his focus on achieving their orderly organization and training. The interruption in Thomas' mission had left matters rather unsettled, and whites, sensing opportunity for promotion, sometimes were eager to get additional black regiments authorized. By late June, Grant had decided that no new units would be established until existing ones were fully manned. His judgment was confirmed by a July 3 letter to his chief of staff, John Aaron Rawlins, from one of the first and ablest of the white officers, Isaac F. Shepard of the Missouri Volunteers, who had responded to Thomas' invitation into the black service. He wrote that, instead of recruits for any new units, there was need for some five thousand blacks to fill ten yet undermanned regiments that Thomas had authorized in the Louisiana-Mississippi-Arkansas area.[29] Indeed, on July 11 Grant wrote Thomas that he had gone so far as to break up all black units except those for which Thomas himself had appointed officers, units that "never could be filled so long as authority was granted to form new ones." Then, very significantly, on July 24 he wrote Halleck that, in order to garrison Vicksburg, he had authorized a regiment of twelve 150-man companies to be used as artillerists and infantry. He had selected one of Thomas' black regiments that formerly had had few troops but that by then was nearly filled, adding: "The negro troops are easier to preserve discipline among than our White troops and I doubt not will prove equally good for garrison duty. All that have been tried have fought bravely. Before raising any new regiments of Colored troops I think it advisable to fill those already organized."[30]

In the meantime Grant had his initial exposure to the way Confederates treated captured black soldiers. Soon after the Milliken's Bend affair there were seemingly reliable reports that Confederates had hanged some captured black soldiers, a white captain, and a white sergeant. On June 22 Grant wrote Maj. Gen. Richard Taylor, the Confederate commander across the river, asking whether he had a policy toward captured black soldiers and their officers different from that toward white units. Assuring Taylor that he was bound to give black soldiers the same protection as whites, he warned that he was ready to retaliate if there was a Confederate policy of no quarter. Taylor replied that no such hangings had occurred, that such an act would be disgraceful. But he added that his government had provided that captured black soldiers and their officers were to be turned over to the civil authorities to be dealt with according to the law of the state where captured. Grant received Taylor's letter on the day of the Vicksburg capitulation; he replied on the same day, accepting the denial of the hangings. But as to turning prisoners over to civil authorities, he sensed that there was an issue beyond his competence. He wrote Taylor that he did not feel "authorized to say what the government may demand" as to the blacks, adding, "[H]aving taken the responsibility of declaring slaves free and having authorized the arming of them, I cannot see the justice of permitting one treatment for them, and another for the white soldiers."[31]

It is unlikely that Grant was surprised by the Confederate government's special treatment of captives from black units. It had been evolving since late 1862. Though occasion for its application had been very rare prior to the Milliken's Bend affair, it was no secret, and it must have been at least discussed between Grant and Thomas, who, as adjutant general, certainly was fully aware of it. It is significant that in January 1863, as Washington was moving toward allowing full-scale black recruitment, President Lincoln had suggested to Secretaries Stanton and Welles that black soldiers be used only "where they would not be liable to be captured." His idea had been that in the Mississippi Valley they take over garrison duty at points in the rear, allowing whites on such duty to "go on more active service."[32] It is all but certain that one factor in Grant's thinking that led to his employment of newly officered and recruited black units other than in front line combat was the concern about Confederate treatment of black captives.

There was another problem that required attention—the antiblack prejudice widespread among the white rank and file. Thomas' impression that his mission had been enthusiastically received by white forces was well short of accurate, despite full support from Grant and most of his top officers. For many Northern troops, initial exposure to blacks was the spectacle of ignorant, illiterate, unkempt refugees; abuse of black soldiers by whites was not uncommon.[33] Doubtless responsive to that problem, on June 15 Grant instructed Brig. Gen. Elias Smith Dennis, commander of his newly designated district west of the river, that "Negro troops should be kept aloof from the White troops, especially in their camps, as much as possible." Only where an enemy threat required concentration should he bring his forces together "without regard to color."[34]

Probably a most significant factor affecting Grant's decisions on the best use of black troops was the abrupt increase of military needs in the Mississippi Valley resulting from Grant's success. A vast new area was brought under actual and potential Union dominion. Yet soon after Vicksburg, Grant had to begin returning troops borrowed from other theatres for the siege. Thus it was essential that his white troops be kept available for duty most requiring veterans' experience. With black troops only newly recruited and fresh from slavery and so many of their officers quite inexperienced in command responsibility, the obvious assignments were garrison duty (as Halleck had suggested as soon as he heard of Vicksburg's capture), and guarding refugee camps and those plantation areas where blacks were put to work. Indeed, manpower needs for such duty had so increased on Vicksburg's capture that Grant sent specially selected recruiters of blacks with raiding expeditions into regions west of the river.[35]

Thus on Thomas' early August return to the valley, he resumed work on a program that, while still evolving, had become considerably more coherent. In the meantime Charles Dana, whose "spying" on Grant had made him a fervent admirer, returned to Washington and, as President Lincoln wrote Grant, reported that Grant believed "that the emancipation proclamation has helped" in his military operations. Surely Lincoln was pleased to read Grant's reply on August 23. "I have given the subject of arming the negro my hearty support," Grant wrote. "This, with the emancipation of the negro, is the heavyest blow yet given the Confederacy. . . . [B]y arming the negro we have added a powerful ally. They will make good soldiers and taking them from the enemy weaken him in the same proportion they strengthen us."[36]

Even so, Grant was alert to the need for avoiding the appearance of "negro stealing." Probably the hopes he once had for giving release to an abiding Unionism among numbers of Southern people were not wholly dead. On August 28 he instructed the commander at Natchez that Negroes belonging "to persons of known loyalty only be recruited as free white persons are. That is when they come and offer themselves." As to masters who had not been loyal but who were willing to return to Union allegiance "and employ the negroes in accordance with existing orders," recruiters could visit their blacks "and the option given them to enlist." But as to blacks of persons "who hold out" in loyalty to the Confederacy, recruiters could resort to what amounted to conscription.[37]

At Vicksburg on August 16, Thomas himself issued an order that seemed to authorize recruiters to conscript all able-bodied blacks. He was concerned with the extent of the black refugee problem suddenly created by Grant's success—a problem involving many thousands of women and children and aged or infirm males—and his mission included coping with that problem.[38] An increase in the numbers and efficiency of the black soldiery, of course, would ameliorate the situation.

Thomas kept close to Grant, even going with him on a trip to Memphis and Cairo in late August. As he wrote the secretary of war , Grant gave him "every assistance in [his] work." Indeed, at the end of August he even accompanied Grant on a trip to New Orleans to see Maj. Gen. Nathaniel Prentiss Banks.[39] Banks was in command of the department to the south of Grant's. The Vicksburg capture had caused the immediate fall of Port Hudson, bringing Grant and Banks at last into direct contact and enabling Thomas to extend his work. Their New Orleans trip, intended as a quick one, lasted two weeks because Grant suffered serious injury when his horse fell on him.

After their return to Vicksburg in mid-September, a potentially serious conflict between Thomas and Chaplain Eaton was worked out. Eaton had come to Vicksburg, and it may be that he and Thomas had not met face to face. Thomas, all along, had acted under authority directly from the secretary of war; indeed, his orders recited that they were "By order of the Sec. of War." Eaton's authority was only from Grant. Within the department their missions for the care and employment of black refugees overlapped, but their methods differed. The result, as Eaton put it delicately in his memoirs, was a lack of "orderliness."[40] During Grant's convalescence from his injury in late September and into October he achieved an accommodation between them.

An important item in that accommodation was the adoption of a proposal by Grant. Eaton was commissioned a colonel and authorized by Thomas to organize a black regiment. He would not be required to keep the regiment assembled but could "distribute it in small groups throughout the Valley, wherever the safety and comfort" of the black refugees needed protection. For the regiment Eaton accepted men of a "lower grade of physique" than required of regular soldiers. Grant's proposal proved so apt that, by early November, Eaton was authorized by Thomas to organize a second regiment of such blacks "as may be incapacitated for active service in the field but who are otherwise fitted for ordinary garrison duty." Just as black soldiers had freed veteran white troops for most critical duty, Eaton's troops, acting as "a sort of Home Guard," freed well-trained regular black soldiers for increasing responsibilities. And, affixing the seal of highest authority on the Ohio chaplain's mission, Thomas issued an order on November 5 not only continuing Eaton as general superintendent of freedmen for the department but extending his mission to include Arkansas.[41]

By that time Grant had been called from the valley to meet an emergency in East Tennessee. There he scored his great victory in the Battle of Chattanooga. In East Tennessee there were few blacks, and during the remainder of the winter he would be but rarely involved in matters of black soldiery. In January 1864, however, he did request authorization for one of his generals to organize a black corps. He proposed that recruitment of the corps start in Tennessee and proceed in Alabama and Georgia, the path he then had in mind for his spring 1864 campaign. In aiming at an entire corps he was far advanced in his thinking; the War Department would not create a black corps until nearly the end of 1864, when it was done on Grant's initiative.[42]

But the authority was denied him in January; Santon felt that black organization in the west should remain in Thomas' hands.[43]

In December 1863, Thomas reported to the secretary of war on his black recruitment from April 1 to mid-December. The numbers in service in the area of his responsibility at the end of that period were just over twenty thousand. He estimated that during the period there had been some five thousand more who had been lost by capture, disease, or other casualty.[44] His figures may include numbers enlisted independently of him (as in Louisiana prior to September). In any event it is notable that such a record was accomplished so quickly in an area where conditions had been chaotic and where so many of the blacks had just emerged from field-hand slavery. That record could not have been approached without the aggressive help, indeed initiative, of Grant.

In March 1864, Grant was called to the supreme command of all armies. In that position, on occasion he would be directly involved in the growing use of black troops, but he never played so intense a part in bringing blacks into the army as he had from the spring to the autumn of 1863.

Few other Union leaders, however, contributed more solidly to ultimate success in that effort.

Notes

1. William S. McFeely, *Grant: A Biography* (New York: W. W. Norton & Co., 1981), pp. 58–66; John Y. Simon, ed., *The Papers of Ulysses S. Grant* (Southern Illinois Univ. Press, Carbondale, 1967–), 1:347 (hereafter cited as *Grant Papers*).

2. Ulysses S. Grant, *Personal Memoirs of U. S. Grant* (C. L. Webster, New York, 1885–86), 1:222, 368–69; Grant to Julia Dent Grant, *Grant Papers*, 2:23–24; Grant to Jesse Root Grant, *Grant Papers*, 3:226–28; *Grant Papers*, 5:142–43.

3. U.S. War Dept., *The War of the Rebellion: A Compilation of the Official Records of the Union and Confederate Armies*, 70 vols. in 128 pts. (1880–1901; rpt. National Historical Society, Gettysburg, 1972), ser. 1, 8:370 (hereafter cited as *ORA*); Halleck to Alexander Asboth, *ORA*, ser. 1, 8:465.

4. Grant to John Cook, *Grant Papers*, 3:342–43; William S. Hillyer (Grant's aide-de-camp) to Leonard F. Ross, *Grant Papers*, 3:373–74.

5. Grant's General Order No. 14 for District of West Tenn., *Grant Papers*, 4:290–91; Grant to Philip B. Fouke, *Grant Papers*, 4:377; Grant to William Tecumseh Sherman, *Grant Papers*, 4:382–83; Grant to Elihu B. Washburne, *Grant Papers*, 4:408–9; Grant to John A. McClernand, *Grant Papers*, 4:437–38; *ORA*, ser. 2, 1:810; *Grant Papers*, 4:453–55.

6. *Grant Papers*, 5:263–64, 273–74.

7. *Grant Papers*, 5:310–11; William S. Rosecrans to Grant, *Grant Papers*, 6:32.

8. *Grant Papers*, 6:315–16.

9. Grant's General Order No. 13, Dept. of the Tenn., *Grant Papers*, 6:316–17; John Eaton, *Grant, Lincoln and the Freedmen* (1907; rpt. Negro Universities Press, New York, 1969), pp. 25–28; Grant, *Memoirs*, 1:424–26.

10. Eaton, *Grant, Lincoln*, p. 15.

11. For approval of black enlistment in South Carolina and the related area, see Stanton to Rufus Saxton, Aug. 25, 1862, *ORA*, ser. 1, 14:377–78. Because of a trip north, Brig. Gen. Saxton was unable to begin enlistments until mid-October, *ORA*, ser. 3, 2:663–64. Butler requested approval on Aug. 27, *ORA*, ser. 1, 15:555–57. Having no response, he continued enlistments, and wrote Halleck on Nov. 6 that he assumed Washington's approval; Halleck replied on Nov. 20 that Stanton left the matter to the discretion of the department commander, *ORA*, ser. 1, 15:162, 601. For Butler's organization of black regiments, see Howard C. Westwood, "Benjamin Butler's Enlistment of Black Troops in New Orleans in 1862," *Louisiana History* 26, no. 1 (1985):5–22 (reprinted herein as chapter 3).

12. James D. Richardson, comp., *A Compilation of the Messages and Papers of the Presidents, 1789–1897*, 10 vols. (Published by the Authority of Congress, Washington, 1896–99), 6:158.

13. Grant to Halleck, *Grant Papers*, 7:338–39; Grant to James B. McPherson, *Grant Papers*, 7:415–16.

14. Grant to George W. Deitzler, *Grant Papers*, 7:278–80; Grant's Special Order No. 66 and Rawlins to Stephen A. Hurlbut, *Grant Papers*, 7:417, 339.

15. *Grant Papers*, 7:339.

16. Dudley Taylor Cornish, *The Sable Arm: Negro Troops in the Union Army, 1861–1865* (1956; rpt. W. W. Norton & Co., New York, 1966), pp. 100–101, 105–10.

17. Stanton's instructions to Thomas, dated March 25, 1863, are in *ORA*, ser. 3, 3:100–101. Thomas was informed of them only on the day before, *ORA*, ser. 3, 5:118. An account of the Thomas mission is given in Cornish, *Sable Arm*, pp. 112–26.

18. Lorenzo Thomas, *Orders and Letters, April–November, 1863*, pp. 1, 10–11, Generals' Papers and Books, RG 94, Nat. Arch. Some items in this volume of Thomas' papers appear also in *ORA*. Only the Thomas volume will be cited because it provides coherent context not available in *ORA*.

19. Thomas, *Orders and Letters*, pp. 14, 18–19, 23.

20. *ORA*, ser. 1, vol. 24, pt. 3:156–57; Halleck's letter is also in *Grant Papers*, 8:93–94. *ORA* dates it March 31; *Grant Papers* dates it March 30 and has some other minor differences from *ORA*. There seems to be no clear record of when Grant received it; that he had it by the time of Thomas' arrival seems virtually certain.

21. *Grant Papers*, 8:49–50, 90–92.

22. *Grant Papers*, 8:355–56. The first sixty-five pages of Thomas' *Orders and Letters* describe his progress; his final report to the secretary of war, dated Oct. 5, 1865, also provides, in its forepart, an informative summary, *ORA*, ser. 3, 5:118–24.

23. Thomas, *Orders and Letters*, pp. 26–28.

24. *Grant Papers*, 8:94, 356.

25. Thomas, *Orders and Letters*, pp. 43, 47–49, 51, 53–56, 59–61, 64–71, 87–90.

26. Thomas, *Orders and Letters*, pp. 55–56.

27. Grant to Thomas, *Grant Papers*, 9:23–25.

28. Cornish, *Sable Arm*, pp. 142–45; Ira Berlin et al., eds., *Freedom: A Documentary History of Emancipation, 1861–1867*, ser. 2, *The Black Military Experience* (Cambridge Univ. Press, New York, 1982), p. 518; *Grant Papers*, 8:327–28.

29. For Rawlins' endorsement on applications for appointment as officers of black regiments and Shepard to Rawlins, see *Grant Papers*, 8:565–66.

30. *Grant Papers*, 9:23–25, 108–11.

31. *Grant Papers*, 8:400–401, 468–69.

32. Westwood, "Captive Black Union Soldiers in Charleston—What to Do?," *Civil War History* 28, no. 1 (1982):28–44 at 29–33 (reprinted herein as chapter 6); Howard K. Beale, ed., *Diary of Gideon Welles*, 3 vols. (W. W. Norton & Co., New York, 1960), 1:218.

33. Thomas' reports to Washington during his initial mission in the valley repeatedly indicated white troops' favorable response to the proposed arming of blacks; even in his final report of Oct. 1865, he insisted that whites' "prejudice" finally was "overcome" by "all my efforts to counteract it," *ORA*, ser. 3, 5:199. He probably never realized the persistence of the problem.

34. *Grant Papers*, 8:374–75. By Special Order No. 143, Dept. of the Tenn., May 28, 1863, the area west of the river was designated the District of North Eastern Louisiana, *Grant Papers*, 8:329.

35. Halleck to Grant, *Grant Papers*, 9:111–12; Grant to Lincoln, *Grant Papers*, 9:195–97; Grant's Special Order No. 220, Dept. of the Tenn., Aug. 13, 1863, *Grant Papers*, 9:208–9; Thomas to Stanton, in Thomas, *Orders and Letters*, pp. 98–102.

36. Thomas left Cairo on Aug. 6 for Memphis and thence to Vicksburg, see Thomas, *Orders and Letters*, pp. 88–90; *Grant Papers*, 9:195–97.

37. *Grant Papers*, 9:207–8.

38. For Thomas' Special Orders No. 45 and Thomas to Stanton, see Thomas, *Orders and Letters*, pp. 94–96, 98–102; see also Thomas' later Special Order No. 63, Thomas, *Orders and Letters*, pp. 133–34.

39. Thomas, *Orders and Letters*, pp. 96, 98–102, 106–7, 112–13.

40. Eaton, *Grant, Lincoln*, p. 63.

41. Eaton, *Grant, Lincoln*, pp. 107–11; Thomas, *Orders and Letters*, pp. 194–97.

42. *Grant Papers*, 10:59; 12:418; *ORA*, ser. 1, vol. 42, pt. 3:791. Cornish, *Sable Arm*, p. 281, refers to the corps as "the only all-Negro army corps in American military history." In 1863 General Banks, in Louisiana, had designated the black troops under his command as the Corps d'Afrique (Cornish, *Sable Arm*, pp. 126–29) but it was not recognized by the War Department as an official army corps.

43. *Grant Papers*, 10:59.

44. *ORA*, ser. 3, 3:1189–91.

3

Benjamin Butler's
Enlistment
of Black Troops
in New Orleans
in 1862

I T IS well nigh the fashion to brand Benjamin F. Butler as a self-seeking opportunist. Notable among the chapters in his career felt to reveal that character was his command at New Orleans from May to December 1862. Significant in that chapter was Butler's enlistment of black troops almost before the ink was dry on his order to a subordinate general refusing permission to enlist blacks. A Treasury Department agent, stationed in New Orleans, wrote Secretary of the Treasury Salmon P. Chase at the time that Butler's refusal to his subordinate "was not a matter of principle," that he simply "wanted the credit of doing the thing himself."[1] A respected historian of the Union's black troops says that that verdict "seems to be substantially supported" by the evidence.[2]

I suggest, however, that the evidence points to a very different conclusion. It is quite true that, in this instance, Ben Butler was not moved by "principle." Rather he was intent on practicalities—on following a course that, as a practical matter, would work in Louisiana at that time. He had a near-desperate need for more troops. His subordinate proposed to arm slaves, an abrupt defiance of local institutions. What Butler did was very different. He started with an invitation not to slaves but to free blacks to join his army, virtually copying what

Originally published in *Louisiana History* 26, no. 1 (Winter 1985):5–22. Reprinted by permission of *Louisiana History*.

Confederate Louisiana itself had done before Butler came. In what he evolved there was something more, but never his subordinate's proposed defiance of Louisiana's slavery.

On May 1, 1862, with the way cleared by Flag Officer David G. Farragut and his fleet, Butler's army occupied New Orleans, a city of approximately 170,000, largest in the Confederacy. The army was less than 14,000, never to be reinforced from the North during Butler's command.[3] No other Union army was closer than West Tennessee and the north rim of the state of Mississippi, and exchange of messages between New Orleans and Washington took twenty days or more. In short, Butler and his army were isolated, deep in Rebeldom.

New Orleans, for years, had been turbulent, its governing difficult. Moreover, while its people initially had been by no means unanimous for secession, Unionist voices had become faint, and the land byond was bitterly hostile. So Butler's governing would tax determination and ingenuity. Nor was his mission confined to holding New Orleans. Though the Union's overall military strategy was not clear, Butler was expected to thrust onward.[4]

In time—not overnight—Butler's success in controlling the city and its environs was remarkable.[5] Latent pro-Union sentiment emerged sufficiently so that, by July, he was able even to begin enlisting locals in his army, pursuant to authority sent him by Secretary of War Edwin M. Stanton to recruit "loyal white men."[6] Augmenting his little army was most important for his strength had been spread thin. He had had to garrison Ship Island, just off the coast of Mississippi, which had been the base for his expedition; to fortify and guard the way between the city and the gulf; to maintain a protecting screen above the city; and to dispatch a large fraction of his force, with Farragut, to seize the state capital, Baton Rouge, and push on to the verge of Vicksburg, which he hoped to capture if Union arms to the north somehow would cooperate.[7] Left to him, within the city, were fewer troops than the number of recent Confederate soldiers among its populace.[8]

Thus, from the outset, Butler's need to attract loyalty to his rule, or at least acquiescence, was acute. To that end it was essential that he avoid social upheaval. The cornerstone of the society he had to deal with was slavery. Nearly half of Louisiana's population was slave. Nowhere was there any significant abolitionist sentiment. Many of the emerging Unionists in the city were slaveholders; some of the free blacks owned slaves. Were he to encourage, even passively, slaves' flight from their masters it seemed that he could not get the local economy operating on its own steam, that he and his little army would have problems of governing and care for the population greater than they could handle. Butler explained this situation in a long report to the secretary of war at the end of May.[9] What he faced was very different from what had confronted him the previous year when he had comanded at Fort Monroe in Virginia. There he had been maintaining a mere military base with no serious problem of governing and could welcome fugitive slaves as "contraband of war"; he probably never had had on his hands more than a thousand "contrabands" and their care had been no large task.[10]

Butler's problems in Louisiana were further aggravated by the whites' fear of servile insurrection, a fear prevailing in the North. Butler was not unique in believing that, were there such insurrection, he would have to suppress it or at least control it. With his strength spread so thin that would be one problem too many.

For all these reasons Butler's initial policy was to try to avoid disruption of slavery in Louisiana. While he would allow his army to employ blacks on needed labor, beyond that he insisted that fugitive slaves be sent away from his army's camps, left "subject to the ordinary laws of the community. . . ." Though in March 1862 Congress had adopted a new article of war prohibiting the military from returning slaves escaped from their masters, he could refuse fugitives food and shelter and passes into his camps.[11]

But at the protective screen established above the city, the general in charge, Brig. Gen. John W. Phelps of Vermont, was a crusading abolitionist. Though a West Pointer and military veteran, and a spit-and-polish disciplinarian, Phelps proved to have one quality quite unmilitary—a will independent of his commander.[12]

Phelps had served under Butler at Fort Monroe and Butler had asked for him in late 1861, when Butler was first told to organize a Gulf of Mexico expedition. In December 1861 Phelps had been sent with an advance force to establish a base on Ship Island. On his arrival he had issued an extraordinary proclamation. Slavery, he announced, was both unconstitutional and "a social evil which is opposed to moral law." Though that view did not govern the Union's conduct of the war, such rhetoric on the small, barren Ship Island probably was thought harmless.[13] However, before the end of the first month of Butler's occupation of New Orleans he and Phelps were on a collision course respecting fugitive slaves. Phelps was receiving them with open arms. More than that, on occasion he was sending parties of his men beyond his lines to bring back slaves being disciplined on nearby plantations. When Butler cautioned Phelps against interference "in the domestic affairs of the people," Phelps rejoined with a long argument for abolition that he requested "be laid before the President. . . ." In mid-June Butler wrote Stanton, enclosing Phelps' letter, and asked for guidance.[14]

Stanton submitted the matter to the president, and by mid or late July Butler had Stanton's response. Stanton said that fugitive slaves coming to Butler's lines should not be turned away, those capable of working should be employed at reasonable wages, and all should be provided with food and shelter.[15] This greatly concerned Butler. There was a fine line, very hard to draw, between merely receiving slaves coming to the army's camps and encouraging them to challenge and flee their masters. On July 25 Butler wrote his wife, "The Government have sustained Phelps about the Negroes, and we shall have a negro insurrection here I fancy." Three days later he wrote her again, betraying discouragement quite uncharacteristic.[16] Wanting to be sure that the president understood the local feeling on "the Question of Slavery as interwoven with the integrity of the Union," Butler already had sent to Washington one of his generals who had been invested as Louisiana's military governor, and now he sent also a prominent local citizen, a former attorney general of the state, who had been one of the holdouts against secession in the Louisiana convention.[17]

Then, on July 30, Butler received requisitions from Phelps for arms and clothing "for three regiments of Africans" which he proposed to raise; he said that already he had organized more than three hundred blacks. He emphasized his need for troops; disease in unhealthy swamplands was taking a toll among his whites. He went further, sounding the abolitionist's note. It was to the interest of the South as well as the North, he said, that the Africans be permitted to support "the Temple of Freedom."[18]

Phelps' proposed action was most unwelcome. If encouraging slaves to flee their masters would complicate Butler's administration, giving them arms surely would cause infinite trouble, aggravating, however irrationally, the ever-present fear of servile insurrection. Butler decided to try to sidestep the issue. Instead of responding to Phelps' request, he ignored it, with an order sent to Phelps to employ his blacks in felling trees between the flank of his lines and Lake Pontchartrain to open a field of fire for supporting gunboats and in constructing an abatis. Butler was not just dreaming up a job; the work already had been agreed to between Phelps and Butler's chief engineeer as a military necessity.[19] But Butler's ploy did not work. On the evening of the very day the order was sent Phelps fired off a reply. He said, "I am not willing to become the mere slavedriver which you propose. . . ." He tendered resignation of his commission, with a request for leave of absence pending its acceptance.[20]

Instead of exploding at such insubordination, Butler controlled his temper. On August 2 he sent two letters to Phelps, one official, one personal, each patient. The official letter pointed out that under an act of Congress the president alone had the authority to allow arming of blacks. The act had been adopted on July 17; doubtless Butler had just received word of it.[21] The president had given no such authority, said Butler, but he would send Phelps' "application" to the president. (It happened that at cabinet meetings shortly after the congressional act the president had refused to approve arming of blacks that had been undertaken by Maj. Gen. David Hunter at Port Royal, South Carolina.)[22] In the meantime, Butler explained, the arms he had received for recruiting Louisianians had been expressly limited to whites. Thus, wrote Butler, pending the president's action on the "application," Phelps could not make soldiers of the blacks.[23]

Butler's personal letter pointed out the need for the tree cutting and abatis. So to employ the blacks would not be "slave-driving." Army of the Potomac soldiers had done just such work the year before on Arlington Heights. "Are Negroes any better than they?" A leave of absence would not be granted, said Butler; rather, Phelps was to see that orders were complied with.[24] On the same day Butler sent Stanton copies of the correspondence, submitting the whole matter. He told Stanton that the emissaries he had sent to Washington could explain the effect of Phelps' course in Louisiana.[25]

Again Phelps fired off an immediate reply to Butler. He would not submit. He sent his formal resignation to be forwarded to the adjutant general.[26] After a brief wait, Butler wrote Phelps officially that his resignation was being forwarded to the president and demanding to know whether he would have the blacks carry out the work ordered. An unofficial note assured Phelps of Butler's goodwill and suggested a conference.[27] Back came Phelps the next day, August 6, with a long screed. While he would carry out routine duties temporarily, pending action on his resignation, he would not continue his service unless a series of propositions was accepted that he submitted to be sent to the president. These proposals called for abolition of slavery and arming of the blacks.[28]

The president did not approve Phelps' application to arm slaves and by mid-September he had departed. Allowed to resign his commission, he lived out his life as a civilian in Vermont crusading for causes he held dear.[29] Probably nothing gave him greater pride than the recognition he received from the Confederate president in August 1862 as Phelps awaited action on his resignation. Jefferson Davis proclaimed him, along with General Hunter, an outlaw for having armed slaves "for military service against their masters. . . ."[30] That Davis credited him with more than he had succeeded in doing surely did not diminish his pleaseure in having rankled the leader of evil rebellion.

The Phelps controversy had come to a head just as Butler's military operations were at a crisis. The Vicksburg expedition with Farragut had had to be abandoned because Union forces to the north would not give adequate help. By late July Butler's troops, with the navy, were drawing back to Baton Rouge. Weakened by sickness, there they were attacked by Rebel Maj. Gen. John C. Breckinridge on August 5. Though the attack failed, it had been a near success. Had not a breakdown in the machinery of the Rebel ironclad ram *Arkansas* kept her out of the battle, leading to her demise the next day, there might have been a Union defeat for it seems that support by Union gunboats, that would have been vulnerable to the ram, produced the victory.[31]

Butler's intelligence at this time indicated that the Rebels were planning to concentrate on a recovery of New Orleans. Breckinridge's attack probably had been designed as a step in such a move. Butler's own little army, already stretched thin, had been thinned further by the illnesses common in the South at that season. Within a few days after the Baton Rouge battle he would receive letters from both the new general in chief Henry W. Halleck and from his own military governor, one of his emissaries to Washington, saying that for the present reinforcements for him were out of the question.[32] Isolated as he was, his situation surely seemed precarious.

As intelligence mounted that the Rebels contemplated a strike at New Orleans, Butler decided, on August 16, to evacuate Baton Rouge, bringing the men back to the New Orleans defenses. Though his recruiting of local whites had gone well initially, it had slowed as good paying jobs became available in a reviving economy. While by the first of September he would have information that a New Orleans attack had been deferred until the Rebels completed ironclads being built up the river, he had remained eager to add to his strength.[33]

When Butler surveyed his needs after the Baton Rouge battle his mind had turned to a body of free blacks who had been in the Confederate state militia. Of New Orleans' populace, more than ten thousand were free blacks, with about eight thousand more in the rest of the state.[34] Louisiana had become a state on the eve of the War of 1812 and almost immediately had provided for a free black militia. In Andrew Jackson's battling of the British at New Orleans, beginning in late December 1814 and lasting for nearly a month, free blacks had played a commendable part in Jackson's army. While the black militia gradually faded thereafter, and had been formally ended by a militia law of 1834, the black veterans of the War of 1812 always had been honored in Louisiana.[35] With outbreak of the Civil War, free blacks again offered their services to the state and in the spring of 1861 Gov. Thomas O. Moore began their enrollment in the state militia. At a massive Confederate troop review in New Orleans in November 1861, nearly fifteen hundred free black soldiers were prominent in the parade, and, in January 1862, at commemorations of the victory over the British and of the Act of Secession, orders for troop parades made special provision for the participation of the "Regiment of Native Guards," a black militia regiment. However, when the Confederates evacuated New Orleans, the black militiamen had stayed.[36]

Soon after Butler's occupation of the city black militia officers had called on him to ascertain his wishes. He shrugged them off, though he was impressed by their appearance and manner.[37] But now, after the Battle of Baton Rouge with all the demands on his resources and with his continued nervousness about unrest among the slaves, he thought further. On August 12 he wrote his wife, "We have danger here of a negro insurrection. I hardly know whether to wish it or fear it most. I shall arm the 'free Blacks,' I think, for I must have more troops, and I see no way of getting them save by arming the black brigade that the rebels had." It was about then that he received a letter from Secretary of the Treasury Chase, written on July 31, telling him of a growing antislavery feeling, and saying, "It would hardly be too much to ask you to call, like Jackson, colored soldiers to the defence of the Union; but you must judge of this." Two days after his letter to his wife, he wrote Stanton about the indication of attack on New Orleans, saying that if it became imminent "I shall call on Africa to intervene, and I do not think I shall call in vain. I have determined to use the services of the free colored men who were organized by the rebels into the 'Colored Brigade,' of which we have heard so much. They are free; they have been used by our enemies whose mouths are shut, and they will be loyal."[38]

It was at about the time of that letter to Stanton that Butler called together some twenty of the black Confederate militia officers to ask whether they and their men would enlist in the Union army. Their unanimous response was affirmative. So Butler decided to cross the Rubicon.[39] On August 22 he ordered that "free colored citizens" of Louisiana, who had been "recognized" by the Confederate governor "as a portion of the militia of the State" and who would enlist in the United States Volunteer Service, "shall be duly organized . . . subject to the approval of the President of the United States." On August 27 he sent a copy of the order to General-in-Chief Halleck with a covering letter. He explained that prudence had led to his evacuation of Baton Rouge in light of information of a Rebel concentration for a New Orleans attack. He said that since he had been told that

> it was impossible to expect re-enforcements. . . . I have called upon a portion of a brigade of soldiers who were in the Confederate service, and are now ready and desirous of doing loyal service to the Union here.
>
> I have kept clear of the vexed question of arming the slaves. I am fortified by precedents of a half century's standing, acted upon by the Confederate authorities within six months, and I believe I have done nothing of which the most fastidious member of Jefferson Davis' household political can rightfully complain. . . . May I ask the prompt approval of the President of my action in this behalf, as the only drawback to two regiments of these Native Guards (colored) is the fear in their minds that the President will not sustain my action—a story, by the by, which is industriously circulated by the rebels here to prevent the enlistment of these loyal citizens.[40]

In response to Butler's call, one black regiment was quickly assembled, to be formally mustered into the Union army on September 27. A second regiment was mustered in on October 12. Each was composed of ten companies, totaling for each regiment a strength of about one thousand. For the first regiment the field officers were chosen from Butler's white army, but the line officers were blacks; for the second it seems that, while the commanding colonel was a white, at least one of the field officers and all or nearly all the line officers were blacks.[41]

In the meantime the military outlook had changed dramatically. Perhaps due to Breckinridge's defeat at Baton Rouge, the Rebels' cry of "on to New Orleans" had faded; principal Confederate arms were preoccupied elsewhere, far to the north. Within the city and its environs, moreover, Butler's authority finally seemed securely established. In October Butler was able to plan a sustained offensive move on his own. Galvanized into action by Rebel attacks on Union shipping plying the Mississippi above New Orleans, Butler decided to drive into the rich plantation lands west of the city with a force commanded by Godfrey Weitzel, a brilliant young man who as a lieutenant had been Butler's chief engineer and now had been promoted to brigadier general of volunteers.[42] Launched on October 26, the move met with considerable success. Needed were troops to guard and repair the railroad from New Orleans into the western country. Though the black regiments by then had had but minimal training, they were assigned, with some white units, to that task. Weitzel was informed that they would be a part of his command.[43]

Once more there was a clash between Butler and a subordinate general, but this one differed from the clash with Phelps. Weitzel wrote headquarters, declining a command including black troops. On November 6 Butler had Weitzel informed that "these colored regiments of free men, raised by the authority of the President, and approved by him as the Commander-in-Chief of the Army, must be commanded by the officers of the Army of the United States like any other Regiments."[44] In having Weitzel told that the president had approved the black regiments, Butler was stretching things. He never had received the president's "prompt approval" that he had requested in his letter of August 27 to General Halleck. He had received only silence; he was taking silence to mean consent. To buttress that position, Butler wrote Halleck, also on November 6, enclosing copies of the exchange with Weitzel. He said to Halleck that "more than 70 days since" he had reported his organizing of the blacks "subject to the approval of the President," that he had had many communications from the department thereafter but none "approving of that organization," and concluded, "I must therefore take it to be approved, but would prefer distinct orders on this subject." Two weeks later, on November 20, Halleck wrote in reply that the August order, with its transmittal letter, "was submitted to the Secretary of War for his instructions, and he replied that no instructions were necessary, as the whole matter was left to the judgment and discretion of the department commander."[45]

Thus, finally, were Butler's free black regiments approved. But by the time Halleck's word reached Butler at the end of November or early December his days at New Orleans were nearly done. In mid-December Maj. Gen. Nathaniel P. Banks arrived to take over his command.[46] In the meantime Butler had organized a third black regiment, mustered in on November 24. Its commander, too, was a white; the other officers included both whites and blacks.[47] So by the end of Butler's tenure at New Orleans he had threee black regiments; their total strength, officers and men, was 3,122.[48]

Can it be concluded that, as one writer has put it, "Butler had done what he had censured Phelps for earlier"—that he wanted to hog the credit?[49] Not so. In the tense conditions Butler faced in the summer of 1862, with the fear—very real, whether or not well grounded—of slave insurrection, with his hold on the populace only in process of being securely established, with intelligence at hand of an intended Confederate attack, with reinforcements denied him and his small army weakened by summer's ills, it would have been foolhardy to invite to arms the slaves of the very people whose loyalty to the Union Butler was seeking to promote. What he did was very different. The people of Louisiana, and especially of New Orleans, long had honored the memory of the free blacks who had helped defeat the British, and the inclusion of free black soldiers in the great Confederate troop parades of November 1861 and January 1862 had been a sight welcome to Louisianians. Their bearing arms was no blow to slavery.

It is true that there was apparent inconsistency in Butler's course in one particular. On the one hand, his refusal to Phelps was on the asserted ground that the recent statute required the president's authorization for blacks' enlistment, which had not been provided, and that arms and equipment furnished him had been limited to white soldiers. On the other hand, he himself had proceeded without prior presidential authorization. But the inconsistency was only superficial. His invitation to the free blacks was explicitly subject to the president's approval, and as soon as he saw that the blacks were responding he reported to Washington and requested "prompt approval." In light of Louisiana history, including its very recent Confederate history, the difference in his course, remote from Washington as he was and facing an apparent immediate emergency, surely was warranted. That enlistments of free blacks presented an issue of no such delicacy as the arming of slaves was eloquently confirmed by a proclamation issued by Jefferson Davis on December 23. In it, in proclaiming Butler an outlaw and his officers as "criminals deserving death," he recited every conceivable violation, real and imagined, under Butler's command, of "the usages of civilization"—but on the arming of blacks it condemned only the arming of "African slaves . . . for a servile war." Strikingly omitted from Davis' litany of Butler's wrongs was any reference to the arming of free blacks.[50]

It has been said, however, that Butler did enlist slaves extensively. That recruiters may have done some winking is likely. But that would not have been the enrolling of slaves willy-nilly as Phelps would have done. Indeed, on September 12, Butler's superintendent of recruiting especially instructed the recruiters that "no man must be enlisted who has failed to obtain his freedom through some recognized legal channel."[51] Strongest testimony that, nonetheless, slaves were freely enlisted is a passage in Joseph T. Wilson's *The Black Phalanx*. He wrote: "Those who made up this regiment [the First] were not all free negroes by more than half. Any negro who would swear that he was free, if physically good, was accepted, and of the many thousand slave fugitives in the city from distant plantations, hundreds found their way into the Touro building and ultimately into the ranks of the three regiments formed at that building."[52] The Touro building was Butler's recruiting post.

Wilson had been a Massachusetts black sailor. In Chile in May 1862 he heard of the war for the first time. He made his way to New Orleans and enlisted in Butler's Second Regiment on September 30. By that time the First Regiment's ranks had been filled for nearly a month and already the unit had been formally mustered in, and the Second Regiment was well along in organization with its formal mustering coming in less than two weeks. Wilson's book, written from memory, was published more than a quarter century later. It should not be taken as definitive. Significantly, a dispatch of September 19 to the *New York Times* from its correspondent reporting regularly from New Orleans, in telling of his visit to the Touro building and witnessing drill of the recruits, referred to the men as "free colored citizens."[53]

Some light on what happened is given in Butler's own testimony in Washington to the Joint Committee on the Conduct of the War in

February 1863, shortly after his return from New Orleans. He insisted that "it was a general order that no slave should be enlisted." But, he explained, there were two classes of blacks not free before the war who had become free and so subject to this enlistment. They were slaves of masters claiming British or French citizenship and slaves of rebel masters in territory invaded by his army after September 1862.[54] Butler's determination of their freedom resulted from his application of the Second Confiscation Act, which had been adopted on July 17, 1862. One section of that act freed slaves of masters who thereafter actively aided the rebellion if such slaves came into the hands of Union forces. Another section provided for the confiscation of the property of rebels who did not return to their allegiance to the United States within sixty days after a presidential proclamation of warning. The proclamation had been duly issued on July 25, so the sixty-day period expired on September 23.[55]

On September 13, as the critical date approached, Butler announced that, since "it may become necessary to distinguish the Disloyal from the loyal citizens and honest foreigners," every alien would be required to register proof of his nationality, and on September 25 there was published a further order, giving citizens a few days' grace, that required all citizens not taking a loyalty oath by October 1 to file a list of all their property.[56]

A substantial number of the populace registered themselves as British or French citizens. In the meantime Butler had ascertained that the laws of both Great Britain and France forbade slavery. So, without questioning the good faith of those who had registered as citizens of those nations, he treated as free, and so subject to this recruitment as Union soldiers, all slaves of those who claimed such citizenship. He testified to the Joint Committee that he had "enlisted one regiment and part of another from men in that condition."[57]

As to the second class of slaves whom he treated as free, he told the Joint Committee of General Weitzel's expedition into the territory west of New Orleans, which began in late October, that brought thousands of slaves of rebels "under our control." The congressional act, he testified, meant that thereby those slaves became free. From that class, he said, there were "enlisted a third regiment and two batteries of heavy artillery. . . ."[58]

It is obvious that Butler's testimony quite overstated the number of aliens' slaves in his regiments, for as early as September 19 some seventeen hundred black recruits already had been assembled in the Touro building[59]—a number well on the way toward completing two regiments—and that was only a few days after Butler's requirement of alien registration had been announced. The exact facts probably never will be known. The scholar who has focused most sharply has concluded that "It seems that the Second and Third Regiments were composed largely of freedmen whereas the First Regiment had a large percentage of free Negroes."[60] But one thing is clear. Butler proceeded in a way very different from the course Phelps had demanded. His course was consistent with the rights of those who were loyal to the Union, and he moved step by step as his control became more assured instead of plunging headlong, as Phelps would have done, at a time when his military position was at a crisis.

If, in the summer of 1862, Butler had let Phelps have his way, it is most unlikely that by December there could have been an election for two members of the United States House of Representatives—as in fact there was—in the area under Butler's control, and that the Emancipation Proclamation, issued on January 1, 1863, could have excluded that area from its scope on the theory that it had returned to Union allegiance.[61] That that could occur in an area then so deep in Rebeldom, so distant from main Union lines, is one of the remarkable facts of Our War. Butler was carrying out precisely the president's own policy. At the very time the Phelps controversy was coming to a head the president was saying that the people of Louisiana were asked to do no more than to "take their place in the Union upon the old terms."[62] Those terms would not have countenanced Phelps' arming of slaves.

A sad footnote is to be appended. Butler's August order for the enlistment of free blacks provided that they would be "paid . . . and rationed as are other volunteer troops of the United States. . . ." That monthly pay for a private was $13, plus a $3.50 clothing allowance. But the July legislation authorizing the president to take black troops had provided that a black soldier would be paid only $10 a month of which $3 could be in clothing.[63] None of Butler's black soldiers received a penny until May 1863. Then they were paid only $6.50 a month for their past service and but $7 a month thereafter.[64] The event was to make bitterly ironical the recruiting advertisements in the New Orleans press addressed to "Colored Men," promising a bounty of $100 or 160 acres of land, $38 to be paid in advance, and monthly pay of $13 to $22, the terms enjoyed by white recruits.[65]

Notes

1. *Private and Official Correspondence of Gen. Benjamin F. Butler During the Period of the Civil War*, 5 vols. (The Plimpton Press, Norwood, Mass., 1917), 2:270–71 (hereafter cited as *Butler Correspondence*).

2. Dudley Taylor Cornish, *The Sable Arm: Negro Troops in the Union Army, 1861–1865* (1956; rpt. W. W. Norton & Co., New York, 1966), p. 66.

3. U.S. War Dept., *The War of the Rebellion: A Compilation of the Official Records of the Union and Confederate Armies*, 70 vols. in 128 pts. (1880–1901; rpt. National Historical Society, Gettysburg, l972), ser. 1, 6:506, 717–20 (hereafter cited as *ORA*, with references to ser. 1, except where otherwise indicated). Joint Committee on the Conduct of the War, *Report of JCCW*, H. of Rep., 37th Cong., 3d Sess. (l863), 3:353, 357 (hereafter cited as *JCCW*); Jefferson Davis Bragg, *Louisiana in the Confederacy* (Louisiana State Univ. Press, Baton Rouge, 1941), p. 34.

4. *ORA*, 6:694–95; Rowena Reed, *Combined Operations in the Civil War* (Naval Institute Press, Annapolis, 1978), pp. 57–63.

5. Notable on Butler's New Orleans regime are Howard Palmer Johnson, "New Orleans under General Butler," *Louisiana Historical Quarterly* 24 (1941):434–536; Thomas Ewing Dabney, "The Butler Regime in Louisiana," *Louisiana Historical Quarterly* 27 (1944):487–536. Notable, too, are treatments in Robert S. Holzman, *Stormy Ben Butler* (Macmillan, New York, 1954); Hans L. Trefousse, *Ben Butler: The South Called Him BEAST!* (Twayne Publishers, New York, 1957); Richard S. West, *Lincoln's Scapegoat General* (Houghton Mifflin, Boston, 1965). Also important, despite apparent pro-Butler bias, is James Parton, *General Butler in New Orleans: Being a History of the Administration of the Department of the Gulf in the Year 1862: With an Account of the Capture of New Orleans, and a Sketch of the Previous Career of the General, Civil and Military* (Mason Brothers, New York, 1864). Parton's book was written in 1863 immediately after Butler's return from New Orleans, with extensive access to his papers. Nor to be ignored, though written long afterward, is Benjamin F. Butler's *Autobiography and Personal Reminiscences of Major-General Benj. F. Butler: Butler's Book* (A. M. Thayer, Boston, 1892), hereafter cited as *Butler's Book*.

6. *ORA*, 15:493–521; *Butler Correspondence*, 2:66. For a document appearing both in *ORA* and in *Butler Correspondence*, I will usually cite *ORA*.

7. *JCCW*, pp. 356–57; Reed, *Combined Operations*, pp. 195–203.

8. Parton, *General Butler*, pp. 298–99; *JCCW*, pp. 354, 356–57; New Orleans *Daily Delta*, Aug. 7, 1862.

9. *ORA*, 15:439–42; William F. Messner, "The Federal Army and Blacks in the Gulf Department 1862–1865" (Ph.D. diss., Univ. of Wisconsin, 1972), pp. 6–18; Parton, *General Butler*, pp. 491–93.

10. Murray M. Horowitz, "Ben Butler and the Negro: 'Miracles are Occurring,'" *Louisiana History* 17 (1976):159, 165–67; Parton, *General Butler*, p. 491; John G. Nicolay and John Hay, *Abraham Lincoln: A History*, 10 vols. (Century Co., New York, 1909), 4:387–89.

11. *ORA*, 15:439–42; ser. 3, 1:937–38.

12. Ezra J. Warner, *Generals in Blue: Lives of the Union Commanders* (Louisiana State Univ. Press, Baton Rouge, 1964), pp. 368–69; Messner, "The Federal Army

and Blacks," pp. 25–28; John W. DeForest, *A Volunteer's Adventures: A Union Captain's Record of the Civil War*, ed. by James H. Croushore (Yale Univ. Press, New Haven, 1946), pp. 28–29.

13. *ORA*, 6:465; ser. 3, 1:637; Parton, *General Butler*, pp. 197–201. The Union navy in the area refused to have Phelps' proclamation taken from Ship Island for circulation on the mainland. *Official Records of the Union and Confederate Navies in the War of the Rebellion*, 27 vols. (Washington, 1894–1927), ser. 1, 17:17–20.

14. *ORA*, 15:446–47, 464, 485–90. For the course of Butler's controversy with Phelps regarding harboring of fugitives, see C. Peter Ripley, *Slaves and Freedmen in Civil War Louisiana* (Louisiana State Univ. Press, Baton Rouge, 1976), pp. 26–33; Peyton McCrary, *Abraham Lincoln and Reconstruction: The Louisiana Experiment* (Princeton Univ. Press, Princeton, 1978), pp. 82–84.

15. *Butler Correspondence*, 2:41–42.

16. *Butler Correspondence*, 2:109, 115–17. By midsummer slave unrest and flight were mounting. John W. Blassingame, *Black New Orleans, 1860–1880* (Univ. of Chicago Press, Chicago, 1973), pp. 26–30.

17. *ORA*, 15:532–33; *Butler Correspondence*, 2:109, 123; Ripley, *Slaves and Freedmen*, pp. 33–34.

18. *ORA*, 15:534–35.

19. *Butler Correspondence*, 2:126; *ORA*, 15:534, 536–37.

20. *ORA*, 15:535.

21. 12 *U.S. Stat.* 599.

22. David Donald, ed., *Inside Lincoln's Cabinet: The Civil War Diaries of Salmon P. Chase* (Longmans, Green & Co., New York, 1954), pp. 95–100.

23. *ORA*, 15:536.

24. *ORA*, 15:536–37.

25. *ORA*, 15:534.

26. *Butler Correspondence*, 2:145–47.

27. *ORA*, 15:542–43; *Butler Correspondence*, 2:155.

28. *Butler Correspondence*, 2:155–57.

29. *Butler Correspondence*, 2:207, 286–87; Warner, *Generals in Blue*, pp. 368–69. On General Halleck's recommendation, Stanton approved Phelps' resignation on Aug. 21. Endorsements on Butler to Stanton of Aug. 2, 1862, Records of Hdqrs. of Army, Letters Rec'd (1862), B 1646, RG 108, Nat. Arch. There is an inaccuracy in Ira Berlin et al., eds., *Freedom: A Documentary History of Emancipation, 1861–1867*, ser. 2, *The Black Military Experience* (Cambridge Univ. Press, New York, 1982), pp. 43, 44, where it is stated that the War Department "took no immediate action, and Phelps' resignation stood" and that Butler "had drummed the abolitionist out of the service." Halleck and Stanton acted very promptly on receipt of Phelps' resignation. And Butler had urged Phelps, for whom he had high regard, to stay in the service.

30. *ORA*, 14:599.

31. *Butler Correspondence*, 2:124; *ORA*, 15:39–40, 76–81; Fletcher Pratt, *Civil War on Western Waters* (Henry Holt and Co., New York, 1956), pp. 119–20; Shelby Foote, *The Civil War, A Narrative*, 3 vols., (Random House, New York, 1958–74), 1: 578–81; Reed, *Combined Operations*, pp. 202–3, 209–21.

32. *ORA*, 15:544, 548–49, 552–53; *Butler Correspondence*, 2: 147–48; Butler testimony of May 1, 1863, Testimony Taken by the American Freedmen's Inquiry

Commission, 1863–64, File 5, Letters Rec'd by the Office of the Adj. Gen. 1861–1870, Nat. Arch., RG 94, M 619, Roll 200, Frame 0490.

33. *ORA*, 15:548–49, 552–53, 559 (date of this Butler letter to Stanton was illegible as received; *Butler Correspondence*, 2: 243–44, shows date as Sept. 1), 564; *Butler Correspondence*, 2: 278–79; *JCCW*, p. 357; Mary F. Berry, "The History of the 73d and 75th United States Colored Infantry Regiments" (M.A. thesis, Howard Univ., 1962), p. 18.

34. Bragg, *Louisiana in the Confederacy*, p. 36.

35. Roland C. McConnell, *Negro Troops of Antebellum Louisiana: A History of the Battalion of Free Men of Color* (Louisiana State Univ. Press, Baton Rouge, 1968), pp. 50–54, 66–90, 97–104, 108–15.

36. Donald E. Everett, "Ben Butler and the Louisiana Native Guards, 1861–1862," *Journal of Southern History* 24 (1958):202–4; Mary F. Berry, "Negro Troops in Blue and Gray: The Louisiana Native Guards, 1861–1863," *Louisiana History* 8 (1967):166–70; Blassingame, *Black New Orleans*, p. 34; Horace Greeley, *The American Conflict: A History of the Great Rebellion in the United States of America, 1860–'65*, 2 vols. (O. D. Case & Co., Hartford, 1866), 2:522; War Department Collection of Confederate States Records, Records of the Louisiana State Gov't, Records of the First Division and of Volunteer Reg'ts, 1861–1863, Entry 69, Gen. Orders, 1st Div., La. State Troops, 1861–1862, v. 149, Hdqrs. 1st Div. La. Volunteers, General Order No. 1, Jan. 3, 1862 (celebration Battle of New Orleans), General Order No. 5, Jan. 21, 1862 (celebration Act of Secession), Nat. Arch., RG 109, M 359, Roll 24. It has been said that by early 1862 there were some 3,000 blacks in the Louisiana state militia. See, for example, John D. Winters, *The Civil War in Louisiana* (Louisiana State Univ. Press, Baton Rouge, 1963), p. 34. Apparently such statements are based on Joseph T. Wilson, *The Black Phalanx* (1890; rpt. Arno Press, New York, 1968), p. 482. The figure seems high for the number of available free blacks. Wilson's authority is questionable, as we will note below. Andrew B. Booth, comp. *Records of Louisiana Confederate Soldiers and Louisiana Confederate Commands*, 3 vols. in 4 pts. (New Orleans, 1920), 1:12, lists only one regiment of the Louisiana Native Guards. In testifying to the American Freedmen's Inquiry Commission Butler referred only to one black Confederate militia regiment, Nat. Arch., M 619, Roll 200, Frames 0491–92.

37. *ORA*, 15:439–42.

38. *Butler Correspondence*, 2:131–35, 185–86; *ORA*, 15:548–49.

39. *Butler's Book*, pp. 492–93, tells of this meeting, saying it was about a month prior to the mustering in of the first of his black regiments, but erroneously dates the mustering in as August 22; in fact it was, as we shall see, September 27. August 22 was the date of Butler's order providing for the enlistment of the blacks. On August 16 Butler ordered the evacuation of Baton Rouge because of "the evident preparations to attack the City of New Orleans," and so reported to Stanton, *ORA*, 15:552–53. That the meeting occurred at about that time is indicated by Butler's testimony to the American Freedmen's Inquiry Commission that he had the meeting after writing Stanton that he would "call on Africa," Nat. Arch., M 619, Roll 200, Frames 0490–92. As we have noted, he had so written on August 14.

40. *ORA*, 15:555–57.

41. Compiled Records Showing Service of Military Units—U.S. Colored Troops, Nat. Arch., RG 94, Office of the Adj. Gen., M 594, Roll 213, Field and Staff Muster Rolls for 73d Infantry Regiment and 74th Infantry Regiment; Regimental

Papers, 73d U.S. Colored Infantry and 74th U.S. Colored Infantry, Nat. Arch., RG 94, Office of the Adj. Gen., Box 44, List of Officers, 73d Reg., Sept. 26, 1862, and List of Officers, 74th Reg., Oct. 1862. (Butler's First and Second Regiments Louisiana Native Guards, were redesignated, some time later, as the 73d and 74th U. S. Colored Infantry Regiments.) Everett, "Ben Butler and the Louisiana Native Guards," 210; Berry, "Negro Troops in Blue and Gray," 174–75. Butler testified to the American Freedmen's Inquiry Commission that one of the field officers of the second regiment was a black of exceptional talent, Nat. Arch., M 619, Roll 200, Frame 0493.

42. *ORA*, 15:158–60; Warner, *Generals in Blue*, pp. 548–49.

43. *ORA*, 15:161–63; Regimental Papers, 73d U.S. Colored Infantry, Nat. Arch., RG 94, Office of the Adj. Gen., Box 44, Col. S. H. Stafford to Maj. Gen. N. P. Banks, Jan. 3, 1863; Compiled Records Showing Service of Military Units—U.S. Colored Troops, Nat. Arch., RG 94, Office of the Adj. Gen., M 594, Roll 213, Field and Staff Muster Roll for 74th Infantry Regiment for Oct. 12 to Dec. 31, 1862; Berry, "Negro Troops in Blue and Gray," 176–78.

44. *ORA*, 15:164–66, 171–72. Parton, *General Butler*, p. 521, and Wilson, *Black Phalanx*, p. 199, say that Butler left the blacks under a separate command. The end of December departmental organization shows the black regiments among the "Independent Commands," *ORA*, 15:627–28. Eventually, a major general, Weitzel would command the only all-black army corps in American military history, Cornish, *Sable Arm*, p. 281.

45. *ORA*, 15:162, 601. In Herman Hattaway and Archer Jones, *How the North Won: A Military History of the Civil War* (Univ. of Illinois Press, Urbana, 1983), pp. 270–71, it is erroneously stated that the secretary of war, with the president's approval, on August 25, 1862, authorized Butler to receive and train "Negro soldiers up to 5,000 in number." The August 25 authorization was to Brig. Gen. Rufus Saxton in South Carolina; it had nothing whatever to do with Butler, *ORA*, 14:377–78. Indeed, as we have seen, Butler's request to Halleck for approval of his enlistment of blacks was not even written until August 27.

46. *ORA*, 15:610–11.

47. Regimental Papers, 75th U.S. Colored Infantry, Nat. Arch., RG 94, Office of the Adj. Gen., Box 45, Mustering Officer Return for the Third Regiment of Louisiana Native Guards (Free Colored) for Nov. 26, 1862. (The Third Regiment, Louisiana Native Guards, was redesignated, some time later, as the 75th U.S. Colored Infantry Regiment.) Berry, "Negro Troops in Blue and Gray," pp. 174, 175. Butler testified to the American Freedmen's Inquiry Commission that officers of the Third Regiment were appointed on the basis of merit without regard to race, Nat. Arch., M 619, Roll 200, Frame 0494.

48. Elon A. Woodward, *The Negro in the Military Service of the United States, 1639–1886: A Compilation* (1888), Office of the Adj. Gen., Nat. Arch., RG 94, M 858, Roll 1, p. 1010.

49. Horowitz, "Ben Butler and the Negro," p. 179.

50. James D. Richardson, comp., *A Compilation of the Messages and Papers of the Confederacy, Including the Diplomatic Correspondence, 1861–1865*, 2 vols. (United States Publishing Co., Nashville, 1905), 1:269–74.

51. *Butler Correspondence*, 2:270–71; *Daily Delta*, Sept. 14, 1862, and following days.

52. Wilson, *Black Phalanx*, p. 195.

53. Preface to *Black Phalanx*, and Sara D. Jackson, Foreword to 1968 reprint; *New York Times*, Sept. 29, 1862.

54. *JCCW*, pp. 357–58.

55. 12 *U.S. Stat.* 589–92; James D. Richardson, comp., *A Compilation of the Messages and Papers of the Presidents, 1789–1897*, 10 vols. (Published by the Authority of Congress, Washington, 1896–99), 6:93.

56. *Daily Delta*, Sept. 14, 1862 (General Order No. 71), Sept. 25, 1862 (General Order No. 76); *JCCW*, p. 360.

57. *JCCW*, pp. 357–58.

58. *JCCW*, pp. 358–59. On Sept. 24, in writing Secretary Chase about a conference he had just held with Butler, the Treasury agent in New Orleans reported that Butler was treating as free, and so eligible for enlistment, all blacks "who come in from the enemy's lines," *Butler Correspondence*, 2:328–29. This seems to refer to Butler's proposed application of the Confiscation Act after Sept. 23, the date of expiration of the sixty-day period after the presidential proclamation of warning; probably it was not until Weitzel's expedition that significant numbers of slaves began falling into that category.

59. *New York Times*, Sept. 29, 1862.

60. Berry, "Negro Troops in Blue and Gray," 175–76. See also Roland C. McConnell, "Louisiana's Black Military History 1729–1865," in Robert R. Macdonald, et al., eds., *Louisiana's Black Heritage* (Louisiana State Museum, New Orleans, 1979), pp. 48–49.

61. McCrary, *Abraham Lincoln and Reconstruction*, pp. 94–109; John R. Ficklen, *History of Reconstruction in Louisiana (Through 1868)* (1910; rpt. Peter Smith, Gloucester, 1966), pp. 40–42; Parton, *General Butler*, p. 595; *Butler's Book*, p. 523; Richardson, *Messages and Papers of the Presidents*, 6:157–59.

62. *ORA*, 53:528–29. A copy of the president's statement was sent Butler by Secretary Chase with Chase's letter of July 31, *Butler Correspondence*, 2:131–36.

63. 12 *U.S. Stat.* 599.

64. So it is recorded for the Second Regiment. Compiled Records Showing Service of Military Units—U.S. Colored Troops, Nat. Arch., RG 94, Office of the Adj. Gen., M 594, Roll 213, Field and Staff Muster Roll, Oct. 12 to Dec. 31, 1862, and the several Company Muster Rolls for periods from Oct. 1862 onward for the 74th Infantry Regiment. The comparable records for the First and Third Regiments seem to contain no such pay information, but their pay experience must have been the same as that of the Second. The long delay by Congress in correcting the inequity in black troops' pay is recounted in Cornish, *Sable Arm*, pp. 184–95. It is not clear whether the pay of the regiments' black officers was similarly curtailed; in 1864 the attorney general opined that the July 1862 limitation applied only to "the humbler kinds of service," not to black officers, Case of Rev. Samuel Harrison, 11 *Ops. Atty. Gen.* 37.

65. *Daily Delta*, Aug. 30, 1862, and following days. There was irony, too, in the name given by one of the recruiters to the unit he advertised, "Phelps Guards," *Daily Delta*, Sept. 6, 1862, and following days.

4

Generals
David Hunter
and Rufus Saxton
and Black Soldiers

"HUNTER was not suited to the work and . . . Rufus Saxton was."

That, says Dudley Cornish in his superb *Sable Arm*, probably was the "conviction" of Secretary of War Edwin M. Stanton that caused him to refuse to recognize a regiment of blacks recruited by Maj. Gen. David Hunter on South Carolina's coastal islands in the summer of 1862, but at the same time to authorize Brig. Gen. Rufus Saxton to enlist blacks of that region into the army. Cornish finds Stanton's action "hard to understand."[1] Understanding is increased by a close look at what was happening on the Sea Islands. It was a time when the president was tiptoeing toward a change in the nation's traditional policy that only whites would be allowed to be soldiers. Hunter did not smooth the way; Saxton did.

At the end of March 1862, Hunter had arrived at Hilton Head to take command of a newly designated Department of the South, defined to include the states of South Carolina, Georgia, and Florida.[2] The department resulted from a navy-army expedition, commanded by Commodore Samuel F. DuPont and Brig. Gen. Thomas W. Sherman, that in early November 1861 had captured Port Royal about midway between Charleston and Savannah. By the time of Hunter's coming, DuPont and Sherman had occupied the strip of coastal islands from twenty or so miles short of Charleston to the vicinity of Savannah, and

Originally published in *South Carolina Historical Magazine* 86, no. 3 (July 1985):165–81. Reprinted by permission of *South Carolina Historical Magazine*.

some coastal points beyond in Georgia and northeast Florida. All along
the Union had held Key West and soon after Hunter's arrival other
Union forces took Apalachicola and then Pensacola on the Florida
panhandle. The troops in Hunter's department never would number
more than about eighteen thousand. Probably no general's command
throughout the war was spread so thin over an area so wide.[3]

The Union's position seemed to offer opportunity to attack Savannah
or Charleston or both, each an important Confederate port. Even
before his relief by Hunter, Sherman had forces poised for an assault
on Fort Pulaski, which guarded Savannah's outlet to the sea. Within
days after Hunter took over, that assault was made with complete
success. But a greater force would be required for capture of either
port. The Union high command's priorities were elsewhere: Virginia,
West Tennessee, and an imminent move on New Orleans. The Port
Royal expedition had been designed initially only to secure anchorages
for the Union's blockading fleet. That purpose had been more than
fully achieved.[4]

General Hunter, however, was hungry for further conquest. While
en route to supersede Sherman, he had written Secretary of War
Stanton that if he were reinforced by only one division he could almost
guarantee that he would have the Stars and Stripes waving over Fort
Sumter by the anniversary of its surrender to the Rebels.[5] One of the
first things that impressed him, on his arrival, was the presence within
his lines of a reservoir of loyal manpower that would need only arms
and training to augment his army were he able to draw upon it. That
reservoir was many hundreds of blacks, lately slaves on the Carolina
Sea Island plantations.

When General Sherman's army had landed, nearly all the whites for
many miles on either side of Port Royal had fled, but their slaves had
stayed. It is said that only one white man had remained in Beaufort, the
"metropolis" of the area. The blacks were nearly as many as Sherman's
invading troops. The problem of care and governing of a large slave
population was then quite without precedent for a Union army, and
for some weeks the blacks seemed to Sherman a baffling burden. But
he and his quartermaster, Rufus Saxton, then a captain, bent to the
task. In time, Sherman made imaginative provision for the blacks'
employment on the plantations and their education.[6] Moreover, help
came from the Treasury Department, which was given responsibility
for abandoned properties. In early March a Treasury agent of excep-

tional vision, Edward Pierce, brought a band of fifty-three people, including a dozen ladies, supported by private associations in the North, to take on plantation management and the teaching of the blacks, adult and children. They are known to history as Gideon's Band, their program as the Port Royal Experiment.[7]

When Hunter arrived he found that program well begun, with busy communities loyal to the Union. It was in their menfolk that he saw potential Union soldiers. More than that, he envisioned attracting thousands more blacks, escaping masters beyond the Union lines. On April 3, only the fourth day after his arrival, he wrote Secretary of War Stanton asking for fifty thousand muskets "with authority to arm such loyal men as I can find in the country, whenever, in my opinion, they can be used advantageously against the enemy." To distinguish such men he asked for fifty thousand pairs of scarlet pantaloons.[8]

Immediately thereafter, on consultation with a dynamic black preacher, Abram Murchison, Hunter arranged for a meeting of black men on Hilton Head to get names of those willing to "take up arms in defense of the Government and of themselves." The meeting, on April 7, was conducted by Murchison and two whites, one a plantation superintendent. Response, at first, was favorable. Hunter soon had a list of 150 willing blacks not too old for military service. While evidence is fragmentary, it appears that the early response encouraged Hunter to continue such solicitation into early May.[9] Though he had no reply to his April 3 request to Stanton—indeed, there never would be a reply—the *New York Times* reported on May 1, in a dispatch from its correspondent at Port Royal, that the War Department's original instructions to General Sherman had conferred "fullest power" to employ blacks "even in arms" and that it seemed that Hunter would exercise that power.

While the instructions to Sherman did continue to apply to Hunter, the *Times* man overstated them. Issued in October 1861, just before embarkation of the Port Royal expedition, they provided that Sherman could avail himself of the services of anyone willing, "whether fugitives from labor or not," either as "ordinary employees, or, if special circumstances seem to require it, in any other capacity, with such organization (in squads, companies, or otherwise) as you may deem most beneficial to the service; this, however, not being a general arming of them for miltary service." The phrase after the semicolon had been inserted by the president himself when the draft was submitted for his approval.

Thereafter the War Department had construed the instructions to mean that blacks could be armed "in cases of great emergency" but "not under regular enrollment for military purposes."[10]

Thus it was clear, in the spring of 1862, that the Union high command had allowed no departure from the policy prevailing after the War of 1812 that the black man, free or slave, could not become a United States soldier. There always had been black sailors; already during the Civil War even fugitive slaves had been taken into the navy. But the army was a different matter. Hunter, as the army's fourth-ranking major general, knew that full well.[11]

Still, Hunter was authorized to arm his blacks "in cases of great emergency" otherwise than "under regular enrollment." There were obvious possibilities of "great emergency." On April 22 Hunter wrote Stanton that the enemy had sixty-five thousand troops at Charleston, Savannah, and Augusta who could be quickly combined against him. Were he not reinforced, he warned, he might have to draw his troops back into very limited enclaves.[12] That, of course, could expose to the Rebels some of the plantations. Then on May 3 came an occurrence that could lead to another kind of "emergency." On that day the barge of the Confederate commander at Charleston was delivered by its slave crewmen to Union blockaders. The crewmen gave information regarding the Charleston defenses that prompted one of Hunter's chief subordinates, Brig. Gen. Henry W. Benham, to propose a Charleston attack. Benham was told to perfect a plan.[13] Any such move would require concentration of Hunter's forces on approaches to Charleston, drawing from the screen protecting the rest of his domain. That would create an "emergency" indeed.

As Benham began his planning Hunter did some thinking on his own. His campaign to list names of blacks willing to "take up arms" had not gone well after the initial response. Though Treasury agent Pierce was cooperative, most of the blacks were so enjoying their new found freedom as employees instead of slaves that they were averse to the restriction and danger of military life; on one island but a single man had agreed to be listed.[14] Hunter decided—evidently without consulting anyone, even his own generals—to intensify this effort and not only to step up his listing campaign but to begin actual organization. As late as May 7 he was still simply having names solicited. But by the next day he had decided "to enlist two regiments to be officered from the most intelligent and energetic of our non-commissioned officers" and had actually named the men from an engineer regiment to be captain and lieutenants of Company A of the first regiment. On the following day, May 9, he issued an order to be transmitted to subordinate commanders in the area "to send immediately to these headquarters, under a guard, all the able-bodied negroes capable of bearing arms."[15]

On the same May 9 Hunter issued another order proclaiming the emancipation of all slaves in South Carolina, Georgia, and Florida, whether or not within Union lines.[16] Back in the summer of 1861 Maj. Gen. John C. Fremont had proclaimed emancipation of the slaves of all enemies of the Union in his command in Missouri. The president had set aside that decree.[17] Nonetheless, Hunter now went Fremont one better. His decree covered slaves not only of enemies but also of masters who might be loyal. There is no evidence of what Hunter deemed his authority to emancipate; he did not even report his action to the War Department.[18] It was, however, reported in the Northern press, and on May 19 the president issued a proclamation announcing that if there had been such a decree it was voided, that whether the Executive's war powers included the power to emancipate and whether it should be exercised "are questions which under my responsibility I reserve to myself." At that time, indeed, heated debated in Congress on a variety of proposals showed that the issue of emancipation, however limited, was explosive, especially among representatives of border slave states.[19]

The coincidence of Hunter's emancipation decree and his order to round up able-bodied blacks suggests that he hoped by the decree to win the confidence of the blacks and so facilitate organization of his proposed regiments. If so, he miscalculated.

Implementing instructions for the roundup reached Treasury agent Pierce and the plantation superintendents late on Sunday, May 11. That night squads of soldiers were deployed to carry out the roundup the first thing the next morning. Pierce was appalled. Hunter's order read as though all able-bodied men were to be conscripted into the military. That would play havoc with work on the plantations. Moreover, Southern masters long had spread the rumor that blacks falling into Yankee hands would be sent off to be sold in Cuba. An abrupt roundup by squads of soldiers would create panic. By the morning of May 12 Pierce was at Hunter's headquarters to follow up a strongly protesting letter he had written the night before. Hunter assured him that only willing men would be enlisted and that plantation foremen and plowmen would not be included in the roundup. But he would not accede to Pierce's plea to defer the roundup.

The scenes on the plantations that morning were fully as sad as Pierce feared. The superintendents, though as appalled as Pierce, loyally cooperated with the military and sought to avert panic. But panic there was. In some places the men fled to the woods, with soldiers trying to hunt them down. Women wailed. And men between the ages of eighteen and forty-five who could be found were marched off under guard. Five or six hundred were brought to Hunter's head-quarters. The next day, May 13, Pierce dispatched to Secretary of the Treasury Salmon P. Chase a full report, with documentation, angrily protesting. One of the supporting documents was a letter to Pierce from a plantation superintendent saying, "Never, in my judgment, did major-general fall into a sadder blunder and rarely has humanity been outraged by an act of more unfeeling barbarity." On May 21 Chase forwarded to Stanton the Pierce report with its documentation in order to give Stanton "a correct view of the state of things." Hunter himself made no report, so just what he was up to was not clear in Washington.[20]

True to his word to Pierce, Hunter confined his "recruitment" to the men who professed to be willing and soon, of those who had been marched off, some drifted back home. But Hunter was persuasive and many remained; organization of a regiment began. Hunter assigned as its colonel one of his own staff officers, his nephew by marriage. The other officers were designated from noncommissioned ones of his army. Recruiting effort continued after the roundup but response was limited. Hunter's original plan to have two regiments was soon abandoned. The one regiment, even weeks later, seems never to have been of more than one thousand and may not have exceeded eight hundred. The strong-arm roundup left a bad impression with the black community that lingered for many months.[21]

Hunter, in any case, had much more than black recruiting to demand attention. At sunrise on May 13, the day after the roundup, the dispatch boat of the Confederate commander at Charleston was delivered to Union blockaders by her slave crewmen, led by a remarkable young black, Robert Smalls. Even more than the crewmen of the Confederate commander's barge who had escaped ten days earlier, Smalls was thoroughly familiar with the Charleston defenses, notably a recent deployment that seemed to leave a wide opening for Union attack. That night Smalls was brought to Port Royal to tell his story to Commodore DuPont. His information was passed on to General Benham for use in his planning of a Charleston attack; on May 17 Benham submitted his final plan.[22]

Hunter soon began preparatory moves toward Charleston. The moves, however, took time. Extensive reconnoitering was necessary, and concentration and advance of Hunter's forces were slow because of inadequate transport on shallow coastal waters and marshy land. Also, eventually, troops had to be brought up from Key West for some protection of uncovered plantations. It was a full month from the time Benham submitted his plan before the moves came to climax. Benham, in field command, at length was in sight of Charleston's spires. Hunter ordered that he establish a secure position for a later attack on the city. In an effort to do so Benham, on June 16, assaulted Confederate works in what became the Battle of Secessionville. The attack was a dismal failure. That ended the moves, though some advanced positions were maintained.[23]

The black regiment had not been even remotely involved in Benham's venture. Benham had wanted it sent to him.[24] But there is no evidence that Hunter had permitted it to leave Hilton Head, its place of encampment. By June Hunter's nephew had been succeeded as its colonel by the son of Maine's powerful Sen. William P. Fessenden. Red pantaloons had come for the blacks' uniforms and they were armed and drilled diligently. But otherwise, apparently, their only employment was on work parties, notably in loading and unloading vessels.[25]

To this point Hunter might have sought to justify his black "soldiers" by stretching somewhat the instructions to General Sherman, now applicable to Hunter, regarding employment of blacks. The instructions allowed organization of blacks "in squads, companies, or otherwise" and, in "special circumstances," their employment not only as "ordinary employees" but otherwise, and, as we have seen, the War Department had construed the instructions to permit arming of the blacks in "great emergency" short of "regular enrollment." It might have been argued that, with all that confronted his white army and with "emergency" threatened, Hunter was authorized to organize and train in the use of arms able black men while employing them in work parties. Whether that indeed was Hunter's rationalization at the time is unknown. He still had not reported his action to Washington. But in late June he was required to report. As we shall see in a moment, that report put him in an untenable position.

It is possible, indeed probable, that Hunter himself never would have had to tender an explanation had not chances of war delayed the implementing of a decision that Secretary of War Stanton made in late April. That was a decision to send back to Port Royal Rufus Saxton, who had been General Sherman's quartermaster, to take charge of the blacks in Hunter's department.

On Hunter's arrival at the end of March, General Sherman and Captain Saxton had returned to Washington for reassignment. Within days each was called to testify on the Port Royal situation by the Joint Committee on the Conduct of the War, a Senate and House joint committee just then exceedingly active and especially intimate with Stanton.[26] As quartermaster, Saxton had been closely involved with the Port Royal blacks. The committee was interested in his appraisal of them; he strongly emphasized their effective cooperation in the work there and his confidence in them.[27] The president already had directed that Saxton be vaulted to the rank of brigadier general, and on April 29, shortly after his testimony to the committee, he had an order from Stanton to return to Port Royal to assume responsibility for the blacks in the department, subject only to Hunter's general authority.[28] Saxton likewise had a conference with Secretary of the Treasury Chase, whose concerns, of course, also were involved. It seems that there had been discussion of Hunter's April 3 request for fifty thousand muskets and scarlet pantaloons and for authority to arm "loyal men" for use "against the enemy," because Chase's diary noted that Saxton told him that Stanton had authorized procurement of "one or two thousand red flannel suits for the blacks, with a view to organization," but no muskets.[29] Thus Hunter's April 3 proposal to add black soldiers to his army had met with no favor in Washington.

Saxton at once busied himself in assembling a staff and preparing to leave. On May 15 he sailed from New York.[30] Word of his mission already had reached Port Royal. When Treasury agent Pierce had his meeting with Hunter on May 12 to protest the roundup, Hunter had recognized that on Saxton's arrival the question of going ahead with the black regiment would be for Saxton to decide.[31] But Saxton did not get there as planned. His ship was wrecked.[32] Then as he prepared to start anew another delay intervened. Stonewall Jackson was threatening Harpers Ferry. Stanton and the president rushed Saxton to command that vital point during its crisis. He met the challenge brilliantly, winning a special commendation from Stanton and in after years a Medal of Honor.[33] Eventually back in Washington, it was not until June 16 that Saxton received a reissue of Stanton's order to proceed to Port Royal. The reissue contained a significant addition giving him police power necessary for the security of the people to be in his charge. This time Saxton did get to Port Royal—but not until the very end of June.[34] By then Hunter long since had organized the black regiment.

Just before Saxton's arrival Hunter, on June 23, had sent to the War Department a report on the regiment. Report finally had been demanded. On June 5 a leading member of the Kentucky delegation in the House of Representatives tendered a resolution directing Stanton to inform the House whether Hunter had been authorized to organize, or had organized, a regiment "of black men (fugitive slaves)." On June 9 the resolution was adopted without objection. On June 14 Stanton responded that Hunter had not been so authorized, that the War Department had "no official information" whether he had done so, and that a copy of the resolution was being sent to him with instructions to report immediately.[35]

Hunter's report could hardly have been better designed to complicate the president's effort to assure the loyalty and support of the Union's border slave states, notably Kentucky. Sarcastic, even arrogant, Hunter said that he had no regiment of "fugitive slaves." He did have "a fine regiment of persons whose late masters are 'fugitive rebels'" and they "are now, one and all, working with remarkable industry to place themselves in a position to go in full and effective pursuit of their fugacious and traitorous proprietors." On July 2 Stanton transmitted the report to the House. On its reading it created merriment among many and its printing was ordered. But Kentuckians saw in it nothing funny. Nor could it be squared with the original instructions to General Sherman for it seemd unmistakably to say that the regiment was about to be used for offensive action, not simply to meet a "great emergency."[36]

In fact, however, the regiment was in no such condition as Hunter seemed to assert. The men had taken to drill and would make a good impression on parade. But since Hunter was treating them as "soldiers"—not the nonsoldiers contemplated by the Sherman instructions—he had no way to pay them; funds simply were not authorized.

Their brother blacks were earning wages as officers' servants and army laborers, to say nothing of the workmen busily engaged on the plantations. It is no wonder, then, that there was rising discontent among the "soldiers." Moreover, the discontent was fed by humiliating ridicule they met with from many white troops. Desertions soon had begun and grew, as Saxton was to find. Some of the "soldiers" even tried to flee to slavery's land. Guards from white units had to be thrown around the regiment's camp.[37]

Why Hunter had never requested Washington's approval of his regiment must be left to speculation. In any event on July 11 occasion arose—he thought—to ask again, as he had on April 3, for general authority to enlist black soldiers. Late that day he received an urgent request to send to Virginia all the troops he could spare. (In Virginia there had been the Seven Days Battles.) That night Hunter wrote Stanton that he was sending six regiments, requiring him to evacuate one of the long-held islands—he actually was to evacuate two—and that he might have to give up Beaufort. "I most earnestly beg that by return mail you give me full authority to muster into the service of the United States, as infantry, all loyal men to be found in my department, and that I be authorized to appoint all officers. This has now become a military necessity in this department."[38] Dispatch of troops to Virginia was to leave Hunter an army of but thirteen thousand in his entire department.[39]

It happened that on July 17, about the time Hunter's request reached Washington, Congress adopted a statute authorizing the president to receive blacks into the service of the United States either as laborers or for "any military or naval service."[40] The president, of course, already had that authority; all along blacks had been in the military service as laborers and, in the navy, not only as laborers but as crewmen, and there had been no law preventing him from also enlisting black soldiers. Hence the statute did not enlarge the president's authority. Moreover, that a congressional majority approved such authority did not mean that its exercise would be any more welcome in the border states or lessen the prejudice against black troops that prevailed in the army, as shown by the ridicule Hunter's regiment was receiving from his own white troops. But the statute did prompt Stanton to present Hunter's request at a cabinet meeting on July 21. Discussion continued the next day. Stanton and Chase, supported by Secretary of State William H. Seward, favored granting the request, and no cabinet member opposed. The president, however, remained "averse to arming negroes." Discussion ended with the president's saying that he would go no farther than to allow local commanders "to arm, for purely defensive purposes, slaves coming within their lines."[41] Hunter's request to rebuild his army with black men was not granted.

Of the "soldiers" in Hunter's black regiment only a fraction remained after persistent skedaddling, and he could not bring himself to deal severely with deserters whom he had never paid. Finally he gave up. On August 9, to the wild joy of the "soldiers" still in camp, he disbanded the regiment, notifying Stanton in a letter the next day.[42]

Hunter had become thoroughly disenchanted with a command charged not with conquest but with little more than maintaining anchorages for the navy. Already he had applied for leave of absence. In late August it was granted. In early September he departed; a superseding commander was coming.[43]

General Saxton, in the meantime, had been a very busy man with a mission then unique in the Union's military experience. On his arrival at the end of June he was well received on the plantations because of a favorable impression left by his service under Sherman. Hardly had he begun to get settled when he had to deal with hundreds of refugees from the two islands evacuated by Hunter's army. Also critical was the problem of the vulnerability of the plantations to Rebel raids. Earlier Hunter had agreed to supply the plantations with arms—well within the Sherman instructions—but it had not been done until Saxton came. Saxton had twenty to thirty muskets distributed to each plantation with orders to instruct the people in their use. On at least one of the plantations the people were delighted and every evening drill in their use was conducted, though on another fear of impressment—lingering from memory of Hunter's May roundup—created suspicion of drill. Nor was threat of enemy raids Saxton's only problem; in time Hunter had to assign Saxton three white companies to deal with pilfering from the black settlements by Union troops.[44]

It was not until early August that Saxton was able to get away from Port Royal to survey his domain down the Georgia coast into Florida. He started on August 5 with his first stop at St. Simons Island, where a special problem had been reported. Then guarded only by the navy and the local blacks with their limited number of muskets, St. Simons was infested with Rebel intruders. Saxton took there additional muskets and Company A of the black regiment. That was the company for which Hunter himself had picked the officers; it was a well-trained, effective unit. On arrival Saxton found that blacks had suffered casualties in fighting the intruders and that Rebels were still in hiding on the island. Company A was needed and Saxton left it there.[45]

Saxton's coastal tour took ten days. On his return he learned of the disbandment of the black regiment but no word of disbandment was sent to Company A. Saxton also found that Hunter had been ordered to ship his only cavalry regiment to Virginia and that this had led Hunter to decide to abandon all the Carolina area beyond the immediate environs of Port Royal, even the town of Beaufort. Gideon's Band was horrified.[46]

Saxton reacted at once. On August 16 he wrote a most important letter to Stanton. He requested authority "to enroll as laborers . . . a force not exceeding 5,000 able-bodied men from among the contrabands . . . to be uniformed, armed, and officered by men detailed from the Army." He described conditions on the islands, including what he had found on St. Simons, and urged that the force he requested could assist in the work on the plantations, guard the people, and "in the event of any emergency" immediately provide aid. Saxton's letter was clever. It did not refer to "soldiers" but only to "laborers." And it seemed within the principles of the War Department's long-standing interpretation of the instructions to General Sherman.[47]

Either the letter or a copy was taken to Washington by Rev. Mansfield French, one of the leading Gideonites, accompanied by Robert Smalls, who had become a national hero. They brought word that the Saxton proposal had the backing of both Hunter and DuPont. In Washington they saw Stanton and Chase.[48] Stanton acted promptly. On August 25 he wrote Saxton, authorizing him to enroll up to five thousand black laborers in the Quartermaster's service. But he went further, and beyond Saxton's request. He added:

> In view of the small force under your command and the inability of the Government at the present time to increase it, in order to guard the plantations and settlements occupied by the United States from invasion and protect the inhabitants thereof from captivity and murder by the enemy, you are also authorized to arm, uniform, equip, and receive into the service of the United States such number of volunteers of African descent as you may deem expedient, not exceeding 5,000, and may detail officers to instruct them in military drill, discipline, and duty, and to command them.

In closing, Stanton's letter noted that a recent act of Congress (the July 17 statute) provided that blacks "received into the service of the United

States who may have been the slaves of rebel masters" would be "forever free" and so would be "their wives, mothers and children." Stanton directed Saxton "and all in your command" so to "treat and regard them." Stanton insisted that French and Smalls deliver the letter in person.[49]

Thus did the Union, for the first time, authorize black troops.

Saxton's letter and the advocacy of French and Smalls had a further effect. An order was sent to Port Royal to keep the cavalry there and "to hold the islands now occupied." When French and Smalls returned, the cavalry regiment, which had boarded ship, was disembarked. The Gideonites' gloom at Hunter's threat to abandon most of the islands was lifted.[50]

For Saxton himself Stanton's authorization meant a renewed commitment to his work at Port Royal. While French and Smalls had been on their mission word had come of Hunter's leave of absence, with indications that he was to be superseded. Saxton assumed that Hunter's next in command would be his successor. With that officer Saxton had been in constant, bitter clash. Perhaps impulsively, Saxton at once had written Stanton asking for assignment elsewhere because of that clash. He had prepared to go north with Hunter on plantation business and, very probably, to pursue his request for transfer. French and Smalls returned to deliver Stanton's letter to Saxton just before Hunter's departure. The authorization for Saxton to recruit and organize black troops meant that he would not be at the mercy of Hunter's successor. That quite changed Saxton's attitude. At first Saxton hesitated about leaving with Hunter, but finally decided to go. It is apparent that face-to-face dealings in the North would facilitate handling all that he now had to accomplish in the South.[51]

Saxton was back by mid-October. One of his first acts was to inform the captain of Company A, who had come up from St. Simons to remind the command of his existence, that the company would become the core of a new regiment, with pay for its men and recognized commissions for its officers. Ultimately that captain became the lieutenant colonel of the new regiment.[52]

Thus, on the issue of black troops, Hunter had been left dangling but, at almost the same time, Saxton was given even more authority than he had requested. That, I submit, is not "hard to understand." Few issues were more delicate for the Union government in 1862. Hunter, heavy-handed, had gone ahead without even reporting his action; then, when required to report, had seemed to say that he was readying blacks for offensive warfare; and finally had persisted in seeking authority to rebuild his depleted army so without limit as to make it possibly even more black than white. Hunter's cause was hopeless; even after the authorization to Saxton, the Executive still was firm in refusal to authorize blacks as all-purpose soldiers.[53] Saxton, on the other hand, with cautious restraint, had sought no more than leave to arm black workmen to help protect the communities from enemy raids. At that not even Kentuckians could cavil. Jefferson Davis himself later was to say to his Congress that "the use of slaves as soldiers in defense of their homes . . . is justifiable."[54]

Thus Saxton gave Stanton the opportunity to push open a bit the door left slightly ajar by the president at the July cabinet meeting where he agreed that slaves could be armed for defense. Stanton allowed a limited black soldiery to protect their homes. And in his letter he added a very ambiguous sentence authorizing Saxton also "to withdraw from the enemy their laboring force and . . . to weaken, harass, and annoy them." This enabled Saxton, as he carefully pursued a course of training of the men being recruited, in November to send some companies raiding into enemy territory. Pridefully he reported to Stanton on their fighting skill and their capturing "from the enemy an amount of property equal in value to the cost of the regiment for a year."[55]

By that time the politics of the war had moved beyond where it had stood in the summer, and the president had moved with it. The Final Emancipation Proclamation of New Year's Day authorized the freed slaves to "be received into the armed service of the United States" for garrison duty and to man vessels. And within days thereafter the Executive was taking further action allowing the black man, whether freed slave or freeborn, to become a full-scale Union soldier.[56]

Saxton the cautious, French the Gideonite, and Smalls the hero had fashioned the first breach in the president's bar. Even after the breach had widened there persisted gross discrimination against the blacks in pay and otherwise. But the breach was a vital opening to the long path the black man would travel to win recognition as a man.

Notes

1. Dudley Taylor Cornish, *The Sable Arm: Negro Troops in the Union Army, 1861–1865* (1956; rpt. W. W. Norton & Co., New York, 1966), p. 53.

2. U.S. War Dept., *The War of the Rebellion: A Compilation of the Official Records of the Union and Confederate Armies*, 70 vols. in 128 pts. (1880–1901; rpt. National Historical Society, Gettysburg, 1972), ser. 1, 6:248, 257 (hereafter cited as *ORA*).

3. Joint Committee on the Conduct of the War, *Report of JCCW*, H. of Rep., 37th Cong., 3d Sess. (Apr. 6, 1863), 3:292–95, 302, 304, 309, 322 (hereafter cited as *JCCW*); *ORA*, ser. 1, 6:237, 263–64; 14:362; George Linton Hendricks, "Union Army Occupation of the Southern Seabord" (Ph.D. Diss., Columbia Univ., 1954, Library of Congress micro.), p. 7; Shelby Foote, *The Civil War*, 3 vols. (Random House, New York, 1958–74), 1:353.

4. *JCCW*, 294–99, 302–6, 309–10; Port Royal, South Carolina, *The New South*, Aug. 23, 1862; Horace Greeley, *The American Conflict: A History of the Great Rebellion in the United States of America, 1860-'65*, 2 vols. (O. D. Case & Co., Hartford, 1866), 2:457–58. Very significantly, Sherman reported on his return to Washington in April that the troops in the Port Royal area were needed far more than merely to hold the Union's position, *JCCW*, 295, 309.

5. *ORA*, ser. 1, 6:254.

6. *JCCW*, 327; *ORA*, ser. 1, 6:203–5, 218, 222–23; Hendricks, "Union Army Occupation," 9–16.

7. Edward Pierce, "The Freedmen at Port Royal," *The Atlantic Monthly* 12 (Sept. 1863):296–98; Hendricks, "Union Army Occupation," pp. 43–54; Willie Lee Rose, *Rehearsal for Reconstruction* (Bobbs-Merrill, Indianapolis, 1964), pp. 19–31, 43–69; Port Royal, *The New South*, March 15, 1862.

8. *ORA*, ser. 1, 6:263–64; ser. 3, 2:292.

9. *New York Times*, May 1, 1862 (dispatch from Port Royal); *ORA*, ser. 3, 2:29–30, 53; Thomas Wentworth Higginson, *Army Life in a Black Regiment* (1870; rpt. Michigan State Univ. Press, East Lansing, 1960), pp. 272–73.

10. *ORA*, ser. 1, 6:176–77; ser. 3, 1:609–10, 626; 2:30; A. Howard Meneely, "The War Department, 1861" (Ph.D. Diss., Columbia Univ., New York, 1928), pp. 341–43.

11. Cornish, *Sable Arm*, Foreword; Fred A. Shannon, "The Federal Government and the Negro Soldier, 1861–1865," *Journal of Negro History* 11 (1926):564–65; Herbert Aptheker, "The Negro in the Union Navy," *Journal of Negro History* 32 (1947):169, 170–74, 179; *Official Records of the Union and Confederate Navies in the War of the Rebellion*, 27 vols. (Washington, 1894-1927), ser. 1, 6:252, 409; Elon A. Woodward, *The Negro in the Military Service of the United States, 1639–1886: A Compilation* (1888), Office of the Adj. Gen., Nat. Arch., RG 94, M 858, Roll 1, pp. 838, 888; Ezra J. Warner, *Generals in Blue: Lives of the Union Commanders* (Louisiana State Univ. Press, Baton Rouge, 1964), p. 244.

12. *ORA*, ser. 1, 14:337.

13. *ORA*, ser. 1, 14:983; John D. Hayes, *Samuel Francis DuPont: A Selection from His Civil War Letters*, 3 vols. (Cornell Univ. Press, Ithaca, 1969), 2:50.

14. *ORA*, ser. 3, 2:53; Elizabeth Ware Pearson, *Letters from Port Royal* (W. B. Clarke Co., Boston, 1906), p. 40; Rupert Sargent Holland, ed., *Letters and Diary of Laura M. Towne* (Riverside Press, Cambridge, 1912), p. 37; Higginson, *Army Life*, pp. 272–73.

15. *ORA*, ser. 3, 2:29–31, 52; Woodward, *The Negro in Military Service*, pp. 846–49.

16. *ORA*, ser. 1, 14:341.

17. Allan Nevins, *The War for the Union*, 4 vols. (Charles Scribner's Sons, New York, 1959–71), 1:331–36.

18. The instructions to General Sherman (applicable to Hunter) directed that he be guided by the "principles" of instructions to Maj. Gen. Benjamin F. Butler at Fort Monroe in the summer of 1861 and attached copies. As printed in *ORA*, ser. 1, 6:176–77, the Sherman instructions give incorrect citation to the Butler instructions; correct citation is *ORA*, ser. 1, 6:243; ser. 2, 1:754–55, 761–62. The Butler instructions forbade interference with slavery, except that a fugitive was not to be returned to his master involuntarily. Nonetheless on April 13, just after the capture of Fort Pulaski, Hunter proclaimed the freedom of all slaves of "enemies" at Pulaski and on its island, Cockspur. Though that decree was reported in the Northern press it evoked no disapproval from higher authority, *ORA*, ser. 1, 14:333; *New York Times*, Apr. 19, 1862.

Thus if Hunter had been one to bother with justification of his actions he might have argued that no disapproval of his Pulaski emancipation indicated a change in War Department policy. Also he might have argued that the presidential action respecting the Fremont proclamation was not an applicable precedent since that proclamation had applied to a loyal state, Missouri, whereas his of May 9 applied to three rebel states.

19. *ORA*, ser. 3, 2:42–43. Consideration of emancipation questions in the 37th Congress is well reviewed in Leonard P. Curry, *Blueprint for Modern America* (Vanderbilt Univ. Press, Nashville, 1968), pp. 36–74. Hunter's blindness to the delicacy of the emancipation question is revealed by the assertion in a Port Royal newspaper, operating under military auspices, that since there had been "no official notification" of the president's disavowal Hunter's emancipation was in full force, and by Hunter's own assertion in later years that the president had "rejoiced" in his action since no word of disapproval had been sent to him. Port Royal, *The New South*, Aug. 23, 1862; David Hunter, *Report of the Military Services of David Hunter*, 2d ed. (D. Van Nostrand Co., New York, 1892), p. 17.

20. *ORA*, ser. 3, 2:50–60; Pearson, *Letters from Port Royal*, pp. 37–42, 51; Holland, *Towne Letters*, pp. 41–54; *National Intelligencer* (Washington), May 28, 1862, quoting May 14 dispatch to Boston *Journal*.

21. Pearson, *Letters from Port Royal*, pp. 50–51, 54; Holland, *Towne Letters*, p. 54; *Cong. Globe*, 37th Cong., 2d Sess. (1862), 3123; *National Intelligencer*, May 28, Aug. 13, 18, 1862; *Washington Evening Star*, Aug. 19, 1862; Hendricks, "Union Army Occupation," p. 67.

22. *Official Records of the Union and Confederate Navies*, ser. 1, 12:807, 820–21; 13:53; *ORA*, ser. 1, 14:983–86; Benjamin Quarles, "The Abduction of the *Planter*," *Civil War History* 4 (Mar. 1958):5–10.

23. *ORA*, ser. 1, 14:41–104, 979–83; Letters Received, Adj. Gen. Office, 1861–70, No. 1063 S, Rufus Saxton to Stanton, June 30, 1862, Nat. Arch., RG 94; *New York Times*, June 28, 1862; Greeley, *American Conflict*, 2:460–62.

24. Register of Letters Received, Dept. of South, from Gen. H. W. Benham, June 11, 1862, Nat. Arch., RG 393.

25. Register of Letters Received, Dept. of South, from Col. N. W. Brown and enclosure, June 24, 1862, Nat. Arch., RG 393; Holland, *Towne Letters*, p. 71; *New York Times*, June 17, July 2, 9, Sept. 15 (Rev. Mansfield French speech in

New York), 1862; *National Intelligencer*, June 28, 1862; Higginson, *Army Life*, p. 73. I have found no formal records of the regiment.

26. Howard C. Westwood, "The Joint Committee on the Conduct of the War," *Lincoln Herald* 80 (Spring 1978): 4–5.

27. *JCCW*, 322–30.

28. Adj. Gen. Office, Register of Letters Received, 1819–1889, 38 (1862):913, Nat. Arch., RG 94, M 711, Roll 35; *ORA*, ser. 3, 2:27.

29. David Donald, ed., *Inside Lincoln's Cabinet: The Civil War Diaries of Salmon P. Chase* (Longmans, Green & Co., New York, 1954), p. 71.

30. Dept. of South—Special Orders, General Orders, Circulars of Gen. Saxton, May 1862–December 1863, special orders at first two unnumbered pages, Nat. Arch., RG 393; *New York Times*, May 16, 1862.

31. *ORA*, ser. 3, 2:52, Pearson, *Letters from Port Royal*, p. 48.

32. *New York Times*, May 22, 1862.

33. Dept. of South—Special Orders, General Orders, Circulars of General Saxton, May 1862–December 1863, note at second unnumbered page and general orders at following eight unnumbered pages, May 26 to June 2, 1862, Nat. Arch., RG 393; Rufus Saxton file, Letters Received by Appointment, Commission and Personal Branch of the Adj. Gen. Office, File No. 1302, ACP 1879 (containing several documents relating to Harpers Ferry episode and Medal of Honor award), Nat. Arch., RG 94; Hendricks, "Union Army Occupation," p. 46.

34. *ORA*, ser. 3, 2:152–53; Letters Received by Adj. Gen. Office, 1861–70, No. 1063 S, Saxton to Stanton, June 30, 1862, Nat. Arch., RG 94.

35. *Cong. Globe*, 37th Cong., 2d Sess. (1862), 2587, 2620–21, 2762; *ORA*, ser. 3, 2:147–48.

36. *Cong. Globe*, 37th Cong., 2d Sess. (1862), 3087, 3102, 3109, 3121–27; H. of Rep., 37th Cong., 2d Sess. (1862), Ex. Doc. No. 143; *ORA*, ser. 3, 2:196–98.

37. Woodward, *The Negro in Military Service*, pp. 907–8; Pearson, *Letters from Port Royal*, p. 100; Higginson, *Army Life*, pp. 43, 273; *New York Times*, July 19, Aug. 22, Sept. 15 (Rev. French speech), Sept. 24, 1862; *National Intelligencer*, May 19, Aug. 13, 16, 18, Sept. 23, 1862; *Washington Evening Star*, Aug. 19, 1862.

38. *ORA*, ser. 1, 14:363–64. Hunter actually sent seven regiments. Though the War Department was to point out to him within a few days that it had sought only what Hunter could "spare," Hunter soon was urging that he be reinforced both to reoccupy the two evacuated islands and to establish new strong positions, *ORA*, ser. 1, 14:365–66.

39. *ORA*, ser. 1, 14:367.

40. 12 *U.S. Stat.* 599.

41. Donald, *Inside Lincoln's Cabinet*, pp. 96, 99–100.

42. *ORA*, ser. 3, 2:346; Holland, *Towne Letters*, p. 84; *National Intelligencer*, Aug. 18, 1862; *Washington Evening Star*, Aug. 19, 1862. Hunter's disbandment of his regiment came abruptly; as late as August 4 he had written Stanton again, this time specifically asking for approval of the regiment, with authority to pay the men, and still insisting that he could organize many more if permitted, *ORA*, ser. 3, 2:292.

43. The leave granted was for sixty days, *ORA*, ser. 1, 14:376. Search for Hunter's application for leave has disclosed only a notation that he had applied for it on July 30. Register of Letters Received by Headquarters of the Army, No. 114, Nat.

Arch., RG 108. So it is unknown whether Hunter also sought a transfer. But on his departure on September 5 it was understood that his return was unlikely, and he was to tell the press that he had sought other assignment because he could not get troops for "offensive service." Holland, *Towne Letters*, p. 90; Port Royal, *The New South*, Sept. 6, 1862; *New York Times*, Sept. 10, 1862. Maj. Gen. Ormsby M. Mitchell was assigned to the department command on September 1; Stanton told him to get to Port Royal promptly, *ORA*, ser. 1, 14:380–85.

44. *ORA*, ser. 1, 14:375–76; Holland, *Towne Letters*, 73–81, 84; Pearson, *Letters from Port Royal*, p. 89; Woodward, *The Negro in Military Service*, p. 929; *New York Times*, July 2, Aug. 26, 1862.

45. *ORA*, ser. 1, 14:375; Woodward, *The Negro in Military Service*, p. 929; Susie King Taylor, *Reminiscenses of My Life in Camp* (1902; rpt., Arno Press, New York, 1968), pp. 12–15; *New York Times*, Aug. 22, 1862.

46. *ORA*, ser. 1, 14:374; Pearson, *Letters from Port Royal*, p. 84. An officer of the troops from Hunter's command sent to Virginia had reported to Stanton that Hunter's remaining army was adequate and its cavalry not needed, *ORA*, ser. 1, 14:368–69.

47. *ORA*, ser. 1, 14:374–76. Rose, *Rehearsal for Reconstruction*, p. 190, mistakenly states that Saxton's letter "envisioned expeditions into coastal districts to capture enemy salt works and to destroy property." It was not Saxton's letter but Stanton's reply that, as we shall see, rather vaguely authorized operations of that nature.

48. Mansfield French to George Whipple, Aug. 23 and 28, 1862, Amer. Missionary Assn. Archives, Nos. HL 4517 and 15901, Amistad Research Center, Dillard University; 17 Cong. Rec. App. 319–20 (1886; speech of Cong. Robert Smalls); *National Intelligencer*, Aug. 30, 1862; Okon Edet Uya, *From Slavery to Public Service: Robert Smalls, 1839–1915* (Oxford Univ. Press, New York, 1971), pp. 17–19. Smalls' national renown was notable, *New York Times*, Oct. 3, 1862.

49. *ORA*, ser. 1, 14:377–78; French to Whipple, Aug. 28, 1862, Amer. Missionary Assn. Archives, No. 15901. Stanton somewhat overstated the statute's emancipation provision for wives and children; their master, too, had to be rebel, 12 *U.S. Stat.* 13:599. On an even more important point Stanton was careless. He said that the black soldiers' pay would be the same as that "allowed by law to volunteers in the service." Understandably Saxton was to interpret this to mean that black pay would be the same as white pay, Woodward, *The Negro in Military Service*, pp. 983–84. But the statute imposed a substantially lower rate of pay for blacks. Had it not been for the statute, black pay would have been the same as white pay, Case of Rev. Samuel Harrison, 11 *Ops. Atty. Gen.* 37 (1864); Pay of Colored Soldiers, 11 *Ops. Atty. Gen.* 53 (1864).

50. *ORA*, ser. 1, 14:378; Holland, *Towne Letters*, p. 90; Pearson, *Letters from Port Royal*, p. 86.

51. Holland, *Towne Letters*, pp. 90–91; Pearson, *Letters from Port Royal*, p. 86; Port Royal, *The New South*, Sept. 6, 1862; *New York Times*, Sept. 10, 1862. Hunter's next in command was Brig. Gen. John M. Brannan, who was left in charge on Hunter's departure, *ORA*, ser. 1, 14:380. Saxton's relations with Hunter had been relatively smooth, but it had been quite otherwise with Hunter's subordinates, notably Brannan. Rufus Saxton Letterbook 1:1–39, Saxton Family Papers, Yale Univ. Saxton's request for reassignment is at pp. 39–40 of this

Letterbook. He did not yet know that Gen. Mitchell, not Brannan, would succeed Hunter.

52. *ORA*, ser. 3, 2:663; Higginson, *Army Life*, pp. 275–76; Taylor, *Reminiscences*, p. 15.

53. Sen. James Lane of Kansas, as recruiting commissioner in that state, had been taking blacks, *New York Times*, Sept. 13, 1862. But in August and September 1862 Stanton insisted to him that he had no such authority, *ORA*, ser. 3, 2:312–13, 445, 582; Cornish, *Sable Arm*, pp. 69–78. On August 22, 1862, Gen. Butler, in New Orleans, ordered enlistment of volunteering free blacks who had been in Confederate Louisiana's state militia, "subject to the approval of the President of the United States." His order provided that they were to "defend their homes." By coincidence that asserted purpose was strikingly similar to the authorization Stanton was about to give Saxton. Butler promptly sought the War Department's approval. But not until late November was a response sent him; then he was told to use his own judgment. In the meantime he had gone ahead, organizing three black regiments without limiting enrollment to prewar free blacks, *ORA*, ser. 1, 15:162, 555–57, 601; ser. 3, 2:436–38; Cornish, *Sable Arm*, pp. 65–67; Howard C. Westwood, "Benjamin Butler's Enlistment of Black Troops in New Orleans in 1862," *Louisiana History* 26, no. 1 (1985):5–22 (reprinted herein as chapter 3).

54. Message to Congress, Nov. 7, 1864, James D. Richardson, comp., *A Compilation of the Messages and Papers of the Confederacy, Including the Diplomatic Correspondence, 1861–1865*, 2 vols. (United States Publishing Co., Nashville, 1905), 1:495.

55. *ORA*, ser. 1, 14:189–93, ser. 3, 4:1027. The training and organization of the regiment are reviewed in Cornish, *Sable Arm*, pp. 81–92.

56. James E. Richardson, comp., *A Compilation of the Messages and Papers of the Presidents, 1789–1897*, 10 vols. (Published by the Authority of Congress, Washington, 1896–99), 6:158; Cornish, *Sable Arm*, pp. 100–101, 104–6.

5

Mr. Smalls:
A Personal Adventure

"ONE OF the most heroic acts of the war," reported the *New York Times* on May 19, 1862. Later, the commander of the Union navy along the South Atlantic coast, Rear Adm. Samuel F. DuPont, pronounced it "one of the coolest and most gallant naval acts of war." Nor was it forgotten in postwar years.

In 1900, the United States Congress recorded it in a statute, providing a reward for the hero of the episode. The statute read: ". . . Robert Smalls, on the thirteenth day of May, eighteen hundred and sixty-two, did capture the steamer Planter, with all the armament and ammunition for Fort Ripley, at the city of Charleston, taking her out and turning her over to the Federal blockading squadron off Charleston. . . ." And in recent years the memory of Smalls' feat was freshened in South Carolina; the state government placed a marker, reciting the act, at a churchyard in Beaufort, where Smalls is buried.

But back in May 1862 Robert Smalls was a twenty-three-year-old illiterate slave. Early on the morning of May 13, 1862, the Confederate commander at Charleston, South Carolina, Brig. Gen. Roswell S. Ripley, was astounded to learn his dispatch boat had disappeared. That boat, the *Planter*, for many months under charter to the army with a civilian crew, had been doing good service on critical missions— inspection, charting, transport—as General Ripley prepared to meet possible Union assault on Charleston, the cradle of the rebellion. The

Originally published in *Civil War Times Illustrated* 25, no. 3 (May 1986):20–31. Reprinted by permission of *Civil War Times Illustrated*.

Articles published in this journal are not annotated. In my research I relied considerably on two biographies of Smalls: Dorothy Sterling, *Captain of the "Planter": The Story of Robert Smalls* (Doubleday & Co., Garden City, 1958), and Okon Edet Uya, *From Slavery to Public Service: Robert Smalls, 1839–1915* (Oxford Univ. Press, New York, 1971).

evening before, May 12, she had been moored, as usual, at the wharf just in front of Ripley's headquarters. Where was she now? The general could find no one who knew.

The regular twenty-man guard had been posted at the wharf during the night, with sentinels a few paces from the boat. They knew only that the *Planter* had moved off about 3:30 A.M. At her rail had been a man who seemed to be her captain, for he had the captain's posture and wore his straw hat and jacket. A Confederate banner and a Palmetto flag had been flying. The *Planter* was scheduled for an early morning chore, so the move seemed quite normal.

But now it was found that the captain had not been with the *Planter*. He and his two brother officers had spent the night ashore. They had no idea what happened. The boat had eight crewmen, all slaves. Robert Smalls was the chief crewman, the wheelman; had he been white he would have been called the pilot. Smalls and all but one of the crewmen were missing. The remaining slave knew nothing.

Anxiously, Confederate officers peered out at the forms of Union blockading ships at sea, well beyond Charleston Harbor's Confederate bastion, Fort Sumter. At first incredulous, finally they were convinced. There was the *Planter*, riding between two of the Union blockaders. General Ripley, furious, ordered an aide to find out how she got there.

The aide's report disclosed little. The boat had moved slowly to a nearby wharf, stopped briefly, whistled, and then turned into the harbor. She had reached Fort Sumter at about 4:15 A.M., where she was reported to the officer of the day. He, thinking her the guard boat, gave her the signal to pass. And so she had gone on into the outer harbor. It was said that during the evening three whites—two men and a woman—had boarded her at the wharf and had not been seen to leave. Though this proved untrue, it did start a long-persisting rumor, amplified by an outraged Southern press, that Union agents had turned the trick.

In the Rebel capital, Richmond, Virginia, government officials were promptly informed of the loss. Confederate Gen. Robert E. Lee opined that the responsible parties should be punished. General Ripley had already preferred charges. The *Planter*'s officers had been arrested, to be tried by court-martial, for violating a general order decreeing officers of vessels moored at the wharves were to remain aboard.

Loss of the *Planter* could not be shrugged off. Some ten days before, Ripley's barge had been spirited out to the Union fleet by slave crewmen; that had been only an annoyance. The *Planter*, however, was not a mere barge. She was a steam-powered side-wheeler. A shallow-draft craft, built as a cotton transport with capacity for fourteen hundred bales, she was ideally suited for moving troops and matériel along South Carolina's labyrinth of coastal waters. Now it appeared that the troops she moved would be Federals.

A Union army had landed the previous November at Port Royal, sixty miles down the coast. Now it was led by aggressive Maj. Gen. David Hunter; threat of attack on Charleston was not academic. But for an assault the Union forces were in great need of shallow-water transport; for them the *Planter*'s value was beyond measure. And there was a dividend. In addition to the *Planter*'s own armament—a 32-pounder cannon on a pivot in the bow and a 24-pounder howitzer in the stern—she had in cargo (to have been delivered to a harbor battery that morning) four fine guns, a large supply of ammunition, and other matériel. (Two of the guns had once belonged to Sumter's defeated Union garrison. Both had been damaged in the April 1861 bombardment opening the war, but were now repaired.)

No wonder, then, that the Charleston press screamed that the *Planter*'s officers' "criminal absence" had been shameful, "disgusting treachery." The press of neighboring cities joined in, condemning the "gross negligence" that called for "the prompt penalty of the halter rigorously enforced," and branding the abduction of the vessel "one of the most shameful events of this or any other war." It had occurred, said the press, because officers seemed to think that the war was "a nice frolic" and neglected "personal attention to their commands."

Union troops were delighted at having secured the *Planter*. But the acquisition had been made only after a very tense moment. That moment came when the tar on watch on the blockading ship nearest to the shore, the *Onward*, screamed an alarm. Approaching through the haze was a Rebel ram, the sailor believed. Quickly, the blockader was swung about to bring broadside guns to bear on the misty target. Just before the command to fire, another sailor cried out that he thought a white flag flew at the Rebel boat's mast. Fire was withheld. Tension eased when a bedsheet was seen billowing where, shortly before, Rebel banners had waved. The *Planter* glided to the *Onward*'s stern.

Leaning on the *Planter*'s rail was a black man wearing the hat and jacket of a Rebel ship captain. Doffing his hat, he shouted, "Good morning, Sir! I've brought you some of the old United States guns, sir!"

On the *Planter*'s deck, yelling triumphantly, were seven other black men. Quickly, the *Onward*'s captain boarded the *Planter*, to be surrounded by joyous blacks begging that the Stars and Stripes be hoisted. That done, eight more blacks climbed from below, five women and three youngsters, one a baby. The mother held the baby high over her head and exhorted him to look at the United States flag, because it was a promise of a better life.

The jacket-clad black was Robert Smalls. After telling his story to the *Onward*'s captain, he was sent on to the squadron commander to repeat it. It was decided that, under a Union crew, the *Planter*, with its black company, should be sent on to Port Royal, base of the blockading fleet. There, at 10:20 that night, as Commodore DuPont (he would become a rear admiral a few weeks later) composed a long letter to his wife, he was interrupted in midsentence; a messenger bore news that a Rebel vessel had just been brought in, delivered that morning to the squadron off Charleston by the vessel's chief crewman. DuPont pushed his letter aside and sent for the "Hero," as he put it, to hear the story. When at length he resumed his letter, that story became a lively addition.

The next day, May 14, DuPont sent a report of the incident to Union Secretary of the Navy Gideon Welles, concluding that, if the government considered the *Planter* a prize, he would "respectfully submit to the Department the claims" of its black company. (Captured Confederate vessels, "prizes," were auctioned off in Northern ports. Half the proceeds went to the United States Government, half to the crewmen who seized the craft.) Also, he could not resist ribbing the Rebel command at Charleston; a civilian caught on another ship captured by the blockaders was sent back to Charleston with word that DuPont found it "mortifying" that the *Planter* should have been purloined from "officers whom he still considered his countrymen."

There was no feigned mortification among Charleston's military men. The outcome of the court-martial of the *Planter*'s officers was proof of that. They were brought to trial in short order. While one of them, the engineer, won a dismissal because the charges against him were faulty, the captain and mate were found guilty and sentenced to fine and imprisonment. Eventually reviewed by department commander Maj. Gen. John C. Pemberton, those sentences were remitted. Pemberton found the order requiring officers to stay aboard vessels moored at the wharf had not been "properly communicated" to the defendants, measures to enforce compliance had been taken, and the *Planter*'s owner, responsible under government charter for his officers, seemed to have been "entirely indifferent" to the order. The general concluded that the public would not "be benefitted by the punishment." He had the officers released.

The real fault was in Charleston's military administration. It had given the Union a great opportunity—or so it seemed. As DuPont put it in his report to Secretary of the Navy Welles, Smalls had brought information "most interesting, and portions of it of utmost importance." Smalls knew the location of the Rebel fortifications all through the area and where torpedoes had been planted in the rivers and creeks. Also, in the *Planter*'s cabin was "the book containing the secret of the signals of the Confederacy," enabling Unionists to "read" the Rebel signal flags wagging around the harbor. Of even greater import was Smalls' word of a Rebel redeployment ordered by Pemberton. Southerners had evacuated Cole's Island and Stono Inlet at the tip of James Island, immediately adjacent to Charleston. Smalls, on the *Planter*, had been engaged in the evacuation and gave DuPont a detailed account. The officer saw at once that, if the Union army could act with sufficient speed and strength, the way was open to get at Charleston by land, up Stono Inlet and through James Island.

DuPont's greatest interest might have been in that information. But what excited the Northern public was the tale of a slave's snatching the *Planter* from under the noses of the Rebels, at the very spot where the war had started. The full story was eagerly sought.

Smalls had been born in Beaufort, near Port Royal. His mother had been a house slave of the prominent McKee family. As a child he had been a favorite of that family. When he was about age twelve, his master took him to Charleston to be hired out. He displayed marked technical ability and progressed from job to job, finally becoming a sailor. He had made a deal with his master, allowing him to keep any earnings above $15 a month. Along the way he married a slave of another family. In 1858, his first child, a girl, was born. She, of course, became the property of his wife's owner. That worried the young father. He persuaded his wife's master to agree to emanicpate wife and child upon payment of $800. By 1862 he had accumulated $700 of that sum. Then, a second child, a boy, was born. Smalls doubtless wondered whether the price of freedom would be increased.

In 1861 Smalls had been hired as a sailor on the *Planter*, and so was with her during her charter to the Confederate military. Though he did not learn to read and write until 1864, he was—as would be said of him in the *Dictionary of American Biography* seventy years later— "good humored, intelligent, fluent, and self-possessed." By the spring of 1862 he had become head crewman. While his regular pay was only $16 a month, with $15 of that going to his master, he accrued considerable personal income—for a slave—by "petty trading." To all appearances he was content with his lot, taking good care of his little family and enjoying the full confidence of the *Planter*'s owners and officers. Their confidence in him was confirmed by Smalls' "reaction" to the theft of General Ripley's barge; he denounced the thieves as "the meanest of mortals."

But appearances deceived. At some time in April 1862 Smalls began planning an escape. When the Union army took Port Royal the previous November and extended influence over the surrounding area, nearly all the white residents fled. But most of their slaves, including Smalls' mother, had stayed. From the mysterious slave "telegraph," Smalls heard that his mother was in her old home in Beaufort, happily engaged as a cook for Union troops. After General Hunter had assumed Union army command at the end of March, the same telegraph brought news that he was disposed to emancipate slaves. Smalls decided Beaufort would be more suited than Charleston for rearing his children.

One of Smalls' fellow crewmen jokingly suggested they should steal the *Planter*. Smalls told him the possibility was no joke. Cautiously, he sounded out others of the crew, save for one who could not be trusted and was left out of the venture. At meetings at Smalls' home a plan matured.

Opportunity beckoned when the boat was wharfside at night and the officers left her in Smalls' care. The wheelman intended to use an excuse to get the distrusted crewman away from the *Planter*. His own wife, four other women, his two children, and another child would go aboard another boat moored nightly at a nearby dock. There, a slave sailor, brought in on the plan, would secrete them. Then on the *Planter*'s approach the women, children, and sailor would join the escape party. The only question Smalls and his conspirators had was when to make their break.

That question was answered at the end of the day on May 12. By late afternoon the *Planter* had been loaded with cargo for delivery to one of the harbor batteries at high water, 6:00 the next morning. The wharf's guard expected the boat to shove off early. And when the boat's officers were leaving at day's end, Smalls was instructed to get ready for the early move. Dutifully he responded, "Aye, aye, sir!"

As soon as the officers were gone, Smalls and his fellows consulted and all agreed: the time had come. Word was sent to the sailor on the other boat and to the women and children: proceed. Quietly, on the *Planter*, Smalls broke into the cabin to secure the captain's straw hat and jacket and any small arms he could find. It was firmly understood among the conspirators that if they met with any interference they would resist and, if it came to that, rather than suffer capture, they would sink the *Planter* and all aboard. If scuttling failed, they "would all take hands . . . and jump overboard and perish together."

At about 3:00 A.M., the boat's steam engine was fired up. Smoke from the stack was blown toward the city. For a short time Smalls feared that someone would think there was a fire near the wharf and sound an alarm. But all remained quiet. When steam pressure was up, the boat's Confederate banner and Palmetto flag were hoisted, and the regular wharf signal blown. In her usual manner, the boat got under way, with Smalls at the captain's post, taking care to imitate that worthy's well-known posture.

The *Planter* sailed to the boat where the women and children were stowed, stopped briefly to pick up the waiting party in the darkness, and turned seaward, sailing on at a slow speed, giving the prescribed signals along the way. She reached Sumter at the normal time harbor traffic began.

Smalls had the captain's hat pulled low, his face averted. He pulled the cord for two long whistles and a short one, as vessels were supposed to do. Permission to pass was signaled from Sumter, and the *Planter* slowly sailed on, seemingly toward the outer forts. But after getting well beyond Sumter, she abruptly picked up speed and swung away, not toward the outer forts, but toward the harbor's bar and the distant blockaders. As she speeded on, Rebel flags came down and up went a white sheet Smalls took from the boat's bunk. So it was that a new day dawned for sixteen slaves.

A few weeks later, Secretary of the Navy Welles was to open a package sent him at DuPont's order; it contained a Rebel naval banner and a South Carolina Palmetto flag. Coincidentally, it was at that time that the commodore was made a rear admiral. In the meantime, Smalls embarked on what was to prove a very busy career.

DuPont immediately passed on wheelman Smalls' information on Rebel deployment to General Hunter. This precipitated a decision by Hunter to begin a move toward a position from which Charleston could be assaulted. Smalls participated in that move, piloting the *Planter* for the Union navy.

The move met only partial success. Union delays enabled the Rebels to prepare a defense. This was not Smalls' fault. In his December 1862 Annual Report, the navy secretary credited Smalls with the information that made it possible to establish on the Stono Inlet and Stono River "an important base for future military operations." This accomplished "virtually a turning of the forces in Charleston harbor."

While Smalls was being launched on a new career, attention in the United States Congress turned to the question DuPont raised about prize money for the *Planter*'s black crewmen. The prize laws did not cover the case. But promptly, on May 19, 1862, a bill was introduced in the United States Senate, directing the secretary of the navy to make an appraisal of the vessel and its cargo and to have half the appraised value apportioned, in cash, equitably among Smalls and his fellows, the equivalent of a prize award. By unanimous consent, reference to a committee was omitted, and the Senate passed the bill that very day. An effort to spur the House of Representatives into action before the day's end was obstructed by dissenting congressmen, but a few days later the measure was brought forward and quickly adopted by a vote of 121 to 9. On May 30 President Lincoln signed it into law.

Secretary of the Navy Welles promptly directed DuPont to carry out the statute. It was DuPont's idea that Smalls and his associates should be paid $20,000, with $5,000 going to Smalls. But at that point the matter reached the hands of penny-pinching appraisers—doubtless not keen about lining the pockets of mere ex-slaves. The *Planter* was appraised at $9,000 and her cargo at $168—ridiculously low figures. The apportionment of half that sum made by DuPont was a payment of $1,500 to Smalls, sums ranging from $348 to $450 to each of the other men, and $100 each to two of the women.

If Smalls realized then the inadequacy of that payment, his actions in his new career never betrayed resentment. Throughout the Civil War he served the Union with distinction, an invaluable pilot on coastal waters he knew well, endowed with indomitable courage. He took part in seventeen engagements. One was the April 1863 naval attack on

Charleston; in it Smalls piloted the ironclad *Keokuk*. Though the attack was a failure, Smalls' performance in it was truly professional.

In the autumn of 1862, the *Planter* was "sold" by the United States Navy to the United States Army. She had done fine naval service, but because she was a wood-burner, the coal-powered navy had difficulty keeping her fueled. For the army, much in need of coastal transport, wood fuel posed no problem. In time, the army hired Smalls as the *Planter*'s pilot.

On a December day Smalls was piloting the boat on a supply mission along one of the waterways near Charleston, with a white captain in command. Suddenly, devastating Rebel artillery fire blanketed the *Planter*. The captain panicked and wanted to surrender. But Smalls defied his captain. Surrender would be grim for him and other former slaves in the crew. The captain slunk down into the hold. Smalls took charge and brought the *Planter* through the shelling. Awaiting him at the landing were thousands of cheering troops. Union Maj. Gen. Quincy A. Gillmore, Hunter's successor, at once promoted Smalls to captain of the *Planter*. And a captain he was to remain, through the rest of the war and after—until the *Planter* was sold by the army in the autumn of 1866.

Although writers in later years said Smalls became an officer either in the navy or army, the fact was that he remained a civilian throughout the conflict. But his was a military career just the same. Though there were cases where civilians on hire as pilots, engineers, or otherwise presented discipline problems, Smalls always took orders exactly as if he had been an enrolled seaman or soldier.

Early in his work with the Union's armed forces, it was foreshadowed that much more than military service was in store for the one-time slave. With the flight of whites from the Port Royal area following the Union's invasion, means had to be devised to support thousands of slaves, "contrabands," remaining behind. What evolved, in the spring of 1862, was a program known to history as the "Port Royal Experiment." A devoted corps of Northern missionaries, teachers, and business managers, under the aegis of the United States Treasury Department and backed by the military, came to organize and lead blacks to a self-sustaining, free existence on plantations around the urban center of Beaufort. Prominent in that program was the Reverend Mansfield French. He saw that Smalls' dramatic theft of the *Planter* and the fame that followed made him a potential asset to the experiment. He

immediately proposed that Smalls be sent to New York City for meetings at the Cooper Union. There, the mayor would preside, to "raise
money for the contrabands" to help meet their needs on the plantations.

DuPont vetoed that proposal. Just then, there was preempting need
for Smalls on the water approaches to Charleston. But a few weeks
later, in August 1862, Smalls was sent to Washington with French to
deliver a plea from the military governor of the Port Royal area, Brig.
Gen. Rufus Saxton, to permit him to arm black workmen on the
plantations for protection from Rebel raids. On that mission Smalls met
both Union Secretary of War Edwin Stanton and President Lincoln. He
also had a long session with Secretary of the Treasury Salmon P. Chase,
who, at the time, had the responsibility for properties abandoned by
their owners in Union-occupied areas of the South. The mission was
a notable success; French and Smalls returned in early September with
authorization for Saxton to help enroll black men as Union soldiers, the
first such authority ever given by the United States War Department.

No sooner was that mission completed than Smalls was off again with
French, this time to New York City with his family. There Smalls
was a drawing card at meetings to solicit support for the Port Royal
Experiment. A high point of that trip was a huge meeting at the Shiloh
Church on October 2. The next morning's *New York Times*, headlined
"The Hero of The *Planter*," reported the house crowded with "the
most intelligent and respectable portion of the Afro-Americans of the
great Metropolis." A choir sang "John Brown's Hymn," "There's a
Better Time a-Coming," and other emancipation songs. At Smalls'
entrance with his family the crowd went wild. He was presented with
a gold medal, embossed with a view of the *Planter* on the way from
Fort Sumter to the blockaders. A resolution was adopted, hailing
Smalls' feat as proof of the "safety, justice and easy possibility" of
immediate, universal emancipation. It was a critical time for the nation's blacks. The Preliminary Emancipation Proclamation had just
been issued, but it remained uncertain whether it would be made final
and how far it would extend.

During the next year and a half, along with his notable service in
the military, Smalls steadily grew in the esteem of the Port Royal
community. In May 1864 a meeting of freedmen and whites in Beaufort
selected a delegation to represent South Carolina at the Republican
National Convention in Baltimore, Maryland. Of the sixteen delegates,

four were blacks. Of those four, one was Smalls. Though the delegation
was not officially recognized at the convention, it is significant that the
first political voice for blacks in South Carolina acclaimed Smalls.

Probably Smalls would not have participated, even had the delegation been seated, for in the late spring he had been ordered to Philadelphia with the *Planter* for a complete overhaul of the vessel. The job
took many months. But while in Philadelphia he achieved literacy and
became prominent in the work of groups in the city aiding the Port
Royal Experiment. He managed also to strike an effective blow against
the discrimination suffered by blacks in the "City of Brotherly Love."

On taking a seat on a streetcar one rainy day, he was ordered by the
conductor to move to the outer platform, as then required of blacks by
Philadelphia law. Smalls left the car and walked on in the rain. The
episode was widely publicized. A Union hero had been humiliated.
Sentiment grew to eliminate race laws in Philadelphia.

When Union Maj. Gen. William T. Sherman captured coastal Savannah, Georgia, in December 1864, at the end of his world-famous
"March to the Sea," Smalls and the *Planter* were kept busy on chores
for Sherman's army as it regrouped for another march northward into
the Carolinas. Isolated by that march, Charleston fell to the Union
on February 17, 1865. Following along was Smalls, en route to an
interesting homecoming, to a confrontation with his past.

A few days after the fall of the city, Smalls brought General Saxton
to Charleston, to be greeted by a crowd of cheering blacks. On the
outskirts of the crowd stood a few whites. Among them Smalls spotted
the original owner of the *Planter*, his former employer. Pushing
through the crowd, Smalls introduced the gentleman to Saxton, an
eloquent sign of Smalls' newfound equality. Two months later, on April
14, the fourth anniversary of the Union's loss of Fort Sumter, Smalls
and the *Planter* took part in the great ceremony in Charleston Harbor.
The old flag was raised again over Sumter. One of a Northern tour
party, in describing the scene in the harbor that day, wrote, "Almost
central in interest, the *Planter*, crowded almost to suffocation" with
freedmen, was commanded by Smalls, "a prince among them, self-
possessed, prompt and proud."

With the war's end Beaufort became Smalls' permanent home. Before the war, his former master's residence, including the quarters
where he was born, had been sold to another Carolinian who, during
the war, was colonel of a Confederate South Carolina regiment. In

1863 United States tax authorities had put up the property for sale for nonpayment of federal taxes, and it was acquired by the United States Government itself. In 1865 Smalls bought it from the government, and lived there the rest of his life. In postwar years the former owner sued to recover the property, contending that the tax sale was invalid. It was a test case affecting many properties in the South, and it went to the United States Supreme Court. There Smalls' land title was defended by the solicitor general of the United States and sustained.

In the meantime, Smalls became a political leader in South Carolina. In the spring of 1867 he helped organize the first Republican Club in that state and soon was on his way to prominence in state offices. Then, in 1874, he was elected as a Republican from the Beaufort district to the United States House of Representatives. In five of the six congresses between that time and 1887 he served in the House. Thereafter, no black had such a long congressional tenure until the 1950s. But in 1886 white supremacists finally stole the election from him, and his subsequent contest of the seat, in a House controlled by Democrats, was in vain.

In 1890, on appointment by Republican President Benjamin Harrison, he became collector of the Port of Beaufort. With an interruption only during the presidency of Democratic President Grover Cleveland, whose second term followed Harrison's, Smalls held that post until 1913. Again, Democratic pressure ended his service. But he would not live much longer. He died in 1915.

Over and over, between 1876 and 1900, there were proposals in Congress to reward Smalls for his outstanding wartime service. In 1883 a House committee report on one measure told in some detail of that service and branded as "absurdly low" the 1862 appraisal of the *Planter* and her cargo; it concluded from evidence it had taken that a fair 1862 valuation would have been more than $60,000. In 1897 a special statute provided Smalls a pension of $30 a month, the pension at the time for a United States Navy captain. That did not still congressional agitation. Finally, in 1900, Congress adopted the statute providing Smalls be paid $5,000, less the amount paid him under the 1862 law. Many then and now believe he received less than his due.

6

Captive Black
Union Soldiers
in Charleston—
What to Do?

"**T**HIRTEEN prisoners Fifty-fourth Massachusetts, black. What shall I do with them?" That message, hastily penned by Confederate Gen. Johnson Hagood on the night of July 16, 1863, near the beginning of the Union attack on Fort Wagner, also noted that two of the blacks were "refugee" slaves, the rest free.[1]

The general's question posed a conundrum. The Confederacy had been struggling with it for months and would continue to struggle with it until the war was dwindling to an end. By mid-1863, the Union, after long hesitation, was taking blacks into its army by the thousands. Inevitably some had become Confederate captives. In time there were many more. Some had been slaves in the state where captured. Some had been slaves in others of the Confederate states. Some had been slaves in Union slave states. Some had been free, residents of Union states or even of the Confederacy (notably Louisiana). Many blacks had donned the Union uniform voluntarily; but not a few, especially among slaves of Confederate states, had been forced into the army, either by formal conscription or by irregular means. Nearly all would be in the ranks, and eventually some would be commissioned. Captive, too, would be some of their white officers. Finally, among captives there would be officers and men of white units operating in conjunction with black units. The law of every Confederate state made slave insur-

Originally published in *Civil War History* 28, no. 1 (March 1982):28–44. Reprinted with permission of The Kent State University Press.

rection or aiding such insurrection a crime; and, as viewed by the Confederate: slaves in arms as Union soldiers were engaged in insurrection. The conundrum: were all these captives regular prisoners of war or were they all common criminals; or were some the former and some the latter? Or were some captives something in between, in some new, unprecedented status? Or were some simply to be slain, without ceremony? Confederate statesmen, politicians, military commanders, judges, lawyers, and ordinary soldiers and civilians were to face this puzzle. Nowhere in the Confederacy was it posed more starkly than in Charleston. For, from late 1862 until almost the end of the war, in Charleston and its near regions there was repeated conflict with Union forces that included slaves of the local citizenry and, by 1863, slaves from elsewhere as well as free blacks.

General Hagood's query, after receipt at district headquarters, was forwarded at once to General Beauregard, commander of the Department of South Carolina, Georgia, and Florida, headquartered in Charleston. With it went word that the captive blacks had been ordered to the city under a strong guard and "without their uniforms."[2] On the next day, July 17, the department sent a copy of Hagood's note to South Carolina Gov. M. L. Bonham. At the same time, Beauregard informed Richmond that he had black prisoners from the Union forces, several of whom "claim to be free, from Massachusetts." He asked, "Shall they be turned over to State authorities with the other negroes?"[3]

It reflected the confusion in the Confederacy at that time—the time of Chancellorsville, Gettysburg, Vicksburg, and Port Hudson—that neither General Beauregard nor Governor Bonham yet knew that on May 1, 1863, President Davis had approved a joint resolution of the Confederate Congress that, as we shall see, answered Beauregard's question. The general and governor both thought that President Davis' proclamation of December 23, 1862, promulgated on Christmas Eve, was still applicable: that "all negro slaves captured in arms be at once delivered over to the executive authorities of the respective States to which they belong to be dealt with according to the laws of said States" and that "like orders be executed in all cases with respect to all commissioned officers of the United States when found serving in company with armed slaves."[4]

Doubtless Beauregard thought that the proclamation had been carefully formulated, for it had followed by less than a month quite different instructions that he had received from Secretary of War Seddon. In mid-November 1862, one of Beauregard's district commanders had captured four slaves, armed and in Union uniform, and Beauregard immediately had sought Seddon's guidance. After checking with the president, Seddon on November 30 had instructed Beauregard to avoid a dilemma. On the one hand, delay and "military inconvenience" would be caused by turning the slaves over to civil tribunals, and, on the other hand, they could not be recognized as "soldiers subject to the rules of war and to trial by military courts." The way between the dilemma's horns, Seddon instructed, was to have the "general commanding the special locality of the capture" inflict on the slaves "summary execution."[5] Obviously, Davis' proclamation, coming so soon after Seddon's harsh instruction, must have been thought through. And notably, it said nothing about free blacks. So Beauregard wanted further guidance. Indeed, as it turned out, most of the black captives claimed that they had not been slaves.

A very recent episode had shown Beauregard that he was in a delicate area. It had been only a month since General Hagood had forwarded a report that several young Confederate soldiers had been captured by Union forces at an observation outpost along one of the coastal waters. They were "sons of wealthy planters or themselves owners of slaves" and were lodged in the Beaufort jail instead of being treated as prisoners of war subject to exchange. It was said that the young men were kept hostage for black Union troops or their officers who might be captured by the Confederates.[6]

It was well for Beauregard to take warning from that report, for the facts behind it were sobering. It seems that the young Confederates were a sergeant and eight privates captured by the Union navy and that the navy had acceded to a demand of Union General Hunter, then army commander in the Sea Islands region, that they be turned over to him. Hunter knew that regiments of former slaves in his command had been one of the causes for the institution of a Confederate policy denying prisoner-of-war treatment to blacks and their officers. When he had found that among the navy's prisoners were "young darlings" of southern families "rich, powerful and malignant," "pets of the aristocracy," he wanted them as hostages.[7] Moreover, on the very day of the report that Hagood had forwarded, Hunter had instructed the commander of one of his black regiments, a onetime Jayhawker, Col. James Montgomery, that "every rebel man you may capture, citizen or soldier, you will send in irons to this place to be kept as hostages for the proper treatment of any of your men who may accidentally fall into the hands of the enemy."[8] While Beauregard would not have known of Hunter's instruction to Montgomery, he did know of a letter that Hunter had written to President Davis as recently as April 23, 1863, that revealed his attitude. Back in August 1862, when Hunter had been first trying to take slaves into his army, Davis had had his War Department issue an order declaring Hunter an outlaw and providing for his execution as a felon, on presidential order, if captured, and the execution of any other captured Union officer engaged in "instructing slaves, with a view to their armed service in this war." In his April letter, Hunter had announced to Davis that if the August order were not revoked, "I will at once cause the execution of every rebel officer and every rebel slaveholder in my possession."[9]

While, by the time of the Union expedition against Fort Wagner, Hunter had been superseded by General Gillmore as the Union army commander,[10] it was obvious enough to Beauregard that measure and contermeasure, retaliation met by retaliation, might soon make war uncivilized, and that he should exercise caution in his treatment of captive blacks. Indeed, there already had been a breakdown of the Union-Confederate prisoner exchange cartel so that any exchange was limited to "special agreements." The Confederate treatment of blacks had been one of the principal causes of the breakdown and would persist as an obstacle to repair.[11]

While Beauregard was writing Richmond, Governor Bonham was asking his state attorney general what evidence was required to render blacks captured in arms "amenable" for delivery to the state's executive under the presidential proclamation. On the next day, July 18, the attorney general opined that, since 1740, "by the laws of South Carolina a negro is presumed to be a slave until the contrary appears." Moreover, he advised, authoritative commentary had declared that "color is prima facie evidence that the party bearing the color of a negro, mulatto or mestizo is a slave." Hence, he concluded, General Beauregard must deliver to the governor all Negroes captured in arms in South Carolina "unless by evidence before him he is satisfied that the prima facie presumption of slavery arising from color has been rebutted."[12]

The governor sent Beauregard a copy of his attorney general's opinion, and they conducted "some informal proceedings."[13] Though more blacks than those first reported by General Hagood were being captured, of the few who did not claim to be free not one was a South Carolinian. The presidential proclamation had ordered that slaves should be turned over to the executive of the state "to which they belong." Also, among the captives, there were white officers of black units, and the proclamation had ordered that "like orders be executed" for such men. Beauregard apparently thought that the proclamation meant what it said, that his slave captives and their officers were not to be turned over to South Carolina authorities, but, presumably, were to be sent to the "belonging" state. The governor—who was a lawyer and formerly had been both a United States and a Confederate congressman[14]—read words not for what they said but for what they intended; in his view, however strained, the state "to which they belong" was intended to be the state where the "offense" of slave rebellion and the capture had occurred—South Carolina. But on the question of the free blacks, Beauregard and the governor did agree that further word from the president was needed.

As a result, on July 21, Beauregard followed up his recent inquiry to Richmond with a wire: "What shall be done with the negro prisoners who say they are free? Please answer."[15] And on the next day the governor wrote Beauregard formally demanding custody of the captured slaves and white officers and asking that the free blacks be retained—not exchanged or paroled—pending word from Richmond. As to the slaves, said the governor, if Beauregard disagreed with this interpretation of "to which [state] they belong," they also should be retained until the president could resolve the question. On the following day, July 23, the governor wrote Secretary of War Seddon, enclosing a copy of his letter to Beauregard, requesting not only the slaves and white officers but also the free blacks; the latter he said, had violated a South Carolina statute of 1805 prescribing death for any person "concerned or connected with any slave or slaves in a state of actual insurrection within this State."[16]

On the day the governor had written Beauregard, Seddon had wired the general that, pursuant to a resolution of the Confederate Congress, "all negroes taken in arms" were "to be handed over to the authorities of the State where captured to be dealt with according to the laws thereof." And on the day the governor wrote Seddon, Beauregard wired the secretary of war that he did not know of the resolution, that, indeed, a congressman had informed him that "it failed to pass."[17] But finally the governor located a copy of the resolution and, on July 27, sent it to the general.[18]

This was the resolution of May 1. It provided, as Seddon's wire had indicated, that all "negroes and mulattoes" (slave or free) who are "engaged in war . . . against the Confederate States" or who "give aid or comfort to the enemies of the Confederate States" shall, on capture, "be delivered to the authorities of the State or States in which they shall be captured to be dealt with according to the present or future law of such State or States."[19] Hence, on July 29, the governor was advised by Beauregard that the blacks, slave and free, were at his disposal. The governor, however, was not yet ready to take custody, and at his request they were kept in Castle Pinckney, the military prison, until August 19, when they were transferred to the Charleston jail.[20]

For a time, however, the governor was confused about the white officers. Perhaps he had not read closely the congressional resolution before sending it to the general. For, on August 8, he wrote Seddon requesting that the officers also be delivered to him.[21] Two days later, though, he had found that the resolution explicitly provided that captured officers from black units would not be turned over to state authorities but would be tried by a Confederate military court and "be put to death or be otherwise punished at the discretion of the court," subject to the president's power to commute sentence.[22] Thus, on August 10, the governor wrote Seddon again, withdrawing his request for the officers. But in this further letter, Bonham raised a question: would it be quite right for a free black to be given one sentence— South Carolina law, as we have seen, prescribed death, subject only to the governor's general power of commutation—but his officer to be given a less severe punishment, as was possible under the congressional resolution? His letter suggested some arrangement between the state and Confederate authorities for uniformity of treatment. Bonham also advised Seddon that he would proceed with the trial of slaves and any free blacks from Confederate states but would delay action on free blacks from the North, hoping to hear word on the question he had raised.[23] The governor was beginning to glimpse something of the conundrum.

In the meantime, there was mounting public outrage that the defenders of Charleston were confronting armed blacks. The press reported that the Confederate troops were indignant at the thought that a white man might one day be exchanged for a Negro. The Northern blacks were described as "a mongrel set of trash." Incidents were reported of blacks, seeking to surrender, being summarily shot. To lend grim humor to the issue, the story was quoted of a Frenchman who begged for quarter from a Scot: " 'I canna stop to quarter ye,' he remarked, 'but I'll cut ye in twa.' And suiting his actions to his words he passed on." Indeed, the account of the opening engagement in the Fort Wagner attack told that the blacks "received no tender treatment during the skirmish, and the marsh in one place was thick with their dead bodies."[24]

One of the local papers, virulently anti-Davis, knowing that the governor had demanded that free black captives be turned over to him, assumed that their continued residence in Castle Pinckney was due to "that serbonian bog of indecision—Richmond."[25] The authorities were quick to correct the paper's misunderstanding; already the governor was preparing for criminal proceedings. On August 10, he had instructed his attorney general to convene a court for the trial of such of the captives as appeared to be slaves or to be free blacks of the Confederate states and on the next day Bonham ordered a three-man commission—two of his staff and another "prominent citizen"—to examine all the black prisoners.[26]

On August 14, the commission reported to the governor. There were, by then, twenty-four black captives other than hospitalized wounded. Each of the twenty-four was questioned separately. One prisoner seemed defiant; all the others were respectful. Only four appeared to be slaves. Of the twenty free men, not one was from a Confederate state (though one seemed to be from Maryland). All were from the Fifty-fourth Massachusetts Regiment (Colored). Questioning disclosed, however, that the entire unit contained not more than fifty or sixty blacks from Massachusetts and but a few more from other New England states; in fact, about a third of the regiment had come from Ohio.

The commissioners had, for the most part, believed the stories they heard, for they were convincingly similar. All but the one defiant captive were utterly disillusioned by their treatment in the Union army and were eager to return to civilian life. In substance their complaints were three: (1) their enlistment had been solicited by the promise that their service would not be for combat but merely for garrison and fatigue duty; (2) promises of bounty and rates of pay had been grossly violated; and (3) in battle they had been put in the forefront "as breastworks for the White Troops," told by their officers that they would be shot from behind if they did not advance. Some said that their officers deserted them. Two prisoners were unarmed officers' servants, carrying into the attack only canteens for their officers.[27]

On August 14, the day the commission filed its report with the governor, Seddon was writing Bonham in reply to the letter of August 8, which had requested custody of the blacks' officers. Seddon pointed out that the congressional resolution superseded the presidential proclamation and that the officers were thus to be handled by the military. He assured Bonham that "appropriate proceedings will be instituted and severe punishment inflicted upon the officers taken in the unworthy and criminal service of commanding negroes, thereby inciting to servile insurrection and all its attendant horrors within your State."[28]

Though Seddon's letter was not in fact a reply to the governor's letter of August 10, in which he had withdrawn his earlier request but had raised the question of uniformity of punishment for free blacks and their officers, it seemed to say that the military would deal harshly with the officers. So, on August 19, with Seddon's letter received, the governor transmitted a copy to his attorney general, telling him to "defer no longer the trial of the free negroes of the Federal States found in arms with slaves."[29] By August 21, the governor had assigned as counsel to the blacks a very able Charleston lawyer, Mr. Nelson Mitchell; on that day Bonham sent instructions to the Charleston sheriff to allow Mitchell and "lawyers associated with him" to have access to the prisoners "for the purpose of preparing for their defence."[30]

Soon—perhaps at Mitchell's request—the governor appointed as his co-counsel Mr. Edward McCrady, also a very able Charleston lawyer. The governor ordered the attorney general personally to prosecute the case, designating as his co-counsel one of the members of the commission that had examined the prisoners.[31] The matter was now coming to a head. On August 25, the court met and organized for the trial.[32] It was the police court for the Charleston District, sometimes called the provost marshal's court, with criminal jurisdiction over slaves and free blacks, and its decisions were not subject to appeal. The proceedings began on September 8; but only the four alleged slaves were brought to trial, despite the governor's instruction of August 19 that the free black captives were to be tried also.[33]

It is not known whether the trial was confined to the four slaves as a result of lawyers' tactics or as a result of the receipt by the governor of a further letter from Seddon, written on September 1, replying to Bonham's letter of August 10.[34] When the governor read this further letter, he was to find new confusion injected into Confederate policy. In Richmond, the complexity of the conundrum was becoming apparent. In early June, Seddon had written an old school friend, who had suggested that captured officers and men of black regiments be put to work "in the Chesterfield coal-pits," that the law required that slaves be turned over to the states and that blacks "without free papers when not claimed by the owners" would "be liable to be sold as slaves."[35] But that easy dictate hardly met the problem. The problem was soon to be posed to Richmond more insistently by Gen. Kirby Smith, commanding the Department of the Trans-Mississippi.

In mid-June, Smith sent to Richmond copies of letters written to Gen. Richard Taylor, one of his district commanders who had custody of some blacks "captured in arms." Smith did not know of the congressional resolution; like Beauregard, he had understood that the legislation had not been adopted, leaving in force the presidential proclamation. One of the letters to Taylor had been sent by Smith's assistant adjutant general; it told Taylor that "no quarter" should be given to slaves in arms, but, if quarter were given, they should be turned over to the executive authorities of the state where captured. (Apparently Smith, like Governor Bonham, interpreted "to which they belong" in the proclamation not to mean what the words said.) The letter went on to say that if such blacks were executed by the military, Union retaliation would be provoked; but the author naïvely added that if they were turned over to the civil authorities to be tried under state law, "no exception can be taken." The other letter to Taylor was from Smith himself, who hoped that Taylor's subordinates "recognized the propriety of giving no quarter to armed negroes and their officers. In this way we may be relieved from a disagreeable dilemma." But if blacks were taken captive, Smith added, they should be turned over to state authorities for trial. In sending copies of the two letters to Richmond, Smith wrote, "Unfortunately such captures were made by some of Major-General Taylor's subordinates."[36]

With Smith's communication in hand by mid-July, Seddon had a reply sent that suggested a different policy. The reply did not mention officers, only the blacks. They, "as deluded victims," ought to be "treated with mercy and returned to their owners." However, "a few examples might perhaps be made," though "to refuse them quarter" would make them, "against their tendencies, fight desperately."[37] If, by the time Smith received this word, he had been informed of the congressional resolution, he must have wondered if his secretary of war intended to follow it; for the resolution was perfectly clear—all blacks, slave or free, were to be turned over to state authorities to be dealt with under state law; it made no provision either for refusing quarter or for the military's return of a slave to his owner.

In any event, Governor Bonham's letters, especially that of August 10 suggesting uniform treatment of free blacks and their officers, forced Seddon to seek instruction from his president. Perhaps he wanted such guidance because of a recent action by the president of the United States. On July 31, the Union's War Department had promulgated a proclamation by President Lincoln announcing that the Union would protect all of its citizens, "of whatsoever class, color, or condition," and that "for every soldier of the United States killed in violation of the laws of war a rebel soldier shall be executed, and for every one enslaved by the enemy or sold into slavery a rebel soldier shall be placed at hard labor on the public works. . . ."[38] When Seddon received Bonham's August 10 letter, he sent it to President Davis for instruction. The president returned it, inviting Seddon to state his own views. On August 23, Seddon resubmitted the letter with his endorsement, saying that "the free negroes should be either promptly executed or the determination arrived at and announced not to execute them during the war." They should not be treated as prisoners of war, said Seddon, but dealt with so as "to mark our stern reprobation of the barbarous employment of such inciters to insurrection." Seddon suggested that the way to do this "effectually" would be "by holding them to hard labor during the war." Seddon did not suggest how this course might be squared with the May 1863 congressional resolution.

On August 25, President Davis returned Bonham's letter to Seddon with his own endorsement added. He noted that the congressional resolution "gives no discretion to the Executive so far as the captured negroes are concerned." But, said Davis, the statute did provide, in the case of "white men serving with negroes" (Davis did not say "officers"), that he had the power "to commute penalty" that might be imposed by a military court. This, Davis noted, indicated "a purpose to make discriminations" among individual cases. So, Davis concluded,

Bonham's suggestion that there be "the same line of action" by the state and by the Confederate governments (in their respective treatment of free blacks and officers) could not be given a definite answer "as each case must depend upon its circumstances"—unless (and here the conundrum surely was confessed), "as you intimate," it be decided "not to bring any case to trial." As to that possibility Davis said that he did "not know how far the power of the Governor extends."[39]

It was with the problem thus back in his lap that Seddon wrote to Bonham on September 1. His letter quoted his own endorsement to the president and the president's return endorsement. To the governor he recommended that "the captured negroes be not brought to trial, or if condemned, that your power of executive clemency be exercised" to allow for the possibility of an "arrangement on this question, so fraught with present difficulty and future danger." The difficulty and danger referred to, of course, was Union retaliation.[40]

Whether or not it was this word from Seddon that prompted the decision not to go forward with the trial of the free blacks when the four alleged slaves were tried, that decision at least was consistent with a position then being taken by the Confederate agent of exchange in a conference with his Union counterpart on the breakdown of the prisoner exchange cartel. At the conference, as the Union agent reported to his superior on August 25, the Confederate agent said that his people would "die in the last ditch" before giving up their right to send captured slaves back to slavery but that they were willing to make "exceptions" for free blacks.[41] Obviously, the seeming neat simplicity of the Confederate Congress' resolution was becoming befogged.

The trial of the four slaves, however, did proceed. It lasted for three days, from September 8 to 10. The court was a five-man tribunal. There were two charges: that, being slaves, the defendants had been in insurrection against the state; and that they had been "concerned and connected with slaves" in insurrection. Allegedly, two of the defendants had been slaves in Missouri and two in Virginia. The second of the two charges presumably was designed to cover the case were it decided that only its own slaves could be deemed to be in insurrection against South Carolina; the evidence was to show that in any case the defendants had been encamped with two Union regiments of South Carolina slaves.

At the trial, the only evidentiary conflict was whether or not one of the defendants in fact had been a slave. Time was largely devoted to lawyers' arguments, chiefly on the question of "the jurisdiction of the court, as a Civil Tribunal, to try offenses committed by persons engaged as soldiers in the act of war, and in the ranks of the enemy." The unanimous decision of the judges, announced without elaboration, was that the court had no jurisdiction. Thereupon the court ordered that the prisoners be recommitted to jail and that the governor be notified of its decision.[42] The captives were subsequently held in the Charleston jail, month after dreary month, along with other captured blacks. Already in the jail when they had arrived were four black Union sailors, as least three of whom were freeborn New Yorkers.

Despite the fact that from the Republic's early days the Union to which the Confederate states had been parties had enlisted blacks in its navy (though not in its army),[43] the Confederates treated these black sailors harshly. As crew members of the Union gunboat *Isaac Smith*, they, with the boat's officers and rest of the crew, had been captured in Charleston's waters in late January 1863. In time, the officers and white crewmen were exchanged. The Confederate exchange agent had included the names of the blacks in the exchange list furnished to the Union agent, but that had been a deception. Not until August did Union authorities hear that the blacks in fact were incarcerated in the Charleston jail. The three black New Yorkers had managed to have smuggled out a note to the United States consul in Nassau telling of their fate: "in close confinement," "almost dead," fed "but a little corn bread and water." Their note was forwarded to Washington, where, on August 3, Secretary of Navy Welles sent it on to Secretary of War Stanton for his "special attention." General Hitchcock, the Union commissioner for exchange, advised Stanton that there had been "other cases like this" and that, in his view, "they can only be effectually reached by a successful prosecution of the war." Stanton then ordered Hitchcock to have three South Carolina prisoners held "in close custody as hostages for the three colored men" and to communicate that action to Richmond.[44] Three captive privates of a South Carolina Confederate cavalry unit were put to "hard labor on the public works" in Washington.[45] But in the Charleston jail the three New Yorkers and a fourth black crewman remained confined.[46]

For Governor Bonham, by mid-September, the conundrum had become most sharply posed. The Confederate Congress had decreed that all captured blacks were to be turned over to state authorities "to be dealt with according to" state law. But the governor's own state court had ruled that a South Carolina crime had not been committed by "persons engaged as soldiers in the act of war," even though they had been slaves. While Bonham later was to write Seddon that "the correctness" of that decision "may be questioned," he could hardly defy it. Aside from its finality under state law, the standing of the counsel involved gave it force. Prosecuted by the attorney general and defended by two of the state's leading lawyers—characterized by Bonham himself as "eminent"—the outcome of the case could not be shrugged off.[47] While the court's ruling, on its face, seemed applicable to slaves of South Carolina as well as other states, the governor in time did have at least some South Carolinian slaves tried before other state courts, and they were executed. But beyond that he did not go; with his president fuzzily suggesting that blacks not be brought to trial and with the secretary of war, obviously troubled by the problem of Union retaliation, recommending that the governor postpone a decision, Bonham simply "suspended further action," leaving the blacks in the Charleston jail at the expense of the state and local civil governments.[48] His bafflement must have increased when he found, as surely he soon did, that white officers of black units were not being given the severe treatment by the military that Seddon had so confidently predicted. With only a few exceptions, nowhere in the Confederacy was the pertinent provision of the congressional resolution actually carried out; the officers were treated rather as prisoners of war.[49]

Nearly a year after the Charleston trial, the governor picked up word from the Richmond press that further complicated the problem. It was reported that recently captured Union soldiers who had been slaves were being delivered to their former owners. Puzzled, on June 24, 1864, the governor wrote Seddon asking for any pertinent regulations.[50] There is no record of a reply. Two months later, on August 23, he wrote Seddon again, saying that, in line with Seddon's letter of September 1, 1863, he had suspended action as to all captive blacks except those who had been South Carolina slaves, but he wanted to bring the question "again to your attention, in order that something definite may be done if practicable." He explained that his term of office would end in December and that he would "be glad" to dispose of the matter before then.[51]

That the governor was in a mood to place the whole business behind him is suggested by the fact that his office had just requested the state auditor to recommend "a suitable and proper fee" to be paid to the lawyers who had conducted the prosecution and the defense in the trial of the previous September. In early September 1864, the auditor, after consulting "eminent members of the bar," recommended that a proper fee would be one thousand dollars "to each of the Council on the part of the State and on the part of the prisoners respectively."[52] This recommendation reached the governor just after he had received a reply from Seddon to his August 23 letter. Seddon's reply, dated August 31, must have made Bonham wonder whether all the trouble and expense undertaken by the state had been worth the candle.

Seddon said, in effect, that the Confederate executive and military were ignoring the congressional resolution of May 1, 1863, because of "embarrassments" from its "rigid enforcement." ("Embarrassments," of course, referred to Union retaliation.) Moreover, some state authorities had objected to having blacks turned over to them and often complained about the "inability . . . to obtain criminal trials." So, said Seddon, captives who had been slaves were being returned to their owners under a statute of October 1862. But "free negroes of the North are held in strict confinement, not as yet formally recognized in any official dealing with the enemy as prisoners-of-war, but, except in some trivial particulars indicative of inferior consideration, are treated very much in the same manner as our other captives." Seddon concluded with advice that the governor deliver slaves to their owners and free blacks "to the Confederate authorities."[53]

The October 1862 statute referred to by Seddon had been adopted at the closing of the second session of the First Confederate Congress as a reaction to President Lincoln's Preliminary Emancipation Proclamation. It had provided that the secretary of war should establish depots in each state to hold slaves captured by the Confederate military. Each slave would be returned to his owner on due proof of the owner's claim; newspaper advertisements of the slave would be published, and until proof of claim was forthcoming the slave would be employed by the military on public works. The bill from whence came the statute had provided also that captured free blacks should be delivered to the governor of the state where captured "to be dealt with according to the laws of such State," but the House committee handling the bill had eliminated that provision.[54] Thus, the measure was very different from the severe congressional resolution of May 1, 1863. Indeed it may be that the 1862 statute had been intended initially to apply only to noncombatant slaves, fugitive or seized by Union forces, captured by the Confederate military; and it certainly had not been designed to cover the case of slaves of a non-Confederate state (Delaware and Maryland).[55] In any case, whatever the intended scope of that statute, and even though the 1863 resolution had not amended it in express terms, the latter most certainly had superseded the former with respect to slaves captured in arms. But now the Confederate executive, by sheer fiat, had superseded the 1863 measure in its entirety with the much narrower and milder 1862 statute.

If, on Governor Bonham's reading of Seddon's August 31 letter, he questioned what the military would do with free blacks "not as yet formally recognized . . . as prisoners-of-war," that uncertainty was removed in a letter sent a few weeks later, at Seddon's instruction, by General Lee to General Grant. This letter, sent on October 19, defended the propriety of the Confederates' returning to their owners captured Union soldiers or sailors who had been slaves of "citizens or residents of the Confederate States," but stated, unambiguously, that all other blacks in the Union armed services "are regarded as prisoners of war, being held to be proper subjects of exchange, as I recently had the honor to inform you. No labor is exacted from such prisoners by the Confederate authorities."[56]

When, if ever, that authoritative word reached Bonham it must have heightened his confusion. Obviously, in his Charleston jail there were many free blacks, and they certainly were not being treated as prisoners of war. Further, he felt that some among his prisoners had been slaves, and Seddon's August 31 letter had advised that they be delivered to their owners, not kept in jail. But from the evidence available to him, Bonham could not identify either the slaves or their owners. Even as to the four who had been tried the year before, there was a problem. As to one, an alleged Virginia slave, evidence of his slavery was not clear; he may have been a freeborn Ohioan. Two of the others were from Hannibal, Missouri, and the third from Norfolk, Virginia.[57] Identifying their owners and returning them would be, to put it mildly, impractical at that state of the war. Finally, as the end of his term loomed near, the governor gave up. On December 8, he wrote Seddon that on that day he had ordered the Charleston sheriff to deliver all the prisoners to the Confederate military. "A few of them, it is supposed, may be slaves," he wrote, "but the State has no means of identifying them or their masters." He told Seddon that he had given the military "the evidence from which it is supposed that some of them may be slaves."[58]

In the meantime, for nearly a year and a half, the blacks had been suffering a jail confinement with the scantiest of fare and the most miserable of conditions.[59] Neither the Confederacy nor the state ever had notified the Union authorities of their identity; they had been nonpersons. While rumors reached the North that there were black prisoners in South Carolina, there was no way for the Union authorities to know who of the missing were dead and who imprisoned. But finally there came in August 1864 another smuggled note brought by an exchanged white officer. The note pleaded that something be done to release the prisoners from their "destitute condition." The note was signed, "Mass.," but appended a list of forty-six blacks in the Charleston jail as of June 13, 1864, most from the Fifty-fourth Massachusetts, including the four who had been defendants in the trial of the preceding September. In a few days the list was published in the New York press.[60] But, as we have seen, the blacks remained in jail until turned over to the Confederate military in December.

From that time, their circumstances, miserable as they had been, worsened. For their destination was the military prison stockade at Florence, South Carolina, which rivaled Andersonville. Disease was rife, and some died, including two of those who had been defendants at the September trial, victims of fever.[61] The Confederacy was disintegrating. By late January 1865, General Winder, in charge of prisons in the area, wanted to move his Florence prisoners; but he was "at a loss to know where," for "in one direction the enemy are in the way. In the other the question of supplies presents an insuperable barrier." He urged "paroling the prisoners and sending them home." Bonham's successor as governor and General Chesnut, a leading South Carolinian, agreed with him.[62] But Winder's proposal was not accepted. Instead the prisoners were moved from place to place in North Carolina.[63] In the meantime, by the end of January the Confederate Congress had drastically amended the May 1, 1863, resolution so that it became nothing more than a condemnation of the employment of Confederate slaves as Union soldiers and a mere authorization to the president to retaliate as he thought proper. President Davis approved the amendment on February 8.[64] Finally, in early March, as General Sherman drove northward, most if not all of the black captives who had survived were released near Goldsboro, North Carolina. It is uncertain from records whether they were paroled, exchanged, or simply released.[65] No matter. The nonpersons had become persons again. And in Charleston, the struggle with the conundrum was no more. On February 18, Charleston had been occupied by the Union army.

Notes

1. U.S. War Dept., *The War of the Rebellion: A Compilation of the Official Records of the Union and Confederate Armies*, 70 vols. in 128 pts. (1880–1901; rpt. National Historical Society, Gettysburg, 1972), ser. 2, 6:123 (hereafter cited as *ORA*); Papers of F. W. Pickens and M. L. Bonham, Library of Congress, 3:519. Hereafter, citation to *ORA* will be to ser. 2 except where otherwise indicated, and citation to the Pickens/Bonham Papers will be to vol. 3.

2. *ORA*, 6:124.

3. Bonham Papers, p. 519; *ORA*, 6:125.

4. *ORA*, 5:795–97. In his message of Jan. 12, 1863, opening the third session of the First Confederate Congress, President Davis said that he would treat the "enlisted soldiers" (meaning whites) as "unwilling instruments" of crime and would release them on parole, James D. Richardson, comp., *A Compilation of the Messages and Papers of the Confederacy, Including the Diplomatic Correspondence, 1861–1865*, 2 vols. (United States Publishing Co., Nashville, 1905), 1:290–91.

5. *ORA*, 4:945–46, 954.

6. *ORA*, 5:970.

7. It is virtually certain that the captives in the Beaufort jail were the Confederate soldiers, captured by the Union navy, whose custody as hostages Hunter had demanded of Admiral DuPont, naval commander in the area, Secretary of the Navy Welles, and President Lincoln, *ORA*, 5:646–47, 659, 666, 697, 698, 708, 711–13. Hence I infer that Hunter's demand had been met.

8. *ORA*, 5:770.

9. *ORA*, ser. 1, 14:448–49, 599; *Charleston Mercury*, June 9, 1863.

10. *Charleston Mercury*, June 9, 13, 1863.

11. *ORA*, 6:136; William Best Hesseltine, *Civil War Prisons* (The Ohio State Univ. Press, Columbus, 1930), pp. 87–89, 112–13, 186–88, 216–30.

12. Bonham Papers, p. 521.

13. *Charleston Mercury*, Aug. 15, 1863.

14. Edward McCrady, Jr., and Samuel A. Ashe, *Cyclopedia of Eminent and Representative Men of the Carolinas*, 2 vols. (Brant & Fuller, Madison, Wis., 1892), 1:88–90; Charles Edward Cauthen, *South Carolina Goes to War* (Univ. of North Carolina Press, Chapel Hill, 1950), p. 166.

15. *ORA*, 6:134.

16. *ORA*, 6:139–40, 145–46; Bonham Papers, p. 523.

17. *ORA*, 6:139, 145.

18. *Charleston Mercury*, Aug. 15, 1863.

19. *ORA*, 5:940–41.

20. *Charleston Mercury*, Aug. 13, 15, 20, 1863; commitment to jail of Alfred Whiting and other Negro soldiers, S.C. Archives, Commitments, 1863, 1864, penal system papers, 1860–65, 7:238, dr. 3.

21. *ORA*, 6:190–91.

22. *ORA*, 5:940–41.

23. *ORA*, 6:193–94; Bonham Papers, p. 535.

24. *Charleston Courier*, July 17, 20, 22, Aug. 1, 1863; *Charleston Mercury*, Aug. 15, 1863.

25. *Charleston Mercury*, Aug. 11, 12, 1863.

26. *Charleston Mercury*, Aug. 13, 15, 1863; Bonham Papers, p. 536.

27. Bonham Papers, pp. 540–41. In the Bonham Papers, pp. 542–49, immediately following the commission's report, are notes of interviews with each of the twenty-four blacks; legibility is difficult. (At that time there were twenty-odd hospitalized wounded black captives in addition to those held in Castle Pinckney; see *ORA*, 6:187–88; *Charleston Courier*, Aug. 11, 1863.) The professed disillusionment of the blacks probably was not feigned. Early in 1863, Governor Andrew of Massachusetts secured authority from the War Department to raise and organize black troops; thus was created the Fifty-fourth Massachusetts. But there were few blacks in Massachusetts or even in all of New England. An intensive recruiting drive was launched throughout much of the North. Unquestionably, recruiters offered strong inducements. The failure to make good on promised compensation is a familiar story. Familiar too is the fact that Col. Robert Gould Shaw, commanding the Fifty-fourth, sought and secured a lead spot in opening assaults in the Fort Wagner operation; see Dudley Taylor Cornish, *The Sable Arm: Negro Troops in the Union Army, 1861–1865* (1956; rpt. W. W. Norton & Co., New York, 1966), pp. 105–10, 150–56, 184–96. Interestingly, though the Preliminary Emancipation Proclamation had not referred to blacks' becoming soldiers, the final proclamation had announced that the freed slaves would be received into the armed service "to garrison forts, positions, stations, and other places and to man vessels"; see James D. Richardson, comp., *A Compilation of the Messages and Papers of the Presidents, 1789–1897*, 10 vols. (published by authority of Congress, Washington, 1896–99), 6: 96–98, 157–59. When general recruitment of blacks began in early 1863, many had the impression that they would be assigned to garrison and fatigue duty; see Cornish, *Sable Arm*, p. 240.

28. *ORA*, 6:202.

29. Bonham Papers, p. 553.

30. Bonham Papers, p. 560.

31. *ORA*, 7:673. The attorney general's co-counsel was Mr. A. P. Aldrich, who had been a member of the examining commission subscribing to the report to the governor, Bonham Papers, p. 541.

32. *Charleston Courier*, Aug. 26, 1863.

33. Bonham Papers, pp. 568–72. This citation is to the report on the trial made to the governor by what appears to have been the five members of the tribunal conducting it. The report refers to the court as "Police Court for Charleston District." The governor referred to it as "the provost-marshal's court for Charleston district," *ORA*, 7:673; see also Bonham Papers, pp. 536, 597; and *Charleston Courier*, Aug. 26, 1863. The court had been recently created. Its creation and

powers are recounted in a letter to the author of October 21, 1980, from Mr. William L. McDowell, deputy director, South Carolina Department of Archives and History.

34. *ORA*, 6:245–46; Bonham Papers, pp. 561–64.

35. *ORA*, 5:960, 966–67.

36. *ORA*, 6:21–22.

37. *ORA*, 6:115. It seems that a little later Seddon wrote Smith suggesting that captured white officers "be dealt with red-handed in the field, or immediately thereafter," Herbert Aptheker, *To Be Free: Studies in American Negro History*, 2d ed., (International Publishers, New York, 1968), p. 94.

38. *ORA*, 6:163; *Charleston Mercury*, Aug. 10, 1863.

39. *ORA*, 6:193–94.

40. *ORA*, 6:245–46, 194; Bonham Papers, pp. 561–64. The South was keenly aware of the threat of retaliation, *Charleston Courier*, Oct. 2, 1863.

41. *ORA*, 6:225–26.

42. Bonham Papers, pp. 568–72.

43. Herbert Aptheker, "The Negro in the Union Navy," *Journal of Negro History* 32 (Apr. 1947):169, 170–74, 179.

44. *ORA*, ser. 1, 14:199–202; *ORA*, 5:708, 823–27; *ORA*, 6:171–72, 188.

45. Elon A. Woodward, *The Negro in the Military Service of the United States, 1639–1886: A Compilation* (1888), Office of the Adj. Gen., Nat. Arch., RG 94, M 858, Roll 5, p. 4224.

46. Luis F. Emilio, *History of the Fifty-Fourth Regiment of Massachusetts Volunteer Infantry, 1863–1865*, 2d ed. rev. (The Boston Book Co., Boston, 1894), p. 413. Emilio's history, though based on painstaking research, including interviews with survivors, was written before records were fully organized and has some errors, including, on. pp. 97 and 406, a mistaken identification of the prisoners tried by the Charleston court.

47. The defense counsel, Nelson Mitchell and Edward McCrady, had been prominent members of the state legislature in prewar days and were leaders of the Charleston bar, *Biographical Directory of the South Carolina House of Representatives*, (Columbia, 1974), 1:356, 360, 364, 369, 373, 376; Mary C. Simms Oliphant and T. C. Duncan Eaves, eds., *The Letters of William Gilmore Simms*, 5 vols. (Univ. of South Carolina Press, Columbia, 1954), 3:221, n. 250; obituary, *Columbia Daily Southern Guardian*, Apr. 21, 1864 (Mitchell); McCrady and Ashe, *Cyclopedia*, 1:151–58 (McCrady). In Emilio, *History of the Fifty-Fourth*, pp. 97, 406–8, it is said that Mitchell suffered obloquy and poverty as a result of his representation of the defendants. The statement is based on hearsay, principally an unsigned letter appearing in *Harpers Weekly* of Apr. 8, 1865. Quite inconsistent with any such statement is the fact that both Mitchell and McCrady were selected as members of a citizens' committee to welcome President Davis on his visit to Charleston in November 1863, several weeks after the trial; see *Charleston Courier*, Oct. 30, 31, Nov. 2, 1863. Inconsistent, too, is the highly commendatory obituary published after Mitchell's death in February 1864; see *Columbia Daily Southern Guardian*, Apr. 21, 1864; Henry A. DeSaussure, "Death Records," *South Carolina Historical Magazine* 59 (Apr. 1958):116. It is notable also that McCrady again was elected to the state legislature in 1864. McCrady, incidentally, had been a member of the state convention of December 1860 and had voted for

secession, *Biographical Directory*, p. 392; McCrady and Ashe, *Cyclopedia*, pp. 151–58; Cauthen, *South Carolina Goes to War*, pp. 65–66.

48. *ORA*, 6:1081–82; 7:673.

49. Brainerd Dyer, "The Treatment of Colored Union Troops by the Confederates, 1861–1865," *Journal of Negro History* 20 (July 1935):273, 282; Aptheker, *To Be Free*, pp. 94–95.

50. *ORA*, 7:409.

51. *ORA*, 7:673.

52. Bonham Papers, pp. 597–98.

53. *ORA*, 7:703.

54. *Public Laws of the Confederate States of America: First Congress, 2d Sess.*, ed. James M. Matthews (Richmond, 1862), pp. 89–90; *Journal of the Congress of the Confederate States of America*, 58th Cong., 2d Sess., Sen. Doc. 234 (1904), 5:537–38.

55. *ORA*, 7:583; Dyer, "Treatment of Colored Union Troops," pp. 275–77.

56. *ORA*, 7:990–93, 1010–12. Grant's reply to Lee refused to discuss "the slavery question," adhering to the position that all captured Union soldiers "regardless of color . . . must be treated as prisoners of war," *ORA*, 7:1018–19, 1029–30.

57. The Charleston court's report to the governor identified the Missourians as Henry Kirk and William Harrison, the Virginians as George Council and Henry Worthington. Evidence conflicted, it said, as to whether Worthington was a slave; see Bonham Papers, pp. 568–72. The descriptive roll of Co. B, Fifty-fourth Massachusetts (Colored), RG 94, Nat. Arch., Washington, shows George Counsel—not "Council." The roll of Co. H shows the other three. The rolls show the residence of each. Worthington is shown as from Ohio, where, according to his Compiled Military Service Record (also RG 94), he was born. There were two men in Co. H named William H. Harrison, one shown as "1st," the other as "2d." The Compiled Military Service Record for each shows the "1st" as having been captured and the "2d" as killed at Fort Wagner in July 1863.

58. *ORA*, 7:673.

59. Emilio, *History of the Fifty-Fourth*, pp. 402–3, 414–15.

60. Emilio, *History of the Fifty-Fourth*, pp. 218, 395, 411–13; Compiled Military Service Records for Henry Kirk, William H. Harrison "1st," and Henry W. Worthington, of Co. H, Fifty-fourth Mass., RG 94, Nat. Arch.

61. Emilio, *History of the Fifty-Fourth*, pp. 419–22, 431. Worthington died on January 12, Harrison on January 26, both at Florence, according to their Compiled Military Service Records.

62. *ORA*, 8:96.

63. Emilio, *History of the Fifty-Fourth*, pp. 422–23.

64. *ORA*, 8:197; *Journal of the Congress of the Confederate States*, 4:501, 503, 507, 510, 520, 545; 7:521, 528.

65. Emilio, *History of the Fifty-Fourth*, pp. 422–23; Compiled Military Service Records for George Counsel, Co. B, Fifty-fourth Mass., and for Henry Kirk, Co. H, Fifty-fourth Mass., RG 94, Nat. Arch.

7

Sherman Marched— and Proclaimed "Land for the Landless"

$\mathbf{W}$HEN General William Tecumseh Sherman undertook to march from Atlanta to the sea we may be sure that it never occurred to him that he would create a heated controversy over whether black men or white men would own thousands of acres of rich plantation lands along the South Atlantic coast. But that happened.

Not long after Sherman occupied Atlanta in early September 1864, he decided that he ought to strike out for salt water. But not until the second of November did his general-in-chief, Grant, after some hesitation, tell him to "go as you propose."[1] The move seemed risky, for Confederate forces, including considerable cavalry under Gen. Joseph Wheeler, if coordinated and divining Sherman's course could seriously cripple him by persistent harassment far from any base. Nor was it possible to send him help, for it could not be known where he would march; at his outset he himself was not sure whether his destination would turn out to be Savannah or Pensacola or Mobile.[2]

The march began on November 15. While the army was large—about sixty thousand infantry, with cavalry of some fifty-five hundred led by Gen. H. Judson Kilpatrick—it was spread wide. There were two wings, each of two corps, each corps in a separate column strung out for miles on different routes, each separated from any of the others by as much as twenty miles. But, though Wheeler's cavalry on occasion kept Kilpatrick busy, deception of the Confederates so succeeded that

Originally published in *South Carolina Historical Magazine* 85, no. 1 (January 1984):33–50. Reprinted by permission of *South Carolina Historical Magazine*.

by December 10, after some three hundred circuitous miles, Sherman had reached the outer defenses of Savannah.[3] Three days later Confederate Fort McAllister, below Savannah guarding a waterway to the sea, fell to his assault and at last he could communicate with the outside world. At once he met with Gen. John G. Foster, heading a small Union army that since November 1861 had been based at Port Royal occupying portions of the Sea Islands. Sherman intended to have Foster move a force to the north of Savannah to complete an investment.[4]

Within Savannah Confederate Gen. William J. Hardee commanded some ten thousand troops. Sherman thought there were more. They were well fortified and watery land would allow attack only over five narrow causeways. Sherman took time to get set. To his surprise and chagrin, on the night of December 20 Hardee slipped away to the north before that route could be blocked. Early the next morning Union troops were entering the city unopposed.[5]

When Sherman had confronted Savannah's defenses his army was in superb condition, its morale high.[6] Though at the beginning of his march he did not know what he would propose on reaching the sea, by the time he got there he had so gained confidence in his army that his conclusion was clear: he wanted to drive on northward and, with Grant, quash the rebellion after administering bitter medicine to the South Carolinians who had started it. Indeed, as he had marched through Georgia some Georgians had urged him to give those Carolinians a good taste of the war they had begun.[7] While Grant had held very different ideas, after he and Sherman exchanged messages Grant agreed to Sherman's wish, and Sherman began to ready a northward drive.[8]

The time from December 21, when he entered Savannah, to the end of January was one of the busiest in Sherman's career. Savannah was to be left in General Foster's hands, for whom Sherman had to get reinforcements from Grant. The fortifications around Savannah had to be adjusted to the Unionist's posture. Supplies had to be gathered for a trip that would be longer and much more contested than the journey from Atlanta. Provision had to be made for the twenty thousand or so of Savannah's civilians whose money had become worthless overnight and whose link with friends had been severed. And, not least of all, something had to be done about thousands of refugee blacks.[9]

Before Sherman left Atlanta, Grant had suggested that he "move

. . . the negroes" from the country he would traverse, adding: "As far as arms can be supplied, either from surplus or by capture, I would put them in the hands of the negro men. Give them such organization as you can. They will be of some use."[10] Though Sherman had some blacks among his pioneer corps when he started, and as he marched on welcomed able-bodied black men as laborers in a variety of functions, he did not arm them as soldiers. That is understandable. Combatant blacks in the Union armies were in units separate from the whites. The last thing Sherman needed for the success of his seemingly dangerous march was untrained, undisciplined units.[11] Also, while he doubtless fully understood Grant's point that he "move . . . the negroes" to mean that he should deprive the Confederates of their labor force, he cautioned his commanders that refugee blacks should not "be encouraged to encumber us on the march."[12] That, too, is understandable. Women, children, and the infirm would clutter and slow the march and would consume food that might be critically needed by the troops. Unquestionably, early in the march effort was made to minimize the refugees, masses of whom did run to the bluecoats, hailing the Day of Jubilee. Unquestionably, too, the effort to minimize met with some success. But as the march proceeded efforts to keep refugees away became lax. There are no reliable figures as to the number who flocked into Savannah with Sherman. There were at least six or seven thousand. But it is quite possible that there were thousands more then or soon thereafter; Sherman once said that one of his wings "reports 17,000 negroes."[13] In any case, the problem of their care cried for Sherman's attention before he moved onward.

Initially, before he entered Savannah, he had assumed that there was a simple solution to the problem—that all he had to do was to order all of the refugee blacks, along with his surplus and broken down horses and mules, sent to Gen. Rufus Saxton who had headquartered at Beaufort, South Carolina, in Foster's department. When the Union landing at Port Royal had occurred in November 1861 the whites had fled the area but their slaves had stayed. In March 1862 the Treasury Department, given responsibility for abandoned property, had launched there what history has called the Port Royal Experiment. Northern businessmen, missionaries, and teachers came to put the blacks to work on the plantations, to teach them, and to introduce them to the way of self-sufficiency as free people. In June 1862 Saxton had been sent there, by special order of Secretary of War Stanton, as the military governor of affairs on the occupied coastal islands. While the experiment had undergone considerable vicissitude and change during the ensuing two and a half years, by December 1864 there were some fifteen thousand former slaves busy in their new life, with Saxton the governor and policeman. Sherman thought it quite appropriate that Saxton take on his refugees, and on December 16 ordered that they be sent to Port Royal "where they can be more easily supplied."[14]

But very shortly Sherman had word from Saxton that the problem was not simple. Saxton told him that "every cabin and house" in the area around Port Royal was already "filled to overflowing." Saxton pointed out, however, that St. Simons Island (below Savannah on the Geogia coast) and Edisto Island (on the Carolina coast between Port Royal and Charleston), once occupied by the Union forces but since vacated, probably were free of Rebels—a sort of no man's land—and had a large number of vacant houses. Saxton thought that those islands could be reoccupied readily by a small force and suggested that the refugees be sent there. It was apparent that Sherman would have to consider the refugee problem more thoroughly.[15]

Then, in early January, Sherman received a personal letter from Gen. Henry W. Halleck, chief of staff in Washington, that certainly made him think twice about black refugees. Halleck wrote that, though Sherman was receiving praise from most people, there were some leading men very critical of his treatment of the blacks, that they thought Sherman rejected the blacks "with contempt." "They say," wrote Halleck, "you might have brought with you to Savannah more than 50,000, thus stripping Georgia of that number of laborers and opening a road by which as many more could have escaped from their masters; but that instead of this you drove them from your ranks, prevented them from following you by cutting the bridges in your rear, and thus caused the massacre of large numbers by Wheeler's cavalry." Halleck knew, of course, that Sherman probably had to discourage refugees because of limited supplies on his march, but, he suggested, perhaps Sherman now could open avenues for the escape of slaves from their masters by arrangement for their subsistence on the coastal plantations. Halleck said that were Sherman thus to foster slaves' escape his critics would be silenced.[16]

If Sherman, on reading Halleck's letter, did not know what was referred to by the charge that he had left refugees to the tender mercy of Wheeler's cavalry, he was quickly to find that the reference was to an incident at Ebenezer Creek about twenty miles from Savannah that had occurred on December 8 and 9 in the march of one of the corps of the left wing. On January 10 Secretary of War Stanton arrived at Savannah to see what was going on; his visit may have been prompted in part by reports of the Ebenezer Creek incident.[17]

The corps involved had been commanded by Gen. Jefferson C. Davis. Not altogether because of his name, Davis was reputed not to love blacks. Nor had he the reputation of a cool head; in the fall of 1862 he had had a quarrel with his former commanding officer and had killed him.[18] Thus any report of Davis' brutal treatment of blacks would be read by Republican politicians with a believing eye. Even today the Ebenezer Creek incident is recalled as "an inhuman barbarous proceeding." But despite testimony seeming to warrrant that label the incident may not have been quite that bad.[19]

Within a week after Sherman's march had started, Davis had warned his corps, "Useless negroes are being accumulated to an extent which would be suicide to a column which must be constantly stripped for battle and prepared for the utmost celerity of movement." Wagons, he said, were too overloaded to allow them to carry also women and children, and he cautioned that "every additional mouth consumes food, which it requires risk to obtain." While, as we have noted, it seems that restraint on numbers of refugees became lax as the march proceeded, this may not have been quite true of Davis' column, especially by December 8 when, being on the extreme left of Sherman's swath, it faced the task of keeping up in the covergence on Savannah. Thus, among the final reports of Davis' units, one regimental report says of refugee negroes: "Large numbers of both sexes and all ages were prohibited from following the command, in obedience to stringent orders issued on that subject from superior headquarters."[20]

In any event on the night of December 7 the column had reached Ebenezer Creek after a hard march on timber-obstructed roads, with Confederate attacks from the rear on Kilpatrick's cavalry and other firing heard in the distance. The creek was wide; the column was entering watery country. Pontoon bridging was required. The bridge was completed at midmorning of December 9, with demonstrations from a Confederate gunboat and troop skirmishing all of the preceding day. After the crossing, heavy cannonading was heard from ahead. Sherman's success in deception had fostered an idea that he might be

headed for Charleston, accounting, perhaps, for attempted Confederate activity over on the Union left.[21]

In the long crossing of the stream an effort had been made to keep
all refugees in the rear, presumably to facilitate the troops' move.
When the troops' crossing was completed the bridge was immediately
pulled across, leaving a mass of blacks, including many women and
children, stranded on the far bank with Wheeler's cavalry soon to come
at them. It is said that the refugees panicked, not a few attempting to
swim across or to get there clinging to logs, with some assistance from
sympathetic soldiers on the other side. Not many made it. Some
drowned. Most eventually were picked up by the Confederates. Rumor
was to spread that the Confederates shot them down. Of that there is
no good evidence and it is most unlikely; much more likely is it that
they were simply returned to slave life.[22]

In assessing this incident it must be kept in mind that Davis' position
at the creek was ticklish, that in watery country he sometimes was
confined to narrow passages that could be blasted by a single opposing
cannon, and that he was under great pressure to maintain coordination
with the rest of the army on the final approach to Savannah's outer
defenses, just then being reached. Indeed over on the Union right wing
an officer had managed, on the evening of the day Davis completed his
crossing of the stream, to go on ahead of the army and soon got all the
way to the coast and reached Foster with word of Sherman's coming.[23]
One should be hesitant about condemnation of Davis for having the
pontoon bridge pulled quickly with Confederates hovering at his rear.
Sherman's own judgment, expressed in a January 12 letter to Halleck
during Stanton's visit and after Sherman had queried Davis about the
creek incident, was that the story of "turning back negroes that Wheeler
might kill them is all humbug." At the watercourse, wrote Sherman,
Davis did "forbid certain plantation slaves—old men, women, and
children—to follow his column; but they would come along and he
took up his pontoon bridge, not because he wanted to leave them, but
because he wanted his bridge."[24]

Whatever the pro or con concerning the Ebenezer Creek incident,
it did make clear that when a Union army was on a swift move black
refugees could not be handled adequately by the mere edict that they
should not be allowed to "encumber us." Some program was essential
for their ultimate disposition that unit commanders could take into

account in meeting the exigencies of invasion and that would promise the blacks a haven more secure than the wake of a marching column. Halleck's letter and Stanton's visit made Sherman focus sharply on such a program. On the evening of January 12, at Sherman's headquarters, he and Stanton had a meeting with twenty black churchmen, all but one Savannah residents, including leaders in the black community; the one was a Maryland free black who had been a missionary for the past two years in connection with the Port Royal Experiment. Nine of them had been slaves until Sherman's coming; one of those nine had been a slave of a leading Confederate, Robert Toombs. At the meeting when asked how the blacks could best take care of themselves and assist the government, their response was that it would be best that they have land to cultivate and so to maintain themselves, with their young men in the meantime enlisting in the army. Then, when asked whether they would rather live in colonies by themselves or be scattered among whites, all but the Marylander said that because of the prejudice in the South they would prefer to live by themselves.[25]

After this meeting, as Sherman explained in a letter to the president a year later, Stanton "was satisfied the Negros could with some little aid from us by means of the abandoned Plantations on the Sea Islands and along the Navigable Waters take care of themselves. He requested me to draw up a plan that would be uniform and practicable. I made the rough draft and we went over it very carefully, Mr. Stanton making many changes."[26] The result was that, on January 16 immediately after Stanton's departure, Sherman issued Special Field Order No. 15. Foster's command was the Department of the South, embracing South Carolina, Georgia, and into Florida, but the department now had been made subject to Sherman's orders.[27] Thus his Order No. 15 was the law for that department. It was among the most notable, if not the most notable, of the several military provisions for refugee blacks made during the war.

It provided as follows:

"The islands from Charleston south, the abandoned rice-fields along the rivers for thirty miles back from the sea, and the country bordering the Saint John's River, Fla., are reserved and set apart for the settlement of the negroes now made free by the acts of war and the proclamation of the President of the United States."

The order was to be administered by General Saxton, given the title of Inspector of Settlements and Plantations, with police and general management power over the area.

Whenever "three respectable negroes, heads of families," selected a locality within the specified area for settlement, Saxton was to give them a license, and, under Saxton's supervision, they would subdivide the land in the locality among themselves and others choosing to join them so that each family would have "a plot of not more than forty acres of tillable ground." Saxton was to provide each family head, "subject to the approval of the President of the United States, a possessory title in writing, giving as near as possible the description of boundaries"; such titles would be treated "as possessory." Their possession would be protected by the military "until such time as they can protect themselves or until Congress shall regulate their title."

On the islands and in such settlements "no white person whatever, unless military officers and soldiers detailed for duty, will be permitted to reside; and the sole and exclusive management of affairs will be left to the freed people themselves, subject only to the United States military authority and the acts of Congress." However, the order would not change the existing settlements "on Beaufort Island" or affect "any rights to property heretofore acquired"—referring, presumably, to the whites engaged in the Port Royal Experiment and to property that had been acquired, mainly by Northern whites, under tax sales by the Treasury Department during the war when the old owners were dutiful to the Confederacy instead of to the United States tax collectors.

Finally, young black men were encouraged to enlist in the Union army. Saxton was given charge of such recruiting and the organization of black military units.[28]

Sherman's January 12 letter to Halleck had said, "I do and will do the best I can for negroes, and feel sure that the problem is solving itself slowly and naturally. It needs nothing more than our fostering care." Nor, indeed, had Sherman ever been blind to the need to make some provision for the blacks. Even before leaving Atlanta, when he had ordered that refugees should not be encouraged to "encumber us," he had added that "at some future time" he would be able to provide for those "who seek to escape the bondage under which they are now suffering."[29] Surely his Order No. 15 provided the basis for the fostering care for all the refugees who had followed him to Savannah and who would flock to him when at last he marched on northward through the

Carolinas. The fact is that on March 14, after Sherman had emerged at Fayetteville, again to make contact with the outside world via a Union force by then at Wilmington, he ordered that the black refugees "that have clung to us during our march through South Carolina" could be sent to General Saxton back at Beaufort.[30]

If the fighting had gone on for another year or so it is very likely that the kind of self-sufficient black communities envisaged in Sherman's order would have become firmly established and that the social and economic development of the blacks in the South Atlantic coastal region would have been very different. The Port Royal Experiment already had shown considerable success but it was limited to the Port Royal–Beaufort vicinity, and, to Saxton's special distress, allowed for but little land ownership by the blacks. Indeed in Saxton's annual 1864 report to Stanton there was a note of his unhappiness on that score.[31] But now Sherman's order gave Saxton what seemed plenary authority, based on the nearly untrammeled war power of the military, to provide land for the landless over a stretch of hundreds of miles of rich plantation lands. With the imprimatur of Sherman, at that time regarded in much of the North as the nation's greatest hero, Saxton was fired with enthusiasm and hope.

Saxton's hope seemed well grounded. He had visited Sherman at the end of December but apparently had not been encouraged about what might happen to the blacks. However, on Stanton's coming the outlook changed. Saxton had gone at once to Savannah to meet with the secretary of war, telling of his recent annual report that Stanton had not yet received in which he had objected to the failure to provide for black land ownership; the interview had been "agreeable" and Stanton had promised Saxton "to put him all right," and had sent him back to Beaufort to return with a copy of the report. Saxton had brought it to Stanton just prior to the secretary of war's meeting with the black churchmen. Then on January 14 Stanton, on leaving Savannah, came to Beaufort for an overnight stay that proved most congenial, highlighted by disclosing to Saxton an advance copy of Order No. 15. As though to seal Saxton's authority, there was delivered to him, just after Stanton's departure, his promotion from brigadier general to major general of volunteers.[32]

But the fighting did not last. In only a few weeks it ended. And as it was ending President Lincoln's assassination brought to the presidency a man who did not share Saxton's vision of land for the black man.

During those few weeks Saxton faced a huge task of administration with a limited staff. By early June he was to report an estimate that he had settled forty thousand blacks under Sherman's order. Later he was to reiterate that estimate. But there is no evidence that Saxton was able consistently to follow the method prescribed in the Sherman order—that is, having three black heads of families mark out a settlement and then, under his supervision, subdivide tracts for self-governing communities, with Saxton issuing precisely defined possessory titles to the settlers. That he could have done so in such a short time seems impossible in view of the chaotic conditions in the vast territory, the limited means of transport, the ignorance of the settlers, the shortage of facilities, and the extent and variety of his responsibilities which included, it will be recalled, recruiting of soldiers. The likelihood is that, working under great pressure, Saxton's procedure was makeshift. [33]

As the fighting dwindled—Charleston itself was evacuated in mid-February as Sherman drove northward and isolated it—some of the former white owners began drifting back to the area, seeming to think that somehow they could resume control of the plantations. On April 22 Saxton issued a circular, publishing the key provisions of the Sherman order and giving "unauthorized persons" thirty days' notice to vacate the area; thereafter trespassers would be arrested, to be punished by sentence of a military commission. [34] But hardly had that thirty-day period lapsed than two things happened that signaled impending change from what Saxton otherwise might have established, that foreshadowed that the nearly all-black enclave from Charleston along the coast into Florida, provided by Sherman's order, would never be realized.

One of these was the implementation of the Freedmen's Bureau Act of March 3, 1865. [35] The act provided that during the war and for one year thereafter a bureau in the War Department, headed by a commissioner, would have charge of the affairs of the freed blacks in the Confederate States. It also provided that the bureau, from land within those states that was abandoned or owned by the United States by confiscation or otherwise, could rent to a male freedman on favorable terms up to forty acres for three years with the freedman's privi-

lege of purchasing "such title thereto as the United States can convey."
But the act did not mention Sherman's order nor did it provide for the
exclusion of whites from any area or even hint at the creation of self-
governing black communities. On May 12, Gen. Oliver O. Howard
took office as the bureau's commissioner. He had been Sherman's right
wing commander. During the time that Sherman was getting ready for
the drive northward from Savannah, Howard had been posted for
a considerable time at Beaufort where he had been most favorably
impressed with Saxton. On May 22, on the very day that Saxton's April
22 circular had provided that unauthorized whites would be arrested
if they had not vacated the area defined in Sherman's order, Howard
wrote Saxton of his appointment as the bureau's assistant commissioner
in charge of South Carolina and Georgia and, temporarily, Florida.
Thus did Saxton lose his autonomy even as the special status of the
Sherman lands was clouded.[36]

The second event occurred on May 29, one week after General
Howard wrote Saxton of his altered office. The new President Johnson
issued a sweeping Amnesty Proclamation for all those who now would
take a loyalty oath.[37] While the proclamation excluded various limited
classes who had "voluntarily participated" in the rebellion, they were
assured that on special application for pardon "clemency will be liber-
ally extended." It was soon to become clear that such assurance was
very real. Needless to say, under a Constitution giving the president
sweeping power to pardon, amnesty to an old owner seemed to destroy
all basis for denying him a return of his abandoned land. The loyalty
oath takers were plentiful, and in hardly more time than it takes to tell
were clamoring for the lands' return. Nowhere was the clamor to be
more persistent than in the area embraced in Sherman's order, and
especially in South Carolina where Saxton's work was most concen-
trated. And it was abandoned lands that were the principal supply for
carrying out that order, or, indeed, the land provision of the more
general Freedmen's Bureau Act.[38]

On the face of things it would seem that these two events would
have ended rather abruptly further administration of the Sherman
order. In fact there is no indication that Saxton attempted to carry out
the bar against white residents in the Sherman area after expiration of
the thirty-day notice in his April circular, and in early June General
Howard wrote him that whites should be no more excluded there than
in other areas where the Freedmen's Bureau operated.[39] Otherwise,

however, Saxton proceeded as though the Sherman order were fully in effect. He had become a crusader for the newly freed blacks. On June 4, in his initial report to Howard as one of the new assistant commissioners of the bureau, he said that his "colonists" under the Sherman order had "many thousands of acres" in cultivation, whence "ample crops will be raised to support the present population, and a large amount of sea island cotton for market will be provided." The crops, he said with pride, "completely astound the former masters who have visited the plantations, while the friends are delighted and encouraged." And in the months following, Saxton continued settling black "colonists" under the Sherman order.[40]

Meanwhile, the clamor of the amnestied whites for a return of their lands mounted, with a sympathetic ear in the White House. It would seem that the president could have eliminated any claim to the lands by the blacks, and cleared the way for the clamoring whites, by simply disapproving any "titles" that had been issued under the Sherman order. For the order itself, it will be recalled, provided that the "titles" were "subject to the approval of the President." But the president did not resort to that provision. If he focused on it, perhaps he hesitated to resort to it lest that imply that he regarded the Sherman order as still in force. Or perhaps—and this is more likely—the president hesitated lest he alienate some members of Congress whose support he wanted on many other issues when Congress came into session in the following December. Congress had not met since the presidency had descended on Johnson; at the coming session his whole program for the nation's reunion would be at stake.

In any event, though the president made it clear that he agreed with the clamoring whites that they should have their lands, he stopped just short of peremptorily insisting to General Howard that all the Sherman lands be restored at once. Instead, he told Howard to try to work out, between the white claimants and the black "title" holders, some accommodation—such as agreement by the black to the white ownership in exchange for employment of the black and some tenancy for him and his family.[41] In the meantime Saxton, though by the end of the summer his authority over Georgia and Florida had been transferred to others, leaving him only South Carolina, had been fighting as hard as ever for his "colonists." He urged, to Howard, that when Congress met it would decide that the Sherman order had "all the binding effect of a Statute."[42] While some lands were restored to the whites, many blacks resisted and Howard vacillated, stalled with support from Stanton, and finally, when Congress met, began working with a leading senator, Lyman Trumbull of Illinois, on proposed legislation that he hoped would be a final solution.[43] At length, in February, Congress did act. It adopted a measure extending indefinitely the life of the Freedmen's Bureau and providing variously for the welfare of the freedmen, including a provision that the holders of Sherman "titles" would be confirmed in their possession for three years.[44] While that at least strongly implied that the white man would have the land restored in three years, that doubtless seemed a long time for the old planters to wait before beginning their recovery from the economic chaos left by the war.

During this time the interest of the white planters had been ably represented in Washington by a lobbyist, William Henry Trescot, the "Executive Agent" of the state of South Carolina. Trescot had come to Washington in the fall of 1865 with authority conferred by the South Carolina Convention, and had been busy at the Executive Mansion, on the Hill, and in the War Department. On January 31 as Congress neared its action, Trescot, with associates, met with the president, telling him that General Sherman was in the city and that they understood he would be willing to state what he had meant by his Order No. 15. The president suggested that they see Sherman. They immediately went to General Grant's headquarters. It happened that Grant was in conference with Sherman and Generals George H. Thomas and George G. Meade. But Grant invited them in, and "they all participated in the discussion of the real meaning of General Sherman's order." The result was that before the end of the day Trescot delivered a note to the president saying that Sherman had said that his order "was meant to be temporary" and that he would "make such a statement . . . upon a reference from you." On the next day the president wrote Sherman asking for a statement of the "purposes" of his order. On the day following, February 2, Sherman replied, "I knew of course we could not convey title to land and merely provided 'possessory' titles, to be good as long as War and our Military Power lasted. I merely aimed to make provision for the Negros who were absolutely dependent on us, leaving the value of their possessions to be determined by after events or legislation."[45] When, a few days later in February, Congress' act reached the president he vetoed it. Among his many objections to the whole measure he stated that the provision for the Sherman "title" holders violated the white owners' Constitutional rights to their property. The veto came to the Senate where the measure had originated. Thirty senators voted to override but eighteen voted to sustain, falling short of the two-thirds required to override.[46]

Surely now all the Sherman lands would go back to the white owners with no further controversy. One problem for the whites—that is, the activity of General Saxton, the aggressive crusader for the blacks—had been solved. From about the time when lobbyist Trescot had begun his work in Washington there had been rumor that President Johnson wanted to be rid of Saxton and hoped he would ask to be relieved. But Saxton was stubborn; he refused to quit. Finally, however, in January the axe fell. Saxton was removed. Though offered a bureau position elsewhere he declined and wound up in army quartermaster duty far from South Carolina.[47] With Saxton out of the way and with the president's veto sustained, Trescot called on General Howard on February 21 and thought he had secured agreement to the issuance of an order for the immediate restoration of the Sherman lands. But Howard worried after their meeting until one o'clock at night; the next day he informed Trescot that he would issue no such order without further instruction from the president. The next day Howard wrote the president that his existing instructions concerning the Sherman lands were that he was to attempt "to make an arrangement mutually satisfactory between the land owners and the resident freedmen." Under those instructions he noted many lands had been restored to the whites. But, said he, "In order not to break faith with these freedmen, who had received possessory titles, or who occupied lands under General Sherman's order, I had hoped to render them some *equivalent or indemnity*; possibly this may yet be afforded them by some future action of Congress." He concluded that he still felt "unwilling to make any sweeping restoration of the lands above named to their former owners without more definite instructions than I have yet received either from yourself or the Secretary of War."[48]

Executive Agent Trescot was very much on the job. General Howard wrote his letter in duplicate, one to go through War Department channels and one to be delivered by Trescot himself to the Executive Mansion. Trescot delivered his copy with a covering letter to the president urging that the regular army authorities in South Carolina (not Howard) should determine whether a white owner was willing to make some fair arrangement with any tenants under the Sherman order, and that Howard should be told to get on at once with all the lands' restoration.[49] While no peremptory order for such restoration was issued, it seems that Trescot's suggestion for having the regular army authorities handle the matter was—or perhaps already had been—substantially adopted, at least for the area in South Carolina. Howard's view was that there should be restoration only if the white owner and the black "title" holder reached a "mutually satisfactory" arrangement. But the regular army authorities would restore if only the white owner tendered a deal that they deemed "fair"—whether or not the black "title" holder was satisfied—and even that condition would be imposed only if they found that the Sherman "title" held by the tenant was technically quite correct in its specification of the land he occupied. Howard protested this interference with his administration. Indeed when by early March he had received no new instructions from the president he ordered Saxton's successor in South Carolina to maintain the possession of the "title" holders "until some definite action is had by the Government." As he had intimated in his February 22 letter to the president, he was hoping for some further action by Congress to provide "some equivalent or indemnity" to the "title" holders if the lands were to be restored to the whites. It is not clear how the conflict between the regular military and the bureau stood when the whole matter finally became academic in July 1866.[50]

At that time Congress again acted. Again it adopted an amendment to the Freedmen's Bureau Act, this time to extend the life of the bureau for a limited period, with various provisions for the freedmen's welfare, and again it addressed the question of the Sherman "title" holders. But this time it gave in to the white owners. It did provide that any Sherman "title" holders still on the lands could not be ousted until they had harvested current crops and had been fairly compensated for any betterments they had made. Otherwise a Sherman "title" holder, whether or not he had yet been dispossessed, was given no relief except the privilege of buying at $1.50 an acre a twenty-acre plot to be provided from several thousand acres in the Port Royal area that the United States had acquired from tax sales during the war. Again there was a veto by a president who seemed to take a dim view of even limited government aid to the blacks. But this time the veto was overridden. So at last the way was cleared for all the abandoned lands to be restored to the white owners, and finally the long controversy having roots reaching as far back as Ebenezer Creek was resolved.[51]

But when at length the dust of controversy had settled there was something pathetic in the outcome. In the haste, tension, and confusion of Saxton's administration of the Sherman order, settlers' "titles" were not always written with required specificity, many settlers never received any "title" papers at all, and others settled elsewhere than on the locations their papers provided for. Still others, through ignorance or discouragement, had simply given up and wandered away. Furthermore, any "title" holder at a point far from the Port Royal area, even if he heard of the opportunity afforded by the July 1866 statute, probably was reluctant to move there to see what might be available to him.[52] The result is that the books of the United States tax authorities, who issued the allotments from the tax lands, show a total of only 1,398 purchases by blacks pursuant to the 1866 statute. Moreover, while the statute provided quite definitely that the plots were to be for twenty acres, any for that amount are almost indiscernible; most were for but ten acres, and not a few for smaller plots, as little as two acres.[53]

How far short that was from the great black enclave that General Saxton thought General Sherman had created.

Notes

1. U.S. War Dept., *The War of the Rebellion: A Compilation of the Official Records of The Union and Confederate Armies*, 70 vols. in 128 pts. (1880–1901; rpt. National Historical Society, Gettysburg, 1972), ser. 1, vol. 39, pt. 3:222, 576–77, 594 (hereafter cited as *ORA*, with references to series 1, except where otherwise noted).

2. *ORA*, 39, pt. 3:660–61.

3. *ORA*, 39, pt. 3:713; 44:7–14, 114, 147–48, 212.

4. *ORA*, 44:10–12, 700–702, 855.

5. *ORA*, 44:10, 12, 727, 728, 771, 786, 959.

6. *ORA*, 44:8, 13–14, 114, 147–48, 152, 159, 700–702, 726–27.

7. *ORA*, 44:727–28, 741–43, 797–800.

8. *ORA*, 38, pt. 1:36; 44:636, 726, 728–29, 740–43, 797–800, 820–21.

9. *ORA*, 44:700–702, 727, 786, 797, 817–18, 841–42; 47, pt. 2:18.

10. *ORA*, 39, pt. 3:222.

11. *ORA*, 39, pt. 3:713–14; 44:59, 159, 166, 212. It was later implied that Sherman might have armed blacks had he been granted his request for assignment of a Union colonel who was experienced in organizing black soldiers, a request not granted, *New York Tribune*, Dec. 24, 1864, p. 4.

12. *ORA*, 39, pt. 3:701.

13. *ORA*, 44:13, 75, 159, 166–67, 203–5, 211–12; 47, pt. 2:36.

14. *ORA*, 44:701–2, 727, 729–30, 817–18; ser. 3, 2:152–53; ser. 3, 4:118–19, 1022–31. A thorough account of the genesis and evolution of the Port Royal

Experiment is Willie Lee Rose, *Rehearsal for Reconstruction* (Bobbs-Merrill, Indianapolis, 1964).

15. *ORA*, 44:787.

16. *ORA*, 44:836–37.

17. Lloyd Lewis, *Sherman: Fighting Prophet* (Harcourt, Brace & Co., New York, 1932), pp. 478–79; Earl Schenck Miers, *The General Who Marched to Hell* (Alfred A. Knopf, New York, 1951), pp. 272–73; Paul M. Angle, ed., *Three Years in the Army of the Cumberland: The Letters and Diary of Major James A. Connolly* (Indiana Univ. Press, Bloomington, 1959), p. 373; Willard Saxton Diary, vol. 26, p. 33, Saxton Family Papers, Yale Univ. Library.

18. Ezra J. Warner, *Generals in Blue: Lives of the Union Commanders* (Louisiana State Univ. Press, Baton Rouge, 1964), pp. 115–16.

19. Angle, *Three Years in the Army of the Cumberland*, pp. 354–55; Burke Davis, *Sherman's March* (Random House, New York, 1980), pp. 91–94.

20. *ORA*, 44:186–87, 502.

21. *ORA*, 44:663, 674; Angle, *Three Years in the Army of the Cumberland*, pp. 349–56.

22. Angle, *Three Years in the Army of the Cumberland*, pp. 354–55; Davis, *Sherman's March*, pp. 91–94.

23. *ORA*, 44:699; *New York Tribune*, Dec. 15, 1864, p. 1.

24. *ORA*, 47, pt. 2:36–37.

25. *ORA*, 47, pt. 2:37–41.

26. W. T. Sherman to President Johnson, Feb. 2, 1866, Andrew Johnson Papers, Library of Congress, Ser. 1, Reel 20.

27. *ORA*, 47, pt. 2:44.

28. *ORA*, 47, pt. 2:60–62.

29. *ORA*, 39, pt. 3:701; 47, pt. 2:37.

30. *ORA*, 47, pt. 2:835.

31. *ORA*, ser. 3, 4:1024–26.

32. Saxton to E. D. Townsend, Asst. Adj. Gen., U.S. Army, Jan. 15, 1865, accepting promotion to major general by brevet, to rank from Jan. 12, 1865, in Rufus Saxton file, Letters Rec'd by Appointment, Commission and Personal Branch of the Adj. Gen., File No. 1302, ACP 1879, RG 94, Nat. Arch.; Willard Saxton Diary, vol. 26, pp. 25–26, 33–40; William S. McFeely, *Yankee Stepfather* (Yale Univ. Press, New Haven, 1968), pp. 47–48.

33. Saxton to O. O. Howard, June 4 and Sept. 5, 1865, Nos. S–14 and S–83, Letters Rec'd & Registers by the Commr., Bureau of Refugees, Freedmen and Abandoned Lands, RG 105, Nat. Arch., M 752, Roll 17; Claude F. Oubre, *Forty Acres and a Mule* (Louisiana State Univ. Press, Baton Rouge, 1978), pp. 46–47.

34. Circular No. 4, Apr. 22, 1865, Orders of Asst. Commr. for S.C., Bureau of Refugees, Freedmen and Abandoned Lands, RG 105, Nat. Arch., M 869, Roll 37.

35. 13 *U.S. Stat.* 507.

36. McFeely, *Yankee Stepfather*, pp. 45–48, 62–64; Howard to Saxton, May 22, 1865, Letters Sent, Endorsements and Circulars by the Commr., Bureau of Refugees, Freedmen and Abondoned Lands, RG 105, Nat. Arch., M 742, Roll 1.

37. James D. Richardson, comp., *A Compilation of the Messages and Papers of the Presidents, 1789–1897*, 10 vols. (Published by the Authority of Congress, Washington, 1896–99), 6:310–12.

38. George R. Bentley, *A History of the Freedmen's Bureau* (Univ. of Pennsylvania, Philadelphia, 1955), p. 74.

39. Howard to Saxton, June 8, 1865, Letters Sent, Endorsements and Circulars by the Commr., Bureau of Refugees, Freedmen and Abandoned Lands, RG 105, Nat. Arch., M 742, Roll 1.

40. Saxton to Howard, June 4, 1865, No. S–14, Letters Rec'd and Registers by the Commr., Bureau of Refugees, Freedmen and Abandoned Lands, RG 105, Nat. Arch., M 752, Roll 17; Oubre, *Forty Acres and a Mule*, p. 68.

41. Bentley, *Freedmen's Bureau*, pp. 97–98; Oubre, *Forty Acres and a Mule*, pp. 51–52.

42. Bentley, *Freedmen's Bureau*, pp. 69, 98–100; McFeely, *Yankee Stepfather*, pp. 126–29; Oubre, *Forty Acres and a Mule*, p. 51; Saxton to Howard, Sept. 5, 1865, No. S–83, Letters Rec'd and Registers by the Commr., Bureau of Refugees, Freedmen and Abandoned Lands, RG 105, Nat. Arch., M 752, Roll 17.

43. Bentley, *Freedmen's Bureau*, pp. 99–100; McFeely, *Yankee Stepfather*, pp. 130–48, 195–200.

44. Sen. Ex. Doc. No. 25, 39th Cong., 1st Sess. (1866):8–10. The measure also included a section authorizing rental and sale to "freedmen and loyal refugees" of public lands in Florida, Mississippi, Alabama, Louisiana, and Arkansas in plots not exceeding forty acres and another section authorizing the bureau, if Congress were to provide appropriations therefor, to acquire land "for refugees and freedmen dependent on the government for support" which the bureau later could sell, presumably to the occupants, at cost. Neither such section made particular provisions for Sherman "title" holders, and the latter section was most ambiguous, Sen. Ex. Doc. No. 25, 39th Cong., 1st Sess. (1866):9.

45. Resolution of Sept. 18, 1865, Committee on Ordinances and Resolutions, Reports and Resolutions, South Carolina Convention (1865), 11–12, S.C. Archives; W. H. Trescot to Gov. Benjamin F. Perry, Oct. 24, 1865, Letters Rec'd and Sent, Sept. 20–Dec. 21, 1865, Benjamin F. Perry Papers, S.C. Archives; Trescot to Gov. James L. Orr, Feb. 4, 1866, Letters Rec'd, Oct. 11, 1865–Apr. 3, 1866, James L. Orr Papers, S.C. Archives; W. H. Trescot to President Johnson, Jan. 31, 1866 (two letters), Letters Rec'd by President Johnson Relating to Bureau Affairs, Bureau of Refugees, Freedmen and Abandoned Lands, RG 105, Nat. Arch.; Johnson to Sherman, Feb. 1, 1866, Andrew Johnson Papers, Library of Congress, Ser. 2, Vol. 3, p. 77, Reel 42; Sherman to Johnson, Feb. 2, 1866, Andrew Johnson Papers, Library of Congress, Ser. 1, Reel 20. Trescot had been prominent in South Carolina affairs for years. R. Nicholas Olsberg, "A Government of Class and Race: William Henry Trescot and the South Carolina Chivalry 1861–1865" (Ph.D. diss., Univ. of South Carolina, 1972), Library of Congress microfilm.

46. Sen. Ex. Doc. No. 25, 39th Cong., 1st Sess. (1866):1–8; Richardson, *Messages and Papers of the Presidents*, 6:398–405; *Cong. Globe*, 39th Cong., 1st Sess. (1866):936–43.

47. Willard Saxton Diary, vol. 26, pp. 218–19, vol. 27, pp. 22–23, 51, 59–61, 68–69; purported copy of letter of Dec. 1, 1865, from Trescot to Johnson, Saxton Family Papers, Letterbook 7 (among loose papers); Brief Sketch of the Military Service of Rufus Saxton, p. 3, in Rufus Saxton file, Letters Rec'd by Appointment, Commission and Personal Branch of the Adj. Gen., File No. 1302, ACP, RG 94,

Nat. Arch.; McFeely, *Yankee Stepfather*, pp. 226–28; Oubre, *Forty Acres and a Mule*, p. 59.

48. Trescot to Orr, Feb. 28 and Mar. 4, 1866, Letters Rec'd, Oct. 11, 1865–Apr. 3, 1866, James L. Orr Papers, S.C. Archives; Howard to Johnson, Feb. 22, 1866, Andrew Johnson Papers, Library of Congress, Ser. 1, Reel 20.

49. Trescot to Orr, Mar. 4, 1866, Letters Rec'd, Oct. 11, 1865–Apr. 3, 1866, James L. Orr Papers, S.C. Archives; Trescott [*sic*] to Johnson, Feb. 22, 1866, Andrew Johnson Papers, Library of Congress, Ser. 1, Reel 20.

50. Bentley, *Freedmen's Bureau*, pp. 123–24; Martin Abbott, *The Freedmen's Bureau in South Carolina* (Univ. of North Carolina Press, Chapel Hill, 1967), pp. 60–62; Oubre, *Forty Acres and a Mule*, pp. 61–67; Trescot to Johnson, Mar. 12, 1866, and copies of Howard to R. K. Scott, Ass't. Commr. for S.C., Mar. 8, 1866, and of Scott's General Order No. 9, Mar. 7, 1866, Letters Rec'd by President Johnson Relating to Bureau Affairs, Bureau of Refugees, Freedmen and Abandoned Lands, RG 105, Nat. Arch.

51. 14 *U.S. Stat.* 173; Richardson, *Messages and Papers of the Presidents*, 6:422–26; Bentley, *Freedmen's Bureau*, pp. 133–34. In June Congress had adopted the Southern Homestead Act opening for homesteading some public lands in Florida, Mississippi, Alabama, Louisiana, and Arkansas. It was assumed that blacks could acquire land under that act. It made no particular provision for Sherman "title" holders. Such lands were of inferior quality; for that and other reasons the act had little practical consequence, Bentley, *Freedmen's Bureau*, pp. 134, 144–46.

52. Probably it will never be known precisely how many "titles" were issued, and when, throughout the Sherman order area from Charleston into Florida because of inadequacy of record keeping at the time, loss of records since, and sheer difficulty in finding what records remain. The most specific effort to tell the story is Oubre, *Forty Acres and a Mule*, pp. 46–71. See also Abbott, *Freedmen's Bureau in South Carolina*, pp. 7–16, 54–63; Carol K. Rothrock Blesser, *The Promised Land* (Univ. of South Carolina Press, Columbia, 1969), pp. 7–12.

53. Heads of Families Certificate Books, Direct Tax Comm. S.C., Nos. D–3 through D–6, Records of Internal Rev. Serv., RG 58, Nat. Arch. Books D–1 and D–2 contain copies of certificates of tax land sales to blacks, numbered 1 through 800, from Dec. 10, 1863, through Nov. 24, 1865. There is a gap between Book D–2 and Book D–3. The latter begins with certificate no. 836 on Sept. 21, 1866, the first reciting issuance pursuant to the July 1866 statute. Each certificate thereafter, consecutively numbered, so recites. The last such certificate is in Book D–6, no. 2234 of Sept. 23, 1871. The 1866 statute provided that the lands to be sold were to be in St. Helena's and St. Luke's parishes. The certificates recited, for the earlier years, that they were for land in Beaufort District and, for the later years, in Beaufort County. The district was changed to county in 1868; each contained the two parishes referred to in the 1866 statute. Letter of June 12, 1981, to the author from William L. McDowell, Deputy Director, S.C. Department of Archives and History.

8

The Cause
and Consequence
of a Union
Black Soldier's
Mutiny and Execution

O_F THE nineteen Union soldiers executed by the Union army for mutiny committed during the Civil War, fourteen were blacks.[1] Since the war was half over before the army began extensive enlistment of blacks, those figures understate the blacks' relative involvement in the most serious military crime. It seems strange that so disproportionate a number mutinously defied the authority that had become engaged in ending slavery.

The first black to be executed for mutiny was William Walker, a sergeant of Company A of the Third South Carolina Colored Infantry. He was charged with leading his company in a strike that protested that the rate of pay to black troops was less than the pay to whites. Rarely have historians done more than note the event.[2] More is merited. However risky it may be to generalize from an instance, the Walker story aids in tracing our society's stumbling advance from slavery toward freedom.

Walker, twenty-three years old when he was enlisted in the spring of 1863, was one of the host of slaves who had come under Union domination in November 1861 in the Port Royal, South Carolina, area.[3] Early in that month a navy-army expedition had occupied Port Royal, roughly midway between Charleston and Savannah. Nearly all the

Originally published in *Civil War History* 31, no. 3 (September 1985):222–36. Reprinted with permission of The Kent State University Press.

white populace for many miles around fled; most of their thousands of slaves remained. During following months the Union achieved control of the entire coast between the vicinities of Charleston and Savannah, with lodgments also below Savannah and in northeastern Florida. Port Royal itself became a busy naval base for a blockading squadron. And, with managers and teachers brought from the North, the Treasury Department organized and launched a program to establish for the blacks a self-sustaining life of freedom on the rich coastal plantations. The program became known to history as the Port Royal Experiment. In June 1862 Secretary of War Edwin M. Stanton sent Rufus Saxton, newly appointed from captain to brigadier general, as military governor, to lead Port Royal's orderly development and government.[4]

Employment by the army, the navy, and the Port Royal Experiment had opened great opportunities for South Carolina blacks. Walker, though illiterate, possessed unusual ability and found employment as a civilian gunboat pilot with the navy.[5] By the spring of 1863 he and his fellow South Carolinians had left far behind their old world of slavery.

A revolutionary opportunity in their new world was the enlistment of blacks into the armed ranks of the United States Army. Just after General Saxton's arrival in late June 1862 a military crisis in Virginia caused the recall of a large fraction of the Port Royal army. That, in turn, led the secretary of war, in a letter of August 25 to General Saxton, to authorize Saxton to recruit blacks as soldiers, under white officers, specifying that they were to "receive the same pay and rations as are allowed by law to volunteers in the service." This was the first time since the War of 1812 that the United States government had allowed any but white men in its army. Conscious of the measure's importance Saxton proceeded with care. After a trip north in connection with his Port Royal affairs, he began recruitment of a black regiment in October. By January 1863 he had one well-trained regiment and had begun assembling a second.[6]

In the previous spring, South Carolina, Georgia, and Florida had been designated the Department of the South. Maj. Gen. David Hunter, who had been the department commander for a few weeks during the previous year, returned as its commander in early 1863 and entered enthusiastically into General Saxton's recruitment campaign. By the spring there were indications that the Union high command might decide to mount an assault on Charleston from the Port Royal base, so recruitment was accelerated; indeed, Hunter had ordered a draft of blacks. On April 24 enrollment of the Third South Carolina Colored Infantry began.[7]

Recruiters for the Third South Carolina persuaded Walker to volunteer, though he was exempt from the draft by a naval "pass," and, in its initial enrollment, he was listed as one of the sergeants of the first company, Company A. Because the regiment had been founded on the secretary of war's authorization to Saxton, recruiters promised Walker and his fellows the same pay and allowances as those of white soldiers. For privates the rate was $13 per month plus an allowance of $3.50 per month when clothing was not furnished in kind. The higher, noncommissioned grades, of course, received higher pay. The initially organized South Carolina regiments were paid at the whites' rates.[8]

By June enough black enlistees and white officers had been assembled to form a regiment, and the Third South Carolina was formally mustered. Lt. Col. Augustus G. Bennett, promoted from captain in a New York unit, was its commander. He was on the job from the beginning of enrollment and put the men to work as they were signed up, without awaiting the formal muster. Indeed, in early May the prospective regiment received, from an interested donor, a "fine flag" as its regimental colors. Its white officers collected quickly with many men promoted from lesser posts; at least one of the officers had been a mere private.[9]

About the time the Third South Carolina was formally mustered, Brig. Gen. Quincy Gillmore relieved General Hunter as the commander of the department.[10] He came with a special mission—to complete preparation for, and then to carry out, a great attack on Charleston that would begin in July, but which, in the event, continued on and on for months until finally reaching stalemate. That move required enormous work at the Port Royal base. The Third South Carolina was assigned to that work, and kept nose to grindstone in details at the docks and in similar fatigue duty. The work details were different from the interesting gunboat piloting that Walker had left to join the army.

In the meantime, back in Washington, the secretary of war was having second thoughts about his promise to the black South Carolinians of pay equal to that of white soldiers. In the early weeks of 1863, with the president's backing, some state officials in the North had been authorized to organize black regiments for the Union army. In the spring the War Department itself had become vigorously engaged in black soldiers' recruitment wherever blacks were available, North and South, save only in the loyal border slave states. The widespread recruitment had caused the War Department to take a hard look at provisions included in a statute adopted by Congress in July 1862, known as the 1862 Militia Act, that might be construed to apply to black soldiers' pay. Those provisions authorized the president to receive "into the service of the United States . . . persons of African descent" for the purpose of "constructing intrenchments, or performing camp service, or any other labor, or any military or naval service," adding that any such person "who under this law shall be employed" was to be paid "ten dollars per month and one ration, three dollars of which monthly pay may be in clothing."[11]

The provisions applied clearly to the navy quite as much as to the army, but the navy, unlike the army, always had enlisted blacks and continued to do so from the outset of the Civil War. It paid them at its regular rates, most of which exceeded $10 a month, and the 1862 Militia Act caused no change in its practice.[12] While that seemed to indicate that the Militia Act's $10 pay provisions did not apply to blacks enlisted as full-scale sailors or soldiers, the secretary of war finally decided, in June 1863, that the provisions did fix the pay for all black soldiers, whatever their duties or rank.[13]

So it was that the army breached the equal-pay promise to the black South Carolinians, even in units where payment at the whites' rates had already begun. In the case of the men of the Third South Carolina the work details were especially hard on clothing, so privates and noncoms often received in cash only $7 a month, while, for whites, even a buck private was paid $13, with clothing in addition. Worse, in the fall of 1862 the War Department's judge advocate general had ruled that the Militia Act's $10 rate did not apply to civilian employees, but only to blacks employed in a "quasi-military" capacity. Hence, black civilians employed by the quartermaster's service, frequently on jobs not as taxing as the Third South Carolina's labor, were paid at prevailing wage rates, which ranged up to $25 a month.[14] Finally, it must have been especially irritating to Walker that the local navy was paying blacks employed as pilots—the very job he had left—$30 and $40 per month.[15]

Even apart from their pay problem, the men of the Third South Carolina faced difficult conditions. Their officers, but freshly promoted, were inexperienced in command. Demands of the emergency work at the base left little or no time for military instruction and training. Contact with white troops and civilians from the North, to many of whom blacks seemed an inferior breed, often was unpleasant; on June 10 Colonel Bennett complained to department headquarters that his men were insulted by whites. On June 20 the colonel requested relief for an overworked company, apparently Company A, from which twenty men had deserted. On July 29 he ordered his officers to stop absenting themselves without permission, and to stop allowing "unsoldiery" marching of their details; and on August 1 he ordered them to stop stealing their men's rations. On August 3 the captain of Company A complained to the colonel, "My men are giving out" from the constant "ardous" fatigue duty in coaling ships and other work. On September 17 General Gillmore (by then a major general) was prompted to issue a general order prohibiting employment of black soldiers "to prepare camps and perform menial duty for white troops," a practice that seems to have continued despite that order.[16] In short, the conditions the South Carolinians faced hardly soothed their anger when the pay they received was much less than had been promised them.

Moreover, even the pay problem was aggravated. At first, by General Hunter's order, the men's families received rations, but later that was stopped, leaving some of the families destitute. At the same time the higher paid civilian blacks employed by the quartermaster received rations for their families and were able to cultivate plots of land on the side.[17] In addition, the Port Royal Experiment was blossoming into a generally happy community, so as the black soldiers witnessed what was happening in the civilian life they had left for nose-to-grindstone labor, resentment at the breach of promise mounted.

That resentment flared on the morning of November 19, 1863. At the beginning of the day, instead of proceeding to their work, the men of Company A (and perhaps some of other companies) marched to their colonel's tent, stacked arms, and hung their accoutrements on the stacks. Colonel Bennett emerged and asked what the action meant. According to the colonel's later testimony, Sergeant Walker replied that they "would not do duty any longer for seven dollars per month," and, when the colonel told them that they would be reported to the post commander and "would be shot down" if they did not return to duty, Walker told the men to leave their stacked arms and go back to their quarters, which they did. That evening Colonel Bennett ordered

Walker's arrest, telling him not to leave his tent. The next day, on hearing that Walker had left his tent that morning without permission, the colonel ordered him into the guardhouse. On November 28 Colonel Bennett demoted Walker to private.[18]

On Saturday, January 9, 1864, Walker was brought before a general court-martial. He requested counsel, and a lieutenanct of a New York unit was invited to represent him. That lieutenant appeared with Walker on Monday, January 11, and the trial began. There were four charges. The first was for mutinous conduct; its specifications had to do with two minor outbursts by Walker on August 23 and October 31. The second charge was for conduct prejudicial to good order and discipline, with a specification alleging that on November 19 Walker had prevented the drum major from arresting one of his drummers. The third charge was for mutiny, with two specifications; the first specification alleged that Walker took command of his company on the morning of November 19, marched them to the front of the colonel's tent, and had them refuse duty at the $7 per month pay rate, and the second alleged that Walker had his company, later that day, release one of the privates from an arrest. The fourth charge was for breach of arrest, with a specification alleging that, though under arrest in his tent, Walker had left it without permission.[19]

The prosecution's case was completed and the defense testimony well along by Monday evening, and the defense was concluded the next morning. Defense then requested two days to prepare Walker's written statement. The court refused, granting recess only until 3:00 P.M. of that day. The statement was prepared, Walker signed it by making his mark, and defense counsel read it to the court upon the afternoon reconvening. After the judge advocate submitted the case "without remark," the court was cleared. Soon it reopened to announce its decision: guilty of each of the four charges and their specifications, except for part of the specifications under the first charge. Then the sentense was pronounced: "to be shot to death with musketry."[20]

We will come later to the question of whether the execution of Walker's sentence was subject to review by higher authority in Washington. But, with that in mind, it is notable that, though defense counsel had only the latter part of Saturday and then Sunday to prepare, his witnesses presented a strong case. The prosecution witnesses had been Colonel Bennett and four other officers of the regiment (not including the commander of Company A), the drum major, and

Company A's first sergeant with whom Walker's relations had been strained. The defense witnesses were three sergeants, at least one being from Company A, and three of that company's privates. The defense testimony took much of the steam out of most of the prosecution's case. For example, in reference to the breach of arrest charge, the defense made it fairly clear that Walker, in his tent under arrest, had asked that a man be sent to escort him to the sink, that his request had been ignored, and that, after an hour, the calls of nature being very pressing, he had gone alone to the sink. In addition, in reference to the first specification under the mutiny charge, alleging that he had led his company in its "strike," the defense testimony indicated that the strike was more a spontaneous revolt by the entire Company A than a move initiated by Walker. Nonetheless, assuming the credibility of Colonel Bennett's testimony, supported by two of his officers, it was Walker who told the colonel that the men would not do further duty at the $7 monthly pay and, despite the colonel's order to return to duty, told the men "to go back to their quarters without their arms." But even Bennett's corroborated assertion was emphatically denied in Walker's statement, and defense testimony supported the denial.[21]

More significant, however, than the denial of specifications and evidence is a passage in Walker's statement questioning the quality of his company's command, and asserting that, "on military law, and the rules of the service, we are entirely ignorant. Never, since the organization of the company, have the 'Articles of War' been read to us nor any part of the 'Regulations' even. We have been allowed to stumble along."[22]

Moreover, events beginning immediately after the November 19 "mutiny" suggest that, belatedly, the Third South Carolina's command was recognizing that the men had serious grievances. Before the day's end on November 19 Colonel Bennett and each of the regiment's officers who was present signed a letter to the adjutant general in Washington protesting that the black troops raised in their department under General Saxton "were enlisted with the promise of the same pay" as whites, that at first they were so paid, but that later the pay was reduced in violation of the government's "plighted honor." The letter insisted that the 1862 Militia Act did not justify that action, and pointed out that civilian blacks employed in the local commissary and quartermaster's service were paid from $12 to $25 per month plus rations. Later, on November 25, General Gillmore issued an order saying that "improper labors" still were being imposed on the black soldiers, and insisting that they were to receive the same treatment as whites, including "the same opportunities for drill and instruction." Then, on November 30, Colonel Bennett wrote to his department's headquarters requesting that rations be furnished the families of his men "until such time as their pay will be raised." He argued that men paid only $7 per month, and having to attend to their military duties, could not support their families. He emphasized that employees of the quartermaster's department were paid from $10 to $25 per month, "with ample opportunity for the cultivation of the soil," and still received "full rations for their families." Bennett's request was denied, but he was recognizing the seriousness of his men's plight. The next month an officer sent by the adjutant general to look into the situation of the black troops in South Carolina reported that, while the men were still assigned excessive fatigue duty, conditions were better than they had been. Finally, in a news report of a ceremony observing the anniversary of the Emancipation Proclamation, the *Beaufort* (South Carolina) *Free South*, on January 9, 1864, commented that the Third South Carolina, "being now relieved and allowed to drill its appearance and discipline is becoming excellent." Coincidentally, that news report appeared on the day Walker's court-martial began.[23]

After Walker's trial ended, the court's decision was to be reviewed by the district commander and then by General Gillmore. But before Gillmore could review the decision the process was interrupted. Gillmore and his command became preoccupied with carrying out a mid-January order from the president to invade Florida. As quickly as possible Gillmore had a force assembled, embarking with it from Port Royal on February 6. He occupied Jacksonville, Florida, and pushed westward. Leaving the expedition in the charge of a subordinate general, Gillmore left on February 13 to return to Port Royal to organize further support.[24] It is a fair guess that he had little time to focus on the Walker matter when it reached him after the court-martial action had been approved, on February 18, by the district commander. On February 20 Gillmore confirmed the sentence, directing that it be carried out as soon as "practicable" at a camp established for black troops near Jacksonville. In the meantime the Third South Carolina had been sent to the camp, presumably for work at the base for the Florida invasion. Though that invasion was abruptly stemmed in the

Battle of Olustee on the very day Gillmore confirmed Walker's sentence, the Jacksonville base was maintained.[25]

Walker was sent to Jacksonville under escort of one of the officers of the Third South Carolina who had been a witness for his prosecution.[26] At Jacksonville Walker was executed on March 1. As reported by a newsman, "He met his death unflinchingly. Out of eleven shots first fired, but one struck him. A reserve firing party had been provided, and by these he was shot to death." Thereafter, on March 3, General Gillmore transmitted the entire record of the court-martial proceeding and sentence to the adjutant general in Washington.[27] Thence the record went to the judge advocate general, but this record did not show that the sentence already had been carried out.

We now reach the question of whether the execution was proper without prior review in Washington. It is conceivable, indeed likely, that upon such a review, perhaps with notice of the steps taken after the "mutiny" showing that the conditions faced by the regiment required correction, Walker's sentence would not have survived.

The 1862 Militia Act included not only the provision regarding the service of blacks and their pay, but also a series of miscellaneous provisions. One of these established the office of judge advocate general, requiring that the records of all court-martial proceedings be filed in that office for review. It added that no sentence of death or penitentiary imprisonment could be "carried into execution until the same shall have been approved by the President." But in March 1863 a provision of another law repealed that section "as far as relates to carrying into execution the sentence of any court-martial against any person convicted as a spy or deserter, or of mutiny or murder," adding that such a sentence could be "carried into execution upon the approval of the commanding-general in the field."[28]

A year later, when the Walker matter reached the judge advocate general—the distinguished Joseph Holt, not known for leniency—he recorded his ruling on the file. "The law invests Commanding Generals with the power to enforce the death penalty only in cases of Desertion, Spies, Mutiny, and Murder," Holt wrote. "Therefore when a person is convicted of other offenses than these, the case should be submitted for the action of the President." Holt pointed out that Walker had been convicted not only of mutiny but of such other offenses as well, and that his death sentence had been based on the entire conviction.

Therefore, the file was to be returned to General Gillmore, obviously for his submission of the case "for the action of the President."[29] But by the time of Holt's ruling there was no case to submit; William Walker lived only in history.

Nevertheless, Walkers' action had impact. Not only did the "mutiny" cause the powers at Port Royal to improve conditions for the black soldiers, but General Gillmore had his department's provost marshal general report on the cases of a number of men in confinement on charges, or convictions, of various crimes. In the case of three prisoners the charges included participation in the mutiny, and in the case of six others mutiny was the only charge. On June 3, 1864, came the report. The mutiny, it said, arose from a determination of several men "no longer to do duty for seven dollars a month," and the leader, Walker, had been executed. It continued that in the summer and fall of 1863 the Third South Carolina "was under bad management, and in a greatly demoralized condition," and that since then several of its officers had been dismissed or were under charges. The enlisted men, the report emphasized, had been slaves; "their great ignorance of their duties and responsibilities as *Soldiers*, led them to commit errors which more intelligent men would have avoided." It insisted that their officers "were more to blame than these men." The report's conclusion was that the regiment, much improved in spirit, had become one of the best in the department, and that the imprisoned men should be restored to duty. And so they were.[30]

Nor was Walker's impact exhausted by the dismissal of blameworthy officers. Even as his execution was impending, news of the mutiny episode reached Washington. The news contributed to the beginning of agitation in Congress to make the pay of black soldiers, whether or not free prior to the war, equal to that of whites. A statute of June 15, 1864, did so as of January 1 of that year. During the Senate's consideration of that measure there had been specific focus on the situation of blacks, like Walker, who had been promised equal pay when they had been enrolled. The result was the Senate's adoption of a provision, advocated by Sen. Henry Wilson of Massachusetts, requiring compliance with that promise for the full period of a promisee's service, not just from January 1, 1864. In his advocacy, Senator Wilson referred to the Third South Carolina's mutiny, Walker's execution, and the arrest of others involved; the mutiny, the Senator said, was "impelled by a burning sense of our injustice." Nonetheless, the House refused to concur in the Senate's provision.[31]

The Massachusetts senator's interest is quite understandable. General Saxton was a Massachusetts man, and it was through him that the secretary of war's equal pay promise had been given. Moreover another Massachusetts man, the very prominent Thomas W. Higginson, had been made the colonel of the First South Carolina regiment; he was outraged at the breach of promise and voiced protest widely. He continued to protest after the June legislation, writing for newspaper publication that officers of the South Carolina regiments would have to continue "as executioners for those soldiers who, like Sergeant Walker, refuse to fulfill their share of a contract where the Government has openly repudiated the other share."[32] Senator Wilson was determined that that repudiation should be corrected. Experience with the June 1864 legislation showed that he could count on the Senate. The problem was in the House.

Congress assembled in December 1864 for its final short session to end with the legislative day of March 3, 1865, which could not be extended beyond noon of calendar March 4. In the course of the session Senator Wilson worked with some key House members, preparing for what would be, most literally, last-minute action. On March 2 he had the Senate adopt a number of miscellaneous provisions as amendments to a minor measure that had come from the House; among the miscellany he included a provision requiring that any authorized promise of equal pay to black soldiers should be complied with retroactively to the time of the soldiers' enlistment, and explicitly requiring compliance with the equal-pay promise in the secretary of war's letter of August 25, 1862, to General Saxton.[33]

On the next day, March 3, the measure as adopted by the Senate was brought to the House floor with some further proposed changes, but none changing the Senate's provision to comply with the equal-pay promise, and in the House's action that provision remained untouched. A conference committee ironed out differences as Congress sat on through the night, and both Houses then agreed. At last the enrolled act was signed by the speaker and the vice president, and, when transmitted to the president, he added his signature, making the act law. By that time noon of calendar March 4 was nearly at hand.[34] At long last there was provision to correct the breach of promise to the

South Carolinians. Colonel Higginson finally would know that officers no longer had to be "executioners for those soldiers . . . like Sergeant Walker."

Back in May 1864, when Senator Wilson of Massachusetts had been trying vainly to have Congress correct the breach of promise of equal pay, Massachusetts Gov. John A. Andrew had sent to his other senator, Charles Sumner, a letter to President Lincoln that he asked Sumner to deliver. It told of the impaired morale among black troops caused by the pay inequality and of the execution of a South Carolinian for mutiny, the Walker case. Wrote the governor, "The Government which found no law to *pay* him except as *a nondescript or a contraband*, nevertheless found law enough to *shoot* him as a *soldier*."[35] One wonders whether the president recalled that letter as he affixed his approval to the measure that Senator Wilson finally had engineered. One wonders, too, whether, when Abraham Lincoln invoked "charity for all" a few minutes later in his second inaugural address, he knew that William Walker's opportunity for charity through having his case "submitted for the action of the President" had been illegally denied.

Be that as it may, there were those in the federal bureaucracy who remained troubled about the basic question of whether it ever had been legal to impose the pay inequality on black soldiers. The second comptroller of the treasury was among the troubled ones. His duties included passing on monetary claims against the government, and by the summer of 1865 he had pending a variety of claims by black soldiers for volunteers' bounty payments. His study of the claims had led him to take a close look at an opinion by the attorney general, of July 14, 1864, that had been issued as a result of a special provision in the June 15 statute that had eliminated the pay inequality from January 1. That special provision had applied to black soldiers who had been free at the beginning of the war. It stated that they were entitled to receive, retroactive from the time of their enlistment even though prior to January 1, both the pay and the bounty "allowed to such persons by the laws existing at the time of their enlistment," and it authorized the attorney general to determine such entitlement. In his ruling the attorney general had carefully considered the $10 pay provision of the 1862 Militia Act. He held that its phrase, "any military or naval service," must be interpreted in light of the "conjoined words," that is, "constructing intrenchments, or performing camp service, or any other labor." So interpreted, he concluded, the $10 limitation did not apply to blacks enlisted as soldiers, for their duties "are essentially of higher nature" than those which the "conjoined words" embraced. He then went on to rule that heretofore there had been no other statute prescribing a color line pertaining to either pay or bounty for free men authorized to be enlisted as soldiers. His conclusion, therefore, was that free blacks should receive volunteers' bounties and retroactive equal pay for the full time since their enlistment.[36]

While the June 1864 statute had made that ruling of the attorney general apply only to blacks who had been free at the war's beginning, the comptroller of the treasury observed that the attorney general's opinion was stated in terms equally applicable to black soldiers who were free at the time of enlistment even if they had been slaves at the war's beginning. Of them there were vast numbers (as William Walker had been) freed by the Emancipation Proclamation and other measures. Apparently they, too, had a right to volunteers' bounties. So, in late September 1865, the comptroller wrote the secretary of the treasury, reviewing the matter, and requesting that the attorney general rule on various specified types of blacks' bounty entitlement. On September 25 the secretary submitted the comptroller's letter to the attorney general, requesting his ruling.[37]

Missourian Edward Bates had been attorney general in July 1864; the attorney general in 1865 was the Kentuckian James Speed. In response to the request of the secretary of the treasury, Speed rendered his ruling on October 17, with a long supporting opinion. Not only did Speed agree with his predecessor but he went even further in his reasoning that blacks had had a legal right to compensation equal to that of whites. On the next day, the comptroller wrote the paymaster general, summarizing the attorney general's ruling and opinion and indicating that all freedmen were "to be placed on a footing with white volunteers." Therefore, he requested the paymaster to direct that bounty be paid to the black soldiers who had volunteered. Shortly thereafter, on October 26, the paymaster general wrote Secretary of War Stanton, giving an estimate of the amount of bounties to be paid "under the ruling of the Second Comptroller." In addition, said the paymaster, "by parity of reasoning" the blacks likewise were entitled to retroactive equal pay, so his estimate gave also the amount of back pay to be provided to blacks, though not free at the war's outset, for service prior to January 1, 1864, the day from which equal pay already had been allowed by Congress in its June 1864 statute that we have previously referred to.[38]

Thus, by the fall of 1865 the bureaucrats had set about correcting most abundantly the inequality in pay that had caused William Walker's "mutiny." That they had actually begun doing so is revealed in an undated note that the paymaster general later penned at the bottom of the original of his October 16, 1865, letter to the secretary of war. The note said that, "till stop'd by your order," the amount paid had been "very inconsiderable" (only a few thousand dollars paid to some District of Columbia and Kentucky troops).[39]

So, in the end, not only had it been determined that William Walker's execution had been illegal, but a decision by the highest legal officer of the government indicated that Walker had been legally right in the grievance that had led him to "mutiny." Nonetheless, when at long last bureaucrats had stepped in to begin rectifying the wrong, Secretary of War Stanton abruptly "stop'd" correction.

Notes

1. *List of U.S. Soldiers Executed by United States Military Authorities during the Late War* (Adj. Gen. Office, 1885). Blacks are listed on pp. 8–11.

2. Of historians' references, *Freedom: A Documentary History of Emancipation, 1861–1867*, ser. 2, *The Black Military Experience* (Cambridge Univ. Press, New York, 1982), edited by Ira Berlin et al., is almost alone in doing more than noting the event. After a summary account on pp. 365–66 it provides some documentation on pp. 388–95.

3. Walker's age appears in the list of initial enlistments, Apr. 24, 1863, of Co. A, 3d South Carolina Colored Volunteers, (hereafter cited as List, Co. A, 3d S.C.) in U.S. Colored Troops, 21st Infantry, Regimental Descriptive, Letter and Endorsement Book, Office of the Adj. Gen., RG 94, Nat. Arch. (hereafter cited as 21st USCT, Reg. Des.). In December 1863 the 3d, 4th, and 5th South Carolina were ordered consolidated into one regiment, the 21st USCT; consolidation was implemented in mid-March 1864. Special Order No. 550, Dec. 11, 1863, Adj. Gen. Office, and Regimental Order No. 1, 21st USCT, Mar. 18, 1864, 21st USCT Regimental Papers, Box No. 21, Office of the Adj. Gen., RG 94, Nat. Arch. (hereafter cited as 21st USCT, Reg. Papers). Thus 3d South Carolina records are filed under the 21st USCT.

4. U.S. War Dept., *The War of the Rebellion: A Compilation of the Official Records of the Union and Confederate Armies*, 70 vols. in 128 pts. (1880–1901; rpt. National Historical Society, Gettysburg, 1972), ser. 3, 2:27, 152–53 (hereafter cited as *ORA*); Ezra J. Warner *Generals in Blue: Lives of the Union Commanders* (Louisiana State Univ. Press, Baton Rouge, l964), pp. 420–21.

5. Statement of William Walker appended to the transcript of his Court-Martial

Proceeding, records of the Judge Adv. Gen., Proceedings of the Courts-Martial, MM 1320, RG 153, Nat. Arch. Walker's signature, by mark, shows his illiteracy. List, Co. A, 3d S.C., 21st USCT, Reg. Des., mistakenly recorded that he had previously been a "laborer."

6. *ORA*, ser. 1, 14:377–78; *ORA*, ser. 3, 3:20.

7. General Orders Nos. 17 and 24, Dept. of South, *ORA*, ser. 1, 14:429–30, 1020–21; List, Co. A, 3d S.C., 21st USCT, Reg. Des.

8. List, Co. A, 3d S.C., 21st USCT, Reg. Des.; Walker Court-Martial Proceeding, appended statement, 1; letter of Nov. 19, 1863, from officers of 3d S.C. to Adj. Gen. in letter book bound in 21st USCT Reg. Des.; *A Compendium of the Pay of the Army from 1785 to 1888* (Paymaster Gen. Office, 1888), 50–51, 57; Sec. 5, *U.S. Stat.*, 12:269–70; *Revised Army Regulations* (1863), 169–72.

9. Various entries in letter book and otherwise in 21st USCT Reg. Des.; regimental orders beginning May 1, 1863, in section containing orders of 3d S.C., 21st USCT Regimental Order and Guard Report Book, Office of the Adj. Gen., RG 94, Nat. Arch. (hereafter cited as 3d S.C., 21st USCT, Reg. Order).

10. *ORA*, ser. 1, vol. 28, pt. 2:3–4.

11. Secs. 12, 13, and 15, *U.S. Stat.*, 12:597–600.

12. *Official Records of the Union and Confederate Navies in the War of the Rebellion*, 27 vols. (Washington, 1894–1927), ser. 1, 5:201, 14:401, 23:638, 25:327–28; Elon A. Woodward, *The Negro in the Military Service of the United States, 1639–1886: A Compilation* (1888), Office of the Adj. Gen., Nat. Arch., RG 94, M 858, Roll 2, p. 1690; David L. Valuska, "The Negro in the Union Navy, 1861–1865" (Ph.D. diss., Lehigh Univ., 1973, Library of Congress), pp. 29, 43–44, 51, 54–55, 65–66.

13. *ORA*, ser. 3, 3:250–52, 404–5, 420.

14. Opinion of Judge Adv. Gen., Oct. 11, 1862, approved by Sec. War, Nov. 7, Consolidated File, "Contraband Fund," Records of Office of the QMG, RG 92, Nat. Arch.; letter of Nov. 19, 1863, from officers of 3d S.C. to Adj. Gen. in letter book bound in 21st USCT, Reg. Des.; letter of Colonel Bennett to headquarters, Department of South, Nov. 30, 1863, Letters Rec'd, 21st USCT, Reg. Papers.

15. *Official Records of the Union and Confederate Navies*, ser. 1, 14:251.

16. Colonel Bennett's letter of June 10 to department headquarters and of June 20 to post commander, in letter book bound in 21st USCT, Reg. Des.; Regimental Orders of 3d S.C., No. 84, July 29, and No. 87, Aug. 1, 21st USCT, Reg. Order; letter of Aug. 3 to Colonel Bennett from captain of Co. A, Letters Rec'd, 21st USCT, Reg. Papers; Herbert Aptheker, "Negro Casualties in the Civil War," *Journal of Negro History* 32 (Jan. 1947):22–23.

17. Colonel Bennett's letter of Nov. 30 to headquarters, Department of South, Letters Rec'd, 21st USCT, Reg. Papers.

18. Colonel Bennett testimony, Walker Court-Martial Proceeding, 12–16. It is impossible to ascertain which men, if any, other than those of Co. A, participated. There are various references to the "regiment" having done so. Bennett testified that it was a "portion" of the command; 3d S.C. Regimental Order No. 121, Nov. 28, 1863, Order Books for 21st USCT Cos. A–K, including orders for 3d S.C., Office of the Adj. Gen., RG 94, Nat. Arch. Demotion dated from Nov. 23, 1863.

19. Walker Court-Martial Proceeding, 7–11.

20. Walker Court-Martial Proceeding, 29, 37, 44, 44–46, appended statement.

21. Walker Court-Martial Proceeding, 30–31, appended statement, 5; Colonel Bennett's testimony is on pp. 12–16, and the two officers' testimony to Walker's "leadership" on pp. 16–18 and 23–24. Walker's denial of his "leadership" is on p. 2 of the appended statement, and the supporting testimony is on pp. 31–32, 34–40.

22. Walker Court-Martial Proceeding, appended statement, 1–2, 6.

23. Letter of Nov. 19 from officers of 3d S.C. to Adj. Gen. in letter book bound in 21st USCT Reg. Des.; Aptheker, "Negro Casualties," 23; Port Royal, South Carolina, *The New South*, Dec. 26, 1863; Colonel Bennett's letter of Nov. 30 to headquarters, and endorsements thereon, Department of South, Letters Rec'd, 21st USCT, Reg. Papers. Significantly, the *Beaufort Free South* item said that the regiment had not been much noticed previously because of its "having to perform constant fatigue duty."

24. Shelby Foote, *The Civil War*, 3 vols. (Random House, New York, 1958–74), 2:899–902.

25. Walker Court-Martial Proceeding, 47–48; that the 3d S.C., in whole or part, was then at Jacksonville is inferred from a recital, in an order fixing the time for Walker's execution, that it would be "in the presence of the Brigade to which his Regt. is now attached." General Order No. 8, Feb. 28, 1864, General Orders, Dist. of Florida, Department of Florida Records, vol. 20, RG 393, Nat. Arch.; Foote, *The Civil War*, 2:903–4.

26. Orders from Headquarters, Department of South, to Colonel Howell, commanding Dist. of Hilton Head, Feb. 26, 1864, to Lieutenant Jacobs, 3d S.C., Feb. 27, 1864, and to General Seymour, commanding Dist. of Florida, Feb. 27, 1864, Nos. 1790, 1792, and 1795, Letters Transmitted, Headquarters, Department of South, Oct. 28, 1863, to Aug. 6, 1864, RG 393, Nat. Arch. The escort was Lieutenant Jacobs. At the court-martial the prosecution's evidence in support of the second of the specifications under the third charge, the mutiny charge, had been Jacobs' testimony that Walker had led his men on the evening of Nov. 19 in releasing a private whom Jacobs was trying to arrest. Walker flatly denied that he even had been present at the incident, and testimony of Private Bryan who was present on guard duty supported Walker. Walker Court-Martial Proceeding, 24–25, 33–34, appended statement, 4–5.

27. Various records differ as to whether the execution occurred on Feb. 29 or Mar. 1; William Wells Brown, *The Negro in the American Rebellion* (1867; rpt., The Citadel Press, New York, 1971), p. 252 (quoting the news item); General Gillmore to Adj. Gen., Mar. 3, 1864, No. 1818, Letters Transmitted, Headquarters, Department of South, Oct. 28, 1863, to Aug. 6, 1864.

28. Act of July 17, 1862, sec. 5, *U.S. Stat.*, 12:598; act of Mar. 3, 1863, sec. 21, *U.S. Stat.*, 12:735.

29. The Holt ruling, dated Mar. 17, 1864, with a notation for the return of the file to General Gillmore, appears on the back of the last page of the Walker statement appended to the Walker Court-Martial Proceeding.

30. Report of Provost Marshal General, Department of South, June 3, 1864, and endorsement thereon, Letters Rec'd, 21st USCT, Reg. Papers. See also the very similar views expressed in a letter of the same date from the superintendent of black recruitment in the Department of the South to the department provost marshal general, based on a conversation wtih Colonel Bennett; it said that as soon "as the worthless officers left & good officers took charge, & explained to the men"

their duties, the men willingly complied with those duties, and the unit was now "one of the best," Berlin, *The Black Military Experience*, pp. 394–95.

31. Sec. 2, *U.S. Stat.*, 13:129; *Cong. Globe*, 38th Cong., 1st Sess., 990, 1030, 1805, 1806, 1813, 2851–54.

32. In Col. Thomas Wentworth Higginson's postwar book about his regiment he included in an appendix, with a prefatory note, the texts of his letters to the press from January to December 1864 protesting the breach of promise, *Army Life in a Black Regiment* (1870; rpt., Michigan State Univ. Press, East Lansing, 1960), pp. 218–28. The reference to Walker is in his letter of Aug. 12, 1864, to the *New York Tribune*, in *Army Life in a Black Regiment*, p. 226.

33. *Cong. Globe*, 38th Cong., 2d Sess., 1294, 1296.

34. *Cong. Globe*, 38th Cong. 2d Sess., 1378–79, 1380, 1386, 1391, 1398–1402. That Congress sat through the night and well into the morning appears at 1389, 1391, 1394–95, 1418, 1420, 1421, 1423–24. The provision as finally adopted is in act of Mar. 3, 1865, sec. 5, *U.S. Stat.*, 13:488.

35. Henry Greenleaf Pearson, *The Life of John A. Andrew*, 2 vols. (Houghton Mifflin Co., Boston, 1904), 2:109.

36. Act of June 15, 1864, sec. 4, *U.S. Stat.*, 13:29–30; *Ops. Atty. Gen.*, 11:53–58. The president sent the attorney general's ruling to the secretary of war on the day of its issuance and on the next day the secretary directed compliance with the ruling as the statute required, *ORA*, ser. 3, 4:493. Herman Belz, "Law, Politics, and Race in the Struggle for Equal Pay During the Civil War," *Civil War History* 22 (Sept. 1976):197–213, is a provocative discussion of the legislative history of the Militia Act, the June 1864 legislation, and the attorney general's opinion. The article seems to view as mistaken the attorney general's ruling that the Militia Act's $10 pay limitation did not apply to black soldiers. It fails, however, to give adequate weight to the statement in the Senate debate, by the original sponsor of the provision that became the $10 pay limitation, to the effect that it did not deal with ordinary soldiers but, rather, with blacks brought into the service only as laborers, *Cong. Globe*, 37 Cong., 2d Sess., 3250–51 (remarks of Senator King of New York in response to an objection to the provision). It is a principle of statutory interpretation that such a statement is nearly determinative of a statute's meaning. While William Walker and his fellows, prior to the "mutiny," had been engaged only in work at the docks and similar duty, their enlistment had not limited them to that duty; they were enlisted and mustered as full-scale soldiers. The article also fails to deal with a later 1865 attorney general's opinion that we are about to refer to.

37. General Accounting Office, Second Comptroller's Office, Misc. Letters Sent, 28:315–17, RG 217, Nat. Arch.; General Records of the Treasury Department, Letters Sent to Executive Officers, 17:168, RG 56, Nat. Arch.

38. *Ops. Atty. Gen.*, 11:365–73; Second Comptroller's Office, Misc. Letters Sent, 28:393–95; Records of the Sec. of War, Letters Rec'd by the Sec. of War from the President, Executive Departments, and War Department Bureaus, 1862–70, M 494, Roll 83, RG 107, Nat. Arch.

39. The paymaster general's file copy of his letter as originally sent does not have the appended note. Letters Sent by the Paymaster General, 1808–89, 49:215, RG 99, Nat. Arch. So it is apparent that the note appended to the letter as received by the secretary of war was added some time later.

9

Company A
of Rhode Island's
Black Regiment:
Its Enlisting,
Its "Mutiny,"
Its Pay, Its Service

O<small>N</small> M<small>ARCH</small> 17, 1864, the men of a company of a Rhode Island black regiment were assembled for a roll call. On the call, all but one noncom stood mute. But in just a few minutes, after a quick exchange between one of the officers and one of the sergeants who had been among the mute, the call was repeated and everyone responded. Nonetheless, that initial muteness caused court-martialing of each noncom understood to have been present (save for the one who had answered the first call) and twenty of the privates. The company was Company A of the First Battalion of the Fourteenth Rhode Island Colored Heavy Artillery.[1] As then was true of all black units, its officers were white.

This March 17 episode and its aftermath have been referred to recently as an illustration of the consequence of imposing on black soldiers a rate of pay drastically lower than the pay of whites.[2] That problem was involved, to a degree, as we shall see. But a close look reveals that there was a deeper problem, that of many white officers' failure, notably in the early days of the blacks' service, to exercise leadership rather than to wield a bludgeon, a failure stemming from the utter alienation between most whites in the free states and the black populace.

The chapter was prepared especially for this book.

142

Blacks in the free states were few; according to the 1860 census they were but little more than 1 percent of those states' population. Many free-state whites hoped that ultimately, somehow, those blacks would disappear. In very few states were they given full citizens' rights. They were generally treated as an alien breed even more fully, in a sense, than a good many slave-state whites treated slaves; in the land of slavery some relations between whites and blacks were close, even cordial.

It is hardly strange, therefore, that exclusion of blacks from the United States Army, which had been in effect ever since the War of 1812, was continued by the Union when the Civil War came. While exclusion never had been by statute, but only by discretion of the Executive, the Union's Executive firmly adhered to it despite repeated proffers by blacks to shoulder arms in suppressing rebellion.[3] After more than a year of warfare, however, army demands on Union manpower had so mounted that here and there among free-state whites it had begun to seem that even the alien breed, however few, should contribute to meeting those demands. That view was entertained notably by the governor of Rhode Island, despite indication in the 1860 census that of the state's 35,881 males between the ages of eighteen and forty-five only 782 were black.[4]

That governor, William Sprague, took a bold step without advance clearance from the War Department. On August 4, 1862, he provided for recruiting blacks for a regiment long before authorized by the War Department but not yet organized. Of course, the authorization had assumed a white regiment, but there had been no explicit prohibition against making it black. The order of the state's adjutant general providing for the recruiting recalled that, in the Revolution, a Rhode Island black unit had been praised by George Washington as equal to any in his service; surely this one could do as well.[5]

On August 6 there was a large meeting of blacks in Providence to consider their response. It was made clear that if the blacks would be accepted as soldiers the response would be enthusiastic. Yet there had been a troubling report that President Lincoln would accept blacks in the army only as laborers, not as soldiers. A committee was designated to consult the governor on that point. On the next evening the meeting resumed for its committee's report. Though unable to see the governor, it had met with the state's officer to be in charge of the recruiting. He had assured the committee that the recruiting would be for a regiment of regular soldiers, at the same pay as for white soldiers, and that, if not so accepted by the Union army, it would be disbanded. Thereupon the meeting, with hardly a dissent, voted to respond "cheerfully" to the call. A recruiting station was opened in Providence on August 14 and soon some three hundred Rhode Island blacks were enrolled, with more in prospect; further, there was definite indication that blacks from neighboring states were ready also to respond to Rhode Island's call.[6] Yet even as this was happening the War Department was refusing black soldiers, and on September 20 the president wrote Governor Sprague that his black regiment would not be accepted.[7] So ended Rhode Island's step away from alienation of blacks.

Variously among the free states, however, sentiment for easing the military demand on whites was growing. By the year's close the Union disaster at Fredericksburg and the thwarting of Gen. U. S. Grant's move into Mississippi made it clear that an end of the war was not in sight. Why blacks, however few in the free states, should be barred from soldiering was becoming incomprehensible. And then, in the president's Final Emancipation Proclamation of January 1, 1863, there was a provision not even hinted at in his Preliminary Emancipation Proclamation of September, a provision that the slaves in the specified territory of the Rebel states not only were freed but those "of suitable condition will be received into the armed service."[8] All through that New Year's Day, and into the evening when finally word came that the proclamation had been issued, there was a spirited meeting of blacks in Providence to celebrate the great event, with much fervent singing by a choir directed by a prominent black musician, John Jenkins. If Jenkins and the others focused on the unanticipated provision that slaves could become soldiers, they must have felt that Rhode Island blacks finally would be allowed to shoulder arms. If so, they were right; almost within days the War Department sent to Rhode Island authorization for a black regiment.[9]

Rhode Island's government, however, did not respond to the War Department's overture. Governor Sprague had been chosen for a seat in the United States Senate and would continue as governor only until March 3, 1863, when he resigned his governorship to go to the Senate. Then there was only an interim governor until an elected successor took office; in early April the successor, James Smith, was elected but he would not be inaugurated until May 26.[10] Thus, during those first months after the Union army's door had been opened to blacks, the

Rhode Island Executive was in flux, not in a position to take any far-reaching step. Moreover, such pressure as there may have been in Rhode Island to recruit blacks was somewhat relieved at that time, because the governor of neighboring Massachusetts had secured authority from the War Department to raise a black regiment that had developed into a recruiting drive reaching into many of the free states, including Rhode Island.[11]

In any case, the new governor, Smith, had not been long in office before focusing on recruiting blacks. Rhode Island already ranked second only to Kansas in the ratio to the state's total population of the soldiers it had provided, and by mid-June there was a still further need.[12] A Confederate invasion into Maryland, aimed at Pennsylvania, was imminent. The governor had concluded that the time was coming when Rhode Island's blacks no longer should be kept at a distance. He sought from the War Department authority to raise a black company of heavy artillery; promptly, on June 17, the authority was given.[13]

At that time, however, a new governor must have been overwhelmed with all he confronted, notably helping meet the mounting emergency in Pennsylvania, so a special arrangement for recruiting and organizing a black unit was not at the fore of his agenda. But the roar of Gettysburg hardly had subsided before the president precipitated the taking of Rhode Island blacks into the army. On March 3, 1863, Congress had authorized the president to draft men into the army, and had imposed no color limitation.[14] By July 6 such conscription had begun in Rhode Island and at once was reaching "quite a number of colored men" along with whites.[15] If Governor Smith ever had had any hesitation about inviting black enlistment, surely that need be no more, for volunteering diminished what would be required by conscription to meet Rhode Island's quota; a black enlisted could mean a white privileged to remain at home. On July 29 the governor had an order issued for recruiting the black heavy artillery company authorized by the War Department back in June. The men, including noncoms, would number about 140, to be enlisted for three years or the war's duration.[16] Appointed captain was a rather prominent Rhode Islander, Thomas W. Fry, who, as a lieutenant, had had considerable experience in the Union's foothold on the South Carolina–Georgia coast.[17]

The state's blacks' response to the call was immediate and enthusiastic, doubtless enhanced by Rhode Island's provision, in June, for a

$300 bounty to a three-year volunteer, available to a black the same as to a white.[18] For that time, that was a generous state bounty, especially for blacks who, however free, generally had a hard economic struggle. The bounty was so attractive that, almost at once, response to Rhode Island's call came also from blacks in other free states. Virtually overnight it was apparent that authorization of only a single company was unrealistic. On August 14 the War Department sent word that a battalion of four companies was authorized; by early September that was extended to a full regiment. A heavy artillery regiment would number some seventeen hundred men, far more than available Rhode Island blacks, but blacks from other states flowed into Rhode Island in a steady stream.[19]

The first company, Company A, had been filled within days after Governor Smith's initial call at the end of July, and was actually mustered into federal service on August 28; by then a second company, Company B, was filled, and soon two more, Companies C and D. The four companies became, for the prospective regiment, the First Battalion, commanded by Major Joseph J. Comstock.[20] Comstock was a Rhode Island native, though he had been in business in New York. Entering the service at the war's beginning, he soon had become a lieutenant in a Rhode Island regiment and later a captain. Along the way he had been severely injured in action on the South Carolina coast. Though physically somewhat impaired he had continued in responsible duty, and in September 1863 was promoted to major to take on the command of the First Battalion.[21]

Enlistments continued steadily through the rest of the year at the rate of completing a new company "about once a fortnight," and as the year's end approached the companies were reaching Company M, so comprising three battalions.[22] In the event, of a total of 2876 Rhode Island enlistments during the entire year of 1863, 1703 were for the colored heavy artillery regiment, all of them within the year's last half. Indeed, in a stretch of four weeks from late September, of a total of 320 recruits accepted in Rhode Island, 264 were blacks, for the colored regiment.[23] The Rhode Island white populace and its officials were enthusiastically applauding a flocking of blacks to the Rhode Island banner that so notably eased meeting the state's quota for the required contribution to Union arms.

In that enthusiasm there was one disturbing note. It was to be charged, with no little supporting evidence, that the leading state recruiter, in vigorously pursuing a recruiting program for the regiment both in Rhode Island and far and wide in the North, often had "milked" into his personal pail no small part of the state bounty money. Officers of the regiment were outraged by what they deemed the recruiter's corruption and after extensive consideration in the State Assembly and legislative committee investigations in 1864 and 1865, the assembly's House, as the war was ending, directed the state's attorney general to institute action against the recruiter.[24]

Such corruption had not occurred, however, in the recruiting of Company A or, probably, Company B. Company A certainly, and very likely Company B, had been filled before that particular recruiter had begun his work. Not only were many of the state's blacks eager to join, but, as we have noted, blacks of other states had begun a rush to Rhode Island from the very outset, attracted by its bounty; even in Company A there were at least sixteen men from elsewhere, mostly New York.[25]

On August 28 Companies A and B did a street parade in Providence, although the B men had received their arms only the day before. It commanded great interest. On September 2 Company A left the recruits' camp at Providence for training grounds at Dutch Island on the state's coast. By the end of September it was joined there by the other three companies of the First Battalion. From time to time in the ensuing weeks, the additional companies were sent on to Dutch Island for training.[26]

On November 19, the day of a ceremony at Gettysburg that included the famous address by President Lincoln, there was another ceremony at Dutch Island. The top state civil and military officials headed by the governor, numerous members of the state's General Assembly and of the city governments of Providence and Newport, the president of Brown University, various of the clergy, and many others were assembled to present the regiment its colors, with a stirring address by United States Sen. H. B. Anthony. Then by December 7, orders had been issued for the First Battalion to be moved from training into the war. So, as the final companies of the regiment were being organized, the first ones would be on their way. Soon there was another ceremony. The black ladies of Providence and its vicinity had prepared a flag for that First Battalion. On December 9 it was presented, with an eloquent address by one of the state's black leaders. He handed the banner to Sergeant Jenkins of Company A, the man who had directed the choir in celebrating the Final Emancipation Proclamation on New Year's

Day; he handsomely responded and handed the banner on to Major
Comstock. The major thanked the ladies and expressed his pride at
being an officer of a colored regiment. Witnessing the ceremony were
the governor, the lieutenant governor, other prominent officials, and
a great crowd. Finally there was a review of the battalion by Governor
Smith, and then a battalion drill, warmly praised by the onlookers.
Ultimately, on December 20, the battalion boarded ship for New
Orleans. After receiving such notable attention in Rhode Island, it was
ready for great accomplishment in fighting the war.[27]

The voyage took ten days. But on reaching New Orleans the men
found they were not to be disembarked. Kept aboard until January
3, 1864, they then sailed on to Matagorda Island, Texas, not to be
disembarked until the morning of January 8.[28] It had been a long trip,
and it is understandable that the men had become restless. While at
anchor at New Orleans some had jumped ship and got into a brawl
with the police. Of that there were exaggerated reports, but in fact the
brawl was quickly quelled, principally by the battalion's own officers.
At last at their destination, surely the men would respond heartily to
Major Comstock's first general order, wherein he called out, "Let us
be second to none, let this Battalion prove that colored men will make
good soldiers."[29]

Matagorda Island was a coastal strip, roughly midway between Gal-
veston and the mouth of the Rio Grande. On and near that strip the
Union had established, during the previous fall, its northernmost Texas
holding, with others on down the coast and just up the Rio Grande to
Brownsville. Around Matagorda several army units were posted. They
were engaged simply in rehabilitating an old fort and otherwise
strengthening the Union's narrow holding. So the battalion's going into
war was hardly exciting. Even so, when the Union commander in
Texas, Maj. Gen. N. J. T. Dana, paid a surprise visit to the battalion
in late January, it most favorably impressed him. He wrote Governor
Smith, "Excellence is the proper term to apply to its condition and
soldierly bearing."[30]

Nonetheless, in but a short time it became evident to the men
of the battalion that, essentially, they were in the midst of nothing
happening. While there were some Confederate forces in the vicinity
they were limited and posed no real threat. Nor was there any indication that the Unionists would make any move. Had the men been ex-
slaves they would have been enjoying the excitement of becoming

free. For the battalion there was nothing of the sort. Indeed, as civilians they had experienced a special freedom, in a sense mastering their own lives, separate from whites. And in their training period in Rhode Island they had been extolled virtually as heroes by the white society, including its highest officials. Now, abruptly, they were mere cogs in a machine, operated at arms' length by their white officers to whom blacks remained an alien breed. With nothing happening that appeared to give purpose to the machine's operation, little things could seem to the men to be big things. On March 17, for Company A, there was a little thing, the first roll call that we referred to at the outset of our account. But it seemed to a few of the men to be possibly a big thing, and that resulted in its becoming truly big.

On that March 17 Company A's Captain Fry was temporarily an acting inspector general of a very recently organized brigade that included the battalion, so the company commander for a time was its first lieutenant, Charles Chace.[31] After the usual duty, the company was assembled for something quite unprecedented, an inspection by Captain Fry and an incident roll call. Lieutenant Chace had the first sergeant do the call, to begin with sergeants, proceed to corporals, thence on to the privates. Four or so names were called without response, though the men were there. Puzzled, Chace had the call stopped, and asked the first sergeant what that meant, but the sergeant was also puzzled. Captain Fry at once reported the matter to Major Comstock, who came over, "made some remark," and left. The roll call then was taken all the way. There was but one response, that by a Sergeant Phinix; from all the others there was utter silence. Baffled, Fry asked one of the sergeants, Humbert, why they were not answering. He was told that it was thought that the unusual roll call might have something to do with a move to have the men of the company receive pay at the low rate being paid blacks instead of the regular soldiers' pay. Fry at once replied that the roll call had nothing to do with pay, that it was merely a step in arms inspection. Immediately Sergeant Humbert announced that Captain Fry was to be trusted, so there should be response to the call. At that, Fry told Lieutenant Chace to have the roll called again, that was done, and there was proper response. It is to be noted, incidentally, that Humbert had been one of the very first to enlist. He had enlisted on July 30, 1863, sacrificing "quite a business" as a tailor. Obviously, the men regarded him as a leader.[32]

On the initial roll call it was the silence of the leading noncoms that caused the silence of the other noncoms and all the privates, who were simply following the leaders with no comprehension of the leaders' reason; the leaders' silence had been spontaneous, almost certainly prompted only by a quick exchange of a word or two between them on being lined up for the roll call and a guess that the unprecedented call possibly was meant to establish their status as low-paid blacks instead of full-paid soldiers.[33] Thus it was that to them a little thing— a mere roll call—seemed a big thing. And the consequence was a big thing indeed: court-martialing. Before we come to the court-martialing some background is needed. Major Comstock, in an April 16 letter to an aide of Governor Smith about this March 17 incident, referred to a key point in that background. He said, "Every man in this Batt. was told, when he enlisted, that it was upon the same footing as white soldiers; that he was to have thirteen (13) dollars pr. month." Although the aide replied that no promise of such full pay ever had been given by the governor, it is true that the initial notice by the state's government of the enlisting of a colored heavy artillery company, appearing in the *Providence Daily Journal* on July 31, 1863, and each day thereafter for a week, had stated that the men of the company not only would receive the state bounty but would be entitled to "the same rights and privileges as are given to other soldiers."[34]

At that time the regular pay for privates and corporals was $13 per month, plus a $3.50 clothing allowance; for sergeants it was considerably more. As we have noted, back at the time of Governor Sprague's abortive 1862 recruiting, the state officer in charge had given assurance that the pay to blacks would be the same as to whites. And in the extensive Massachusetts recruiting in 1863, highly publicized in Rhode Island, equal pay had been promised blacks. It was not until June of 1863 that the War Department finally decided that a July 1862 statute was to be construed to impose on all black soldiers, including sergeants, a special low rate of pay, only $10 a month, *less* a $3 clothing allowance.[35] But it may have taken time for that decision to permeate fully. It certainly had not permeated to the pen of the Rhode Island officer who drafted the official notice that began appearing in the press on July 31, stating that the men of the black company, that would become Company A, would have "the same rights" as other soldiers.

Save for the state bounty, none of the men of the battalion had received any pay by March 17, 1864.[36] (It would be nearly a half year more before their pay would be received.) So it is understandable that to the men of the company, far from the fighting and with time on their hands, any question as to their pay would loom large. The War Department's black pay decision of course had become known in Rhode Island well before completion of all the enlistments in the battalion after Company A; Major Comstock grossly overstated in his April 16 letter to Governor Smith's aide.[37] Certainly the black pay question had come well to the fore during the training period back in Rhode Island, as revealed in what Governor Smith said in introducing Senator Anthony at the great ceremony of November 19, when its colors had been presented to the regiment; he said that the men could look to the senator "to assure your future increased pay," and the senator, in response, had promised that "on his return to Washington" he would attempt to do so.[38] But whether or not all the men of the entire battalion had been told they would receive the same pay as white soldiers, there is no doubt that the leaders of Company A had thought that, whatever might happen generally on the black-pay issue, their company had been assured of such full pay by the state of Rhode Island at the time of their enlistment so that they—perhaps—had some kind of special status.[39]

In any case, Major Comstock was determined that his alien breed, new to war's theatre, should comprehend war's basic requirement: prompt, unquestioning obedience to orders. At once he had court-martialing begun for each noncom, other than Sergeant Phinix, understood to have been present at the first roll call.[40] In each case the accused was charged with conduct prejudicial to discipline, specified as refusing, "in combination with nearly the whole company," to answer when his name was called at the inspection even though he did answer on the second call that had ensued so immediately. The court was headed by Capt. Henry Simon, the commander of Company B; other members were Capt. Joel Metcalf of Company D and officers of another black unit and of a couple of white units in the area.[41]

The court's docket was not confined to these cases; it included all disciplinary cases coming up during its sessions. But it is rather notable that two of Major Comstock's subordinate captains would be judges, one the head judge, for the March 17 cases in which Comstock himself, in reality, was the complainant.

Each man charged was separately tried. The first one wished counsel, "but being unable to procure one, said he was willing the Case should proceed."[42] In none of the later cases is there a record of any request for counsel; probably none of the men fully understood a counsel's possible role, and it is not likely that the court enlightened them. Trials began on March 23, with each of the four sergeants tried on successive days. They included Sergeant Humbert, who, as we have said, after his exchange with Captain Fry following the silence on the first roll call told the men to rely on the captain and to answer the call, and Sergeant Jenkins, who at the ceremony back on December 9 had received the flag prepared by the black ladies. Each of the four pleaded not guilty, but Captain Fry and Lieutenant Chace testified to what had happened on the first roll call and, of course, none of the defendants challenged their account or had any defense to the charge. (Jenkins did attempt a strained argument to the effect that he had enlisted with the promise of $13 pay, "guaranteed to us by the State of Rhode Island," on a call by the Rhode Island Governor, but that no pay had been received from the United States so he had never been mustered into Federal service.) Each was promptly found guilty. On March 28 a corporal, also pleading not guilty, was brought to trial that ran into March 29; he, too, was found guilty after attempting in vain to prove that he had not been present at the roll call. The sentence for each of those five was demotion to private and a year of hard labor without pay at Fort Jefferson (Dry Tortugas), Florida.[43]

On March 30 the court dealt with three more of the corporals. One pleaded not guilty to the charge, but guilty to the specification; testimony was limited to a second lieutenant's vouching for the accused's "pretty good" character and behavior, but the accused was found guilty with the same sentence as had been imposed on the predecessors, save that the hard labor time was six months instead of a year.[44] The other two corporals pleaded guilty to both charge and specification. Testimony dealt only with their good character and their confusion as to the purpose of the first roll call. Their sentences were like the sergeants' but with one very important difference: the hard labor would be for only three months with no indication that it was to be at Fort Jefferson.[45]

On that same March 30 some serious trouble occurred among the battalion at its isolated post. A recent reference to that trouble asserts that the court-martial's sentencing of imprisonment "for as much as one year at hard labor generated seething unrest." Nothing is cited to support that statement.[46] Obviously, though, the men of the battalion knew of the charges and undoubtedly had begun to hear something of the outcome of the court-martialing; certainly, in light of the prominence of the court-martialed sergeants, their trials must have caused some "seething." Also, by then, with the fighting war seeming far away, anything as unusual as such extensive court-martialing would loom large in the men's minds.

In any case, on the night of March 29 there had been a commotion by some of the men who had been drinking. Then, on March 30, 2d Lt. Joseph Potter, of Company D, made officer of the guard for that day, found that some drunks were causing trouble. Toward the end of the afternoon Potter arrested one of the privates; on his refusal to go to the guardhouse Potter had him tied up to be carried there. At that another man caused trouble and Potter ordered him tied, having to use "severe means" to quell him. Thereupon other men rushed up, including a Corporal Cooley of Company A. (Cooley had not been among those court-martialed for the March 17 incident; he had been hospitalized for fever from March 14 to March 23, so was not present at the roll call.)[47] Potter ordered these men away, threatening with his pistol to blow their brains out if they did not obey. On their leaving, Cooley lagged behind, defying Potter to shoot, but, after an exchange of words, left. Later Potter had Cooley come to his tent; Potter intended to "reason" with him. But again Cooley was defiant, daring Potter to shoot. At that Potter, who had been sitting, jumped up, whereupon Cooley raised one hand as though to strike Potter and reached, with his other hand, toward Potter's holstered pistol. Potter pulled another pistol and shot Cooley. This account is based on Second Lieutenant Potter's testimony at a court-martialing of Corporal Cooley that we will come to.[48] A year later there was to be a very different account of the shooting that also we will come to.

In any event, the shooting of Cooley immediately resulted in excited outrage among the men of the battalion, with a number of men rushing into the streets with threatening shouts, one a demand that Lieutenant Potter be taken "off from this Island . . . or by God he will go off a corpse." But Captain Fry and other officers finally got the shouters quieted with no actual violence.[49] On a report of the matter to higher authority the battalion was kept under guard by a white regiment for a day and the unrest subsided.[50] Corporal Cooley was hospitalized; he had a head wound, but it was treated successfully and, on April 9, he was discharged from the hospital.[51] Lieutenant Potter had continued on his regular duty with Company D.

On March 31 Captain Simon's court-martial proceeded with its work. Two of the corporals had not yet been tried but the court turned to the twenty accused privates. Each of them pleaded guilty and all were disposed of by April 5, after character testimony and, in all but three cases, a statement by the accused. That statement generally indicated that his silence on the first call resulted from his not understanding its purpose and his following the leaders. The character witnesses were Captain Fry and Lieutenant Chace, usually both of them in a given case, and a second lieutenant in a couple of cases. In nearly all the cases the character testimony was favorable to the accused, in some very favorable, but in a few it was derogatory. In all but five of the twenty cases the sentence was for only three months at hard labor without pay. Of the five, two were for six months and three for four months at payless hard labor, to be served at Fort Jefferson. The place for service of the three months' sentences was not specified, as in the cases of the two corporals who previously had received three months' sentences.[52]

Court-martial judgments, of course, were subject to review by higher authority, and all these cases were being reviewed promptly at division headquarters. The judgment of the court-martial was approved in every case. As to the fifteen privates and the two corporals whose sentences were for three months it was determined that they would be served at Matagorda Island. Moreover, in the cases of eight of those privates and of those two corporals the hard-labor portion of the sentences was remitted, either in the court's own sentence or on its recommendation to the reviewing authority.[53] For those men, then, the actual punishment was only three months' pay loss, and, for the two corporals, demotion to private. Pay loss must have seemed rather academic, since no pay was yet being received by anyone and, as it turned out, none was in prospect for many months more.

Finally, on April 8, the court reached the two remaining corporals. One pleaded not guilty and was acquitted (the only acquittal) when it developed that, with permission, he had been absent at the roll call.[54] But for the other there was an outcome very different. His was the only case having more than a single charge; in his there were two. The first was the same as in all the others. But the second was a charge of attempting, on March 30, "to excite a mutiny." He pleaded guilty to both. Evidence on the first charge was much like that in the case of the two corporals who had received three month's sentences, followed by remittals; it is very likely that, had that been all of his case, disposition would have been the same as that of those two corporals. But guilt of the second charge caused a very different outcome. Although Captain Fry and Lieutenant Chace gave favorable character testimony, his own statement revealed that when on March 30 he saw that Corporal Cooley was bleeding from a head wound from Lieutenant Potter's shooting he had proclaimed that "if we are to be shot by our own officers I am willing to die now." Although Captain Fry then ordered him to his quarters and he had promptly obeyed, the court's judgment was guilt on both counts, with reduction to the ranks and payless hard labor at Fort Jefferson for ten years. The judgment was duly approved at division headquarters except that the ten years was reduced to the remainder of his enlistment term.[55]

On March 30, obviously prior to the troubles of that day, Major Comstock had left Matagorda to accompany a general on an extensive visit to the Union's Texas footholds; he did not return until April 12. Hence he was not present during the court-martialing from March 30 onward or the shooting of Corporal Cooley that afternoon. But his April 16 letter to an aide of Governor Smith telling of the March 17 incident told also of the following court-martialing and of the March 30 episode. His account was somewhat inaccurate. In any event as to the court-martialing for the March 17 incident he opined that the one-year sentences were "not sufficient punishment, as it was a case of mutiny." And respecting Lieutenant Potter's shooting a man on March 30, he said, "The men needed a lesson and received one," adding, "I should have sustained Mr. Potter, if I shot every man in the Regt; a fact which the men know perfectly well. It is only fear which will keep this class of men in their place and make good soldiers, and the moment they find an officer is afraid of them, they will over run him and put him down."[56]

In the meantime Captain Simon's court-martial had been continuing its sessions, and on April 15, the day before Major Comstock's letter, had reached two of Company A's privates charged with mutinous conduct for their outbursts following the shooting of Corporal Cooley. (Neither of these men had been among those tried for the March 17 incident.) On similar charges the court reached a corporal of Company

C on April 19 and the next day a sergeant and two privates of that company. All these men pleaded not guilty, except that the sergeant's plea was guilty to the specification with a not guilty plea to the charge. As in the trials for the March 17 incident, none of these men had counsel. All were found guilty. Evidence varied considerably as to the intensity of the men's outbursts, some including threats against Lieutenant Potter, nor did every man obey when ordered to go to his quarters. None of the men submitted evidence contradicting the prosecution's case. In sum, the men, except the sergeant, left little doubt that they would not put up with Potter's shooting of Cooley; even the sergeant asserted that in a white regiment an officer would not dare do such a thing. The outcome was payless hard labor at Fort Jefferson for the remainder of their enlistment terms, except that the Company C sergeant and one of its privates received only three months of such labor at Matagorda.[57]

On April 22 Corporal Cooley himself was brought to trial on two charges, contempt toward a superior officer and conduct prejudicial to discipline. He pleaded not guilty. He, too, was without counsel. The principal prosecution evidence was Lieutenant Potter's account that we summarized earlier. On behalf of Cooley the only evidence was the testimony of a second lieutenant of Company A, Cooley's company, who had just resigned for health reasons; he asserted that Cooley's character always had been very good. The court's judgment was guilty on both charges, sentencing him to reduction to the ranks and fifteen payless years at Fort Jefferson with ball and chain. That sentence was approved at district headquarters.[58] It is to be noted that the transcripts of these cases show that while there were some changes in the court's membership after the cases involving the March 17 incident, Captains Simon and Metcalf sat in all the cases. Thus Metcalf, a Company D captain, was a judge in cases stemming from the shooting of Cooley by Lieutenant Potter also of Company D; and in the Cooley case Metcalf was actually judging on the testimony of Potter himself.

A year later, on April 12, 1865, a letter was written to the secretary of war by one of the Company A privates who had been convicted on April 15, 1864, for his outburst at the shooting of Corporal Cooley. That letter asked for the writer's release from imprisonment. It told of the shooting incident, saying that Lieutenant Potter had had Cooley come to his tent for an interview, that after an exchange between them, with no threat by Cooley, Potter had grabbed Cooley by the throat, and Cooley pulled free. Thereupon Captain Fry, who happpened to be outside the tent and heard the fracas, called for Cooley to come out. As Cooley was leaving, Potter shot him in the back of his head. Presumably the letter writer had been given that version by Cooley while they were fellow prisoners at Fort Jefferson. That letter was referred, in due course, to Judge Advocate General Holt. Holt reviewed the transcript of the writer's court-martial, concluding that even if his version of the shooting of Cooley were accurate the writer himself was guilty of mutinous conduct in his protesting outburst after the shooting. On June 21, 1865, word went to the prisoner that his plea for release was denied.[59]

In the meantime the Civil War fighting had ended, and the War Department had begun steps toward a program to release military prisoners.[60] (By then, of course, those convicted only for the incident of March 17, 1864, had served out their time if they had survived illness.) It may be that the Company C private sent to Fort Jefferson for his involvement in the Cooley episode already had been released; back in January 1865 his release had been recommended because of his good conduct during his imprisonment. At length, on January 27, 1866, there was a War Department order for the freeing of the Company A corporal confined at Fort Jefferson for his part in both the March 17 and the March 30, 1864, incidents. Then, a few days later, on February 5, 1866, a War Department order was issued for the release of the Company A privates and the Company C corporal whose Fort Jefferson imprisonment had been imposed for their doings in the March 30 affair. Moreover, the same order released Corporal Cooley himself.[61] Thus all those involved in the March 30 Cooley incident were freed.

One cannot but wonder whether Corporal Cooley would have been released with the others—based as his conviction was on Lieutenant Potter's testimony at the Cooley court-martial that he, Cooley, had attempted to attack Potter, reaching for Potter's pistol—had the very different version of what had occurred not been sent to the secretary of war and on to Judge Advocate General Holt. Although no record has been found indicating any later inquiry into the Cooley case, it would not be surprising were Holt to have been at least disturbed by the statement that Cooley had been shot in the back of his head. Were that so—and surely a hospital record or a head scar would reveal it—Potter's version tendered to the court-martial would have lost credibility. It is true that Cooley had not testified at his court-martial, so his very different account of what had occurred had not then been voiced. But Holt may not have regarded that as making his account incredible. After all, the court-martial had been without counsel, and in an atmosphere that could have confused an unsophisticated accused and left him feeling helpless.

Moreover, any inquiry about Lieutenant Potter would have undermined confidence in him. In October 1864 he had been arrested on charges that since May he had been causing trouble, that he had called a couple of men "damned niggers," that he had been drunk in the presence of enlisted men, and on being ordered to his quarters had been so drunk it had been necessary to keep him under guard. Although shortly released from close arrest he was kept under arrest at the post until, at Major Comstock's request, the charges finally were withdrawn in early December. While, as the senior second lieutenant in the regiment, he was promoted to first lieutenant soon thereafter to fill a vacancy in the latter office, he shortly again was facing charges for being drunk on duty. Ultimately those charges were withdrawn because witnesses were only enlisted men, no officer being found who opined that he had been drunk, and drunkenness was the "hardest of all things to prove." Then by September 1865, as the regiment was awaiting its mustering out, Potter was in trouble again; he had been hospitalized but had left the hospital without permission and his arrest and jailing were ordered pending his muster out, though apparently the matter was dropped. In sum, it seems very likely that Potter was an alcoholic. It is even conceivable that he had been under the influence when he shot Cooley.[62]

Whatever the facts concerning the March 30, 1864, episode, the days thereafter of the battalion's do-nothing time on the Texas coast were soon to come to an end. On the next day after that episode, General Grant had sent to the Union's commander of the western region a direction "That you abandon Texas entirely with the exception of your hold upon the Rio Grande."[63] By the end of May the battalion had been moved to Louisiana. The regiment's Second Battalion had gone to war there many weeks before; more recently the Third Battalion also had arrived there. At long last the three battalions were brought under a single regimental command. Very soon, however, the First Battalion was separately stationed at a fortification on the Mississippi well below New Orleans; its main mission for the rest of the war was to monitor ship movements on the river, enforcing the Union's will with artillery. Never would it experience the thrill of actual combat. But it would find that miasmic disease was as deadly as Rebel bullets. The postwar report of Rhode Island's adjutant general stated that seventy men had died while stationed at the fortification on the Mississippi, noting that, while blacks were good soldiers, "their power of endurance" did not equal the whites'.[64]

There was, however, one event that must have given the men of Company A a special thrill, notably those enduring imprisonment at Fort Jefferson for the March 17, 1864, incident. While the men of the company probably had been but little, if at all, aware of it at the time of that incident, Congress, since early 1864, had been seriously considering the justice of the black pay discrimination. Finally, by summer, Congress ended the injustice. Although for blacks who had been slaves as of the war's beginning the discrimination's end was made retroactive only to January 1, 1864, there was a special provision for blacks who had been free at the war's outset. That was a provision that they were to be paid from the time of their enlistment what the law at that time called for, and that authorized the attorney general to determine what that law had provided. Very promptly the attorney general ruled that it had provided, for such free blacks, full pay, the same as for whites. Thus the War Department's decision, back in June 1863, imposing the $10 less $3 rate of pay on those blacks had been grossly erroneous.[65] At long last, in the fall of 1864, the battalion began receiving pay, and soon Major Comstock was certifying that every man of the battalion had been mustered as free as of April 19, 1861, and so was "entitled to full pay emoluments etc."[66] Those leaders of Company A who, on March 17, had been concerned about possible impairment of the right to full pay must have felt that they had been vindicated. Unhappily a principal one of them, Sergeant Humbert, could not have that feeling; he died from disease during his prison term at just about the time his former brethren were being paid for the first time and finally would receive full pay retroactively, just as Humbert thought they had been promised when Company A had been recruited.[67]

Although Company A's service on to the war's end had continued to fall short of any notable combat, the company was involved in an episode of some historic interest, the surrender of what seems to have been the last white Confederate force to lay down its arms. On June 2, 1865, Confederate Gen. Kirby Smith had signed the capitulation of his west of the Mississippi army, ending Confederate armies' surrenders. But there was a company of Confederate scouts, known as "Rough Riders," led by a Capt. Bailey Vinson, long operating very effectively in an area about midway along the Louisiana coast, that knew only by rumor of the surrenders of the Confederate leaders, and, to the concern of the Union commander of the pertinent district, had not laid down its arms. Lieutenant Chace at the time was on detached duty with that district commander and was assigned to take ship up one of the Louisiana rivers to the vicinity of where Captain Vinson was thought to be, to find him, and to demand his surrender. His ship was to be manned by Company A, led by Captain Fry. On June 3 they took off. In due course, after considerable probing ashore—Fry and the company were left aboard ship—Chace, accompanied only by his servant, located Vinson and persuaded him, with his officers, to board the ship to sail to the Union's district headquarters to confer about a possible surrender. That was done, and the conferring resulted in surrender. It would be nearly another three weeks before the last Confederate force, a battalion of Indians in the Indian Territory, would lay down its arms. The black Company A doubtless took pride in playing a part, however passive, in the last of the white Rebels' surrender.[68]

That episode ended anything of note in the company's service in what had been the theatre of war. In early October 1865 it finally boarded ship, with the rest of the regiment, for a return to Rhode Island. En route it landed in New York City, and there the regiment participated in a street parade to hearty applause by great crowds. Thence it voyaged on to Rhode Island, where it was greeted even more enthusiastically and with much ceremony by Governor Smith and "an immense concourse." In a few days the regiment finally was disbanded, and the men were on the way to their homes, "but a few of them" in Rhode Island.[69]

Years later, in 1898, an elaborate history of the regiment was published. It told nothing of the incidents of March 17 and March 30, 1864, save for a passing reference to the former; that was a mere quotation from a letter written by Captain Fry to a friend on September 21, 1864, when the First Battalion was at its miasmic post on the Mississippi River below New Orleans. He said that a paymaster was expected that day, at last to pay the battalion; he was glad that "the amount of pay is settled." He referred briefly to the refusal of his company to answer a roll call, thinking he "was trying to make them take seven dollars per month," that resulted in court-martials. But, he concluded, he knew of "no white regiment that would have remained in the service thirteen months as my company has, without any pay, that would have given us less trouble."[70]

Although, in more recent years, the pay problem has received considerable notice in histories of black troops, the Rhode Islanders' episodes of March 17 and 30, and what followed, have been nearly overlooked.[71] But they are of importance to history, not only in portraying the matter of pay but also in revealing the problem of establishing understanding rapport between white officers and black men whom many of those officers, at least initially, deemed an alien breed. Had there been such rapport it is most likely that Captain Fry would have had his exchange with Sergeant Humbert at once without reporting to Major Comstock, and that then all would have proceeded without incident. Indeed, Fry himself, in his testimony at the first of the court-martials for the March 17 episode, acknowledged that it was customary, on occasion, to make explanations to soldiers.[72] It may be, too, that then there would not have been the unrest that led to the Potter-Cooley encounter. The basic problem was not that of black pay but of white-black alienation. To two or three of the black sergeants it had seemed that a little thing might be a big thing. Thereupon Major Comstock and Captain Fry, nervously tense in dealing with what then was, to them, an alien breed, turned the seeming big thing into a major confrontation.

Notes

1. This was the initial designation of the regiment. After some changes, the designation finally became 11th United States Colored Heavy Artillery. Most of its records in the National Archives are filed under that final designation.

2. Ira Berlin et al., eds., *Freedom: A Documentary History of Emancipation, 1861–1867*, ser. 2, *The Black Military Experience* (Cambridge Univ. Press, New York, 1982), pp. 366, 396; Joseph T. Glatthaar, *Forged in Battle: The Civil War Alliance of Black Soldiers and White Officers* (Macmillan, Free Press, New York, 1990), pp. 115–16.

3. Opinion of Attorney General William Wirt, Mar. 27, 1823, *Ops. Atty. Gen.*, 1:602–3; Dudley Taylor Cornish, *The Sable Arm: Negro Troops in the Union Army, 1861–1865* (1956; rpt. W. W. Norton & Co., New York, 1966), pp. 2–3; Benjamin Quarles, *Lincoln and the Negro* (Oxford Univ. Press, New York, 1962), pp. 67–68, 71–72; Benjamin P. Thomas and Harold M. Hyman, *Stanton: The Life and Times of Lincoln's Secretary of War* (Alfred A. Knopf, New York, 1962), pp.

132–34; Erwin S. Bradley, *Simon Cameron, Lincoln's Secretary of War* (Univ. of Pennsylvania Press, Philadelphia, 1966), pp. 202–4, 208–10; Roy P. Basler, Marion Dolores Pratt, and Lloyd A. Dunlap, eds., *Collected Works of Abraham Lincoln*, 8 vols. (Rutgers Univ. Press, New Brunswick, 1953–55), 5:356–57.

4. *Providence Daily Journal*, Aug. 27, 1862, p. 2 (hereafter cited as *Daily Journal*).

5. *Daily Journal*, Aug. 5, 1862, p. 2; see also Aug. 6, p. 2.

6. *Daily Journal*, Aug. 7, 1862, p. 2; Aug. 8, p. 2; Aug. 9, p. 2; Aug. 11, p. 1; Aug. 15, pp. 2, 3; Aug. 16, p. 2; Sept. 11, p. 2; Feb. 3, 1863, p. 1.

7. Basler, *Collected Works*, 5:431.

8. James D. Richardson, comp. *A Compilation of the Messages and Papers of the Presidents, 1789–1897*, 10 vols. (Published by the Authority of Congress, Washington, 1896–99), 6:96–98, 157–59.

9. *Daily Journal*, Jan. 2, 1863, p. 2; U.S. War Dept., *The War of the Rebellion: A Compilation of the Official Records of the Union and Confederate Armies*, 70 vols. in 128 pts. (1880–1901; rpt. National Historical Society, Gettysburg, 1972), ser. 3, 3:16, 38–39.

10. *Daily Journal*, Mar. 2, 1863, p. 2; Mar. 4, p. 2; Mar. 5, p. 2; Mar. 11, p. 2; Apr. 2, p. 2; May 27, p. 2.

11. Cornish, *Sable Arm*, pp. 105–10; *Daily Journal*, Feb. 24, 1863, p. 2; Feb. 25, p. 2; Feb. 26, p. 2; Mar. 4, p. 2; Mar. 6, p. 2; Mar. 11, p. 3; Mar. 27, p. 2.

12. *Daily Journal*, Apr. 14, 1863, p. 2.

13. *Daily Journal*, June 17, 1863, p. 2; *Annual Report of the Adjutant General of the State of Rhode Island for the Year 1865* (Providence, 1866), 2:587.

14. 12 *U.S. Stat.* 731.

15. *Daily Journal*, July 8, 1863, p. 2; July 9, p. 2.

16. General Order No. 24, Rhode Island Adj. Gen., *Daily Journal*, July 30, 1863, p. 2; repeated at p. 3 of each subsequent issue through Aug. 5.

17. William H. Chenery, *The Fourteenth Regiment, Rhode Island Heavy Artillery (Colored)* (1898; rpt. Negro Univ. Press, New York, 1969), pp. 284–85; *Daily Journal*, July 31, 1863, p. 2.

18. *Daily Journal*, Mar. 7, 1865, p. 1; the bounty was specified in the official notice of the enlistment for the company, *Daily Journal*, July 31, 1863, p. 2; repeated at p. 3 of each subsequent issue through Aug. 6.

19. *Daily Journal*, Aug. 14, 1863, p. 2; Aug. 15, pp. 1, 2; Aug. 17, p. 2; Aug. 20, p. 2; Aug. 21, p. 2; Aug. 22, p. 2; Aug. 24, p. 2; Aug. 25, p. 2; Aug. 28, p. 2; Aug. 29, p. 2; Aug. 31, p. 2; Sept. 2, p. 2; Sept. 3, p. 2; Sept. 8, p. 2; C. W. Foster, Asst. Adj. Gen., War Dept., to Governor Smith of Rhode Island, Aug. 14, 1863, Box No. 5, Office of Adj. Gen., U.S. Colored Troops (hereafter USCT), Regimental Papers, 11th U.S. Colored Heavy Artillery, RG 94, Nat. Arch.; Chenery, *The Fourteenth Regiment*, p. 9.

20. *Daily Journal*, Aug. 15, 1863, p. 1; Aug. 28, p. 2; Aug. 29, p. 2; Sept. 8, p. 2; Sept. 29, p. 2; Office of Adj. Gen., Volunteer Organ. Civil War, USCT, 11th Heavy Artillery, Field & Staff, muster-in roll of Company A, Box 5295, RG 94, Nat. Arch.

21. Chenery, *The Fourteenth Regiment*, pp. 273–74.

22. *Daily Journal*, Oct. 24, 1863, p. 2; Dec. 24, p. 2.

23. *Daily Journal*, Oct. 21, 1863, p. 2; Jan. 9, 1864, p. 2.

24. *Daily Journal*, Mar. 19, 1864, p. 1; Mar. 22, pp. 1, 2; Mar. 24, p. 2; Mar. 26, p. 2; Mar. 29, pp. 1, 2; Mar. 30, p. 2; Mar. 31, p. 2; June 6, p. 1; Aug. 12, p. 2; Major Comstock to Col. Charles E. Bailey (Rhode Island governor's staff), Apr. 16, 1864, Berlin, *The Black Military Experience*, p. 397 (from USCT, Regimental Letters Sent, Endorsement, Misc. Book, 11th Heavy Artillery, unpaginated, RG 94, Nat. Arch.); *Daily Journal*, Jan. 11, 1865, p. 1; Jan. 12, p. 2; Jan. 13, p. 2; Jan. 14, p. 1; Jan. 18, pp. 1, 2; Jan. 21, p. 1; Mar. 7, p. 1; Mar. 11, p. 1.

25. *Daily Journal*, Mar. 7, 1865, p. 1; Aug. 15, 1863, p. 1; Sept. 1, p. 2. There is some uncertainty as to the precise number in Company A from other states; one record shows 20 from New York and 2 from Massachusetts, USCT, 11th Heavy Artillery, muster-in roll of Company A, Box 5295, RG 94, Office of Adj. Gen., Volunteer Organ. Civil War, Nat. Arch. *Annual Report of the Adjutant General of the State of Rhode Island for the Year 1865*, 2:595–705, gives purported residences of the regiment's men up to the time of discharge; it shows, for Company A, Rhode Island residence for 113 men and 40 with residence unspecified. Of course, by the time of discharge there had been replacements for vacancies occurring during the war, notably by deaths, and replacements likely had come from non–Rhode Island residents.

26. *Daily Journal*, Aug. 29, 1863, p. 2; Sept. 3, p. 2; Sept. 29, p. 2; Chenery, *The Fourteenth Regiment*, pp. 11–12. From time to time to the end of the year the *Journal* notes departures of other companies for Dutch Island.

27. *Daily Journal*, Nov. 20, 1863, p. 2; Dec. 7, p. 2; Dec. 10, p. 2; Dec. 21, p. 2.

28. *Daily Journal*, Jan. 11, 1864, p. 1; Jan. 16, p. 2; Chenery, *The Fourteenth Regiment*, p. 20.

29. *Daily Journal*, Jan. 13, 1864, p. 1; Mar. 29, p. 2; Chenery, *The Fourteenth Regiment*, pp. 21–22; General Order No. 1, Jan. 11, 1864, Hdqrs. 1st Batt., 14th Reg. R.I.H.A., by order of Comstock, USCT, Order Book Cos. A to G, 11th Heavy Artillery (not paginated, portion on Company A), RG 94, Nat. Arch.

30. Chenery, *The Fourteenth Regiment*, pp. 22–25.

31. Case of Sergeant Melville Graham, pp. 3, 5, LL 1815, Box 636, Office of the Judge Adv. Gen., General Courts Martial 1812–1938, RG 153, Nat. Arch.

32. Our account is a summary of testimony of Captain Fry and Lieutenant Chace in the Cases of Sergeants George E. Wilson, Melville Graham, William L. Humbert, and John A. Jenkins, in LL 1815 of the Courts Martial file cited in n. 31, above, and in the Case of Corporal Howard Edwards in NN 1526, Box 1012, of that file. There are minor differences in the testimony from one case to another, so in no single case does the testimony fit our account precisely. As to Humbert's prominence, see *Daily Journal*, Aug. 29, 1863, p. 2; Chenery, *The Fourteenth Regiment*, pp. 10, 157.

33. This is our inference, based on the testimony in the cases following those cited in n. 32, above; we refer to them later.

34. Berlin, *The Black Military Experience*, p. 396; Col. Charles E. Bailey to Major Comstock, May 2, 1864, p. 15 of section on Letters Received, USCT, Regimental Letters Received and Guard Report Book, 11th Heavy Artillery, RG 94, Nat. Arch.; *Daily Journal*, July 31, 1863, p. 2; Aug. 1–6, p. 3 of each.

35. The course of the government's handling of the matter of pay to black soldiers is reviewed in Howard C. Westwood, "Lincoln's Position on Black Enlistments,"

Lincoln Herald 86, no. 2 (Summer 1984):107–9 (reprinted herein as chapter 1); and "The Cause and Consequence of a Union Black Soldier's Mutiny and Execution," *Civil War History* 31, no. 3 (Sept. 1985):222 (reprinted herein as chapter 8). And see Cornish, *Sable Arm*, pp. 183–96.

36. Case of Melville Graham, p. 8 (appended statement); Case of John A. Jenkins, p. 3; Chenery, *The Fourteenth Regiment*, p. 66.

37. *Daily Journal*, Aug. 22, 1863, p. 2.

38. *Daily Journal*, Nov. 20, 1863 p. 2.

39. Case of John A. Jenkins, p. 3.

40. Berlin, *The Black Military Experience*, p. 396.

41. The court was constituted by a March 20 order of district headquarters, set forth at the beginning of the transcript of each case. The charge and specification appear in each transcript; those in each case were identical, save that in one case, which we will come to, there were a second charge and specification. Chenery, *The Fourteenth Regiment*, pp. 287, 288, identifies the company commands of Simon and of Metcalf.

42. Case of George E. Wilson, p. 2.

43. These five cases are those of the four sergeants and one corporal that we have previously cited. Citation to those cases, and to the others that we are about to refer to, is to the documents that are transcripts of the proceedings, including the testimony and judgment.

44. Case of Corporal John A. Cravat in NN 1526, Box 1012, of the Courts Martial file.

45. Cases of Corporals Valentine Paine and Benjamin C. Gardner, also in NN 1526.

46. Berlin, *The Black Military Experience*, p. 366.

47. Regimental Hospital record for Charles Cooley, Company A, 14 Reg't R.I. Col'd H.A., USCT, 11 H. Art'y, Entry 534, Carded Medical Records, Volunteers, Mexican and Civil War, Office of the Adj. Gen., RG 94, Nat. Arch..

48. Case of Corporal Charles Cooley, pp. 7–9, in NN 1688, Box 1023, of the Courts Martial file.

49. These happenings are recounted in the court-martialing of men involved in the outbursts that we come to below.

50. Berlin, *The Black Military Experience*, p. 396.

51. Regimental Hospital record for Charles Cooley.

52. The court-martial records do not appear in chronological order. The Courts Martial file NN 1526, Box 1012, has Charles H. Gardner, James Lecompt, Simon Niles, and William H. Hector; NN 1500, Box 1011, has Charles Johnson, Randall King, Silas Lyons, Solomon Miltier, George Lippitt, Jacob Myers, George H. Johnson, and George C. Hull; LL 1830, Box 637, has Benjamin G. Gardner, Robert Houck, Joseph S. Hicks, William H. Jackson, James Madison, William Myers, Jeremiah Noca, and Martin Van Howland. (Names sometimes are variously spelled.) Houck and Hicks received the six months sentences; Miltier, Jacob Myers and William Myers the four months sentences.

53. The eight privates were Charles H. Gardner, Lecompt, Hector, Benjamin G. Gardner, Jackson, Madison, Noca, and Van Howland.

54. Case of Corporal Isaac Smith, LL 1830, Box 637. Only a couple of months later Smith was court-martialed for drunkenness and striking an officer; he pleaded

guilty, was reduced to the ranks, and imprisoned for thirty days without pay. Box 40618, Adj. Gen. Office, Civil War Compiled Service Records, 11th U.S. Col'd Heav. Art., RG 94, Nat. Arch.

55. Case of Corporal John B. Lane, also in LL 1830.

56. Berlin, *The Black Military Experience*, p. 396. Some weeks later, Major Comstock, in an affidavit that apparently was intended to explain the troubles that eventuated in the shooting of Cooley, asserted that they were caused by a delay in the payment by a Rhode Island agent of the last 10 percent of the state bounty. Comstock stated that, on leaving Rhode Island in December 1863, the men were promised that the payment would be made at their destination, but that the payment was not made during the time in Texas but only after the battalion had been moved to Louisiana—a move that, as we will note, did not occur until late May 1864—and that payment was not completed until June 16. The Rhode Island agent in Louisiana had the money available, but it was earning interest; the interest would not be paid to the men but would be retained by the agent. Hence, Comstock concluded, it was to the state agent that "I lay all blame for the disturbance which occurred some time since in the 1st Battalion, and which sent some of the men to Tortugas." *Daily Journal*, July 19, 1864, p. 2; see also related items, June 22, p. 1; June 25, p. 2; July 26, p. 2; July 27, p. 2. (Incidentally, the *Journal* had been mistaken in reporting that the state bounty had been fully paid at the time of the battalion's sailing from Rhode Island. *Daily Journal*, Dec. 21, 1863, p. 2.) We would observe that "all blame" doubtless was an overstatement; Comstock probably was inclined to grope for a cause of the March 30 troubles beyond the severe treatment he had imposed for the March 17 incident.

57. The Company A men: Case of Samuel A. D. Douglass and Case of William H. Smith, both in LL 1891, Box 646, of the Courts Martial file; the sentence for Douglass was ten years and for Smith five years of hard labor without pay at Fort Jefferson, but district headquarters reduced both terms to the remainder of their enlistment times. The Company C men: All are in NN 1688, Box 1023, of the Courts Martial File. In Case of Corporal John Wheeler and Case of George Kelley the sentences were ten years of payless hard labor at Fort Jefferson, but reduced by district headquarters to the remainder of their enlistment terms. In Case of Sergeant William D. Harris and Case of Daniel Townsend the sentences were two years of payless hard labor at Fort Jefferson, but on recommendation of a majority of the court, district headquarters shortened the terms to three months of payless hard labor at Matagorda. Presumably Corporal Wheeler and Sergeant Harris were reduced to the ranks. (It is possible that there were additional cases that we have not found.)

58. Case of Corporal Charles Cooley, also in NN 1688.

59. Case of William H. Smith, in LL 1891, documents attached to the transcript.

60. Illustrative are General Orders No. 98, May 27, 1865, and No. 104, June 2, 1865, of the Adj. Gen. Office.

61. List of prisoners in confinement at Ft. Jefferson, Florida, whose good conduct while in confinement renders them fit subjects for executive clemency, Jan. 30, 1865, Entry 463, Lists of Prisoners Remaining at Various Prisons, 1865–1893, RG 94, Nat. Arch.; on the list is George Kelly, Company C, 14th Rhode Island Heavy Artillery. Special Order No. 36, War Department, Adj. Gen. Office, Jan. 27, 1866; sec. 21 lists men confined at Ft. Jefferson, Florida, whose release

is ordered, the list including John B. Lane, Company A, 14th Rhode Island Heavy Artillery. Special Order No. 49, War Department, Adj. Gen. Office, Feb. 5, 1866; sec. 12 lists men confined at Dry Tortugas, Florida, being released, the list including Cpl. Charles Cooley, Samuel A. D. Douglas, and William H. Smith, all of Company A, and Cpl. John Wheeler, of Company C, 14th Rhode Island Heavy Artillery.

62. Charles H. Potter, 11th U.S. Colored Heavy Artillery, Compiled Military Service Record, Office of the Adj. Gen., RG 94, Nat. Arch.; Charles H. Potter, P 163, Box 28, Colored Troops Division 1863, Office of the Adj. Gen., RG 94, Nat. Arch.

63. General Grant to Maj. Gen. Nathaniel P. Banks, Mar. 31, 1864, in John Y. Simon, ed., *The Papers of Ulysses S. Grant* (Southern Illinois Univ. Press, Carbondale, 1967–), 10:242–43.

64. *Annual Report of the Adjutant General of the State of Rhode Island for the Year 1865*, 2:588–91; Chenery, *The Fourteenth Regiment*, pp. 63, 66; Cornish, *Sable Arm*, pp. 286–87. Documents at the National Archives are replete with records of hospitalization and deaths from disease, including some for the men who were court-martialed.

65. Westwood, "The Cause and Consequence of a Union Black Soldier's Mutiny and Execution," *Civil War History* 31:234.

66. Muster Roll of Company A for Aug. 31 to Oct. 31, 1864, Box 5295, 11th Heavy Artillery, USCT, Volunteer Organ. Civil War, Office of Adj. Gen., RG 94, Nat. Arch.; Chenery, *The Fourteenth Regiment*, p. 66; Maj. J. J. Comstock to Lt. J. C. Whiting, Adj., 11th U.S.C.A. (Hy), Oct. 21, 1864, Box 5, Regimental Papers, 11th U.S. Colored Heavy Artillery, USCT, Office of the Adj. Gen., RG 94, Nat. Arch.

67. Adj. Gen. Office, Civil War (Union) Compiled Service Records, 11th U.S. Colored Heavy Artillery, Box 40608, William L. Humbert, RG 94, Nat. Arch.

68. Chenery, *The Fourteenth Regiment*, pp. 135–39; Shelby Foote, *The Civil War: Red River to Appomattox* (Random House, New York, 1974), p. 1022.

69. Chenery, *The Fourteenth Regiment*, pp. 147–48; letter of Oct. 3, 1865, from Providence Mayor Thomas A. Doyle to Governor Smith, Box No. 5, and Capt. J. A. York report to Lt. Col. C. C. Gilbert, Chief Mustering Officer, Providence, Oct. 20, 1865, Box No. 6, Office of Adj. Gen., USCT, Regimental Papers, 11th U.S. Colored Heavy Artillery, RG 94, Nat. Arch.

70. Chenery, *The Fourteenth Regiment*, p. 66.

71. The only more recent references to the Rhode Islanders' episodes are those cited in n. 2, above. Incidentally, the reference in Berlin, *The Black Military Experience*, asserts that in March 1864 the men of Company A had "refused to accept their pay." So, too, it had been stated in *Annual Report of the Adjutant General of the State of Rhode Island for the Year 1865*, 2:589; that report even says that there had been such a refusal also by Companies C and D. But, as we have seen, at that time no pay yet had been tendered to the battalion. That report also says that the companies "were under arrest" for such refusal. But the so-called "arrest"—it included Company B—consisted in having the battalion under guard of a white regiment for a day to quell the unrest caused by the shooting of Corporal Cooley, not for refusing pay. See n. 50, above.

72. Case of George E. Wilson, p. 5, in LL 1815.

10

The Reverend Fountain Brown: Alleged Violator of the Emancipation Proclamation

THE FIRST conviction for violating the Emancipation Proclamation to come to the president for his review was that of Fountain Brown, an esteemed preacher and elder of the Methodist Episcopal church in Arkansas. Browns' alleged crime was his sale back into slavery of some blacks he had owned until they had been freed by the proclamation. Few, if any, criminal cases occurring during the Civil War were so persistently pressed for presidential pardon. The pressing was in vain. In after years the case has been all but forgotten. It merits recalling as an illustration of the problem faced by the people of a seceded state as the war was suddenly moving them back into the Union.

Brown, once a resident of Tennessee, was one of a small number of Methodist preachers who had come to Arkansas a few years before its 1836 statehood to spread the gospel. His home had become the village of Flat Bayou, about a dozen miles northeast of Pine Bluff. In that region he was in the traveling ministry and "was one of the most popular and successful preachers. . . . He was a charming singer, and powerful in exhortation, and his gifts and graces qualified him admirably for great usefulness." Also, as shown in the 1860 census, he owned a substantial amount of farmland, which was worked with six-

Originally published in *The Arkansas Historical Quarterly* 49, no. 2 (Summer 1990):107–23. Reprinted by permission of *The Arkansas Historical Quarterly*.

teen slaves, of whom nine were aged sixteen to forty, the others
younger; he had nine slave houses. There were some forty slaveowners
in his township (the Plum Bayou township) at that time, about half of
whom owned more slaves, half fewer, so he was median among them.
In 1860 he was a widower; later he was remarried. The 1860 census
listed seven children, aged two to sixteen, but there also were two
older ones, then or soon married.[1]

With the secession of Arkansas, and the coming of war, Brown's
activities were not changed. In 1863 he was aged fifty-seven; he had
simply continued his preaching and farming, taking no active part in
the rebellion. Until September of that year Union arms had not reached
his area, so he had carried on under Confederate government, maintaining his slave ownership. By that time the number of his slaves may
have somewhat increased for one slave mother, Lucy, had four children
of six years and younger, two of whom had been born since the 1860
census, and another mother, Delia, had two children, each born since
that census, one indeed newborn. Both women had slave husbands;
Lucy's was owned by a neighbor of Brown's, Delia's by Brown himself.[2]

In September 1863 an important change suddenly came in the
governing of the area where Brown resided. A Union army, commanded by Gen. Frederick Steele, captured Little Rock, about fifty
miles up the Arkansas River from Pine Bluff, and Steele promptly sent
a force on south to occupy Pine Bluff. There, the very able Col. Powell
Clayton took command. While, in late October, Confederates attacked
Pine Bluff, they were quickly repulsed. Union arms controlled the
Little Rock–Pine Bluff area. Although troops were not posted at Flat
Bayou, it was evident that the village had become Union governed.[3]

So it was that Parson Brown deemed that his slaves had been freed.
President Abraham Lincoln's Final Emancipation Proclamation had
been issued months before, on January 1, 1863. It specified the area
where all slaves were freed as provided in the Preliminary Emancipation Proclamation of September 1862. The area included Arkansas.
While some would argue that the Union's law applied according to its
terms, even if Confederate governing prevented its enforcement, that
view was questionable. But certainly it applied wherever Union governing was reestablished. Hence, with Rebel power no longer prevailing in his part of Arkansas, the parson told his blacks that they had
ceased being his property and could go as they willed. How many of
them left is uncertain. In any case it is clear that Delia's husband left,

going to Pine Bluff, but Lucy and Delia, with their children, remained. Also Lucy's husband remained with the parson's neighbor.[4]

Soon after the Union army had secured its control of the Little Rock–Pine Bluff region Arkansans there began what would become a strong movement to establish a civil government loyal to the Union. The movement was enhanced by the return to Union loyalty of an Arkansan of prominence, Edward W. Gantt, who had been a Confederate officer; after a special pardon by President Lincoln, he would become a Union army officer. And most certainly enhancing was the president's amnesty proclamation of December 8, 1863. With limited exceptions it pardoned any participant in rebellion who took an oath of loyalty to the Union. Further, it provided that, whenever in any of the Confederate States (except Virginia) the oath was taken by persons qualified to vote by the law of such state as it had existed prior to secession and numbering at least 10 percent of the number in that state who had voted in the 1860 presidential election, they could establish a state government that would be recognized as "the true government of the State." Arkansas was a state that the president especially had in mind. In his annual message to Congress, also on December 8, he had named Arkansas, along with Tennessee, as "substantially cleared of insurgent control," with "influential citizens" declaring "openly for emancipation" in the state. By that time pro-Unionists in Arkansas were well on the way to having a constitutional convention to begin a new state government loyal to the Stars and Stripes and with slavery no more. The convention would convene in January 1864.[5]

With these happenings in his region. Parson Brown was troubled by something he had done in November. On December 24 he went down to Pine Bluff and called on the Union army's post adjutant. He asked the adjutant whether any charges had been filed against him. The adjutant knew of none. Thereupon the parson told the adjutant what troubled him.[6]

According to the testimony of the adjutant at a trial of Brown, which we are about to recount, Brown told him that in late November he had sold Negroes to a white man named McAfee who had come to Brown asking to be allowed to "let him run my negroes off." Brown at first refused because "it was contrary to the rules of the Military Authorities" and "he did not want to do anything contrary to the rules." But again McAfee came, this time wanting to buy the Negroes. "I would not sell them," said Brown, "as it was contrary to the rules." Yet again McAfee came, this time offering to pay $7,000 for the Negroes. At that Brown told him to take them; McAfee did so, and took off, Brown supposed to Texas, having paid Brown $4,000 with a promise later to pay the additional $3,000. Brown told the adjutant at the time "he did not know he was doing wrong," but that he now "knew it was wrong."

Soon, perhaps at once, Brown was arrested by the military for trial by a military commission. The commission, established by an order previously issued, was headed by a lieutenant colonel and began a sitting in Pine Bluff on January 6, 1864. Two days later Brown's case came to trial on two charges. One was kidnapping free citizens "inside lines occupied by the Army of the United States" and sending them, without their consent, "outside the territory occupied by the Army." The "free citizens" were named: they were Lucy and her four children and Delia and her two children. The second charge was selling blacks who had been freed by the Final Emancipation Proclamation, a sale to McAfee for $7,000 with intent to reduce them to slavery, though at the time they resided within the lines of the army. The blacks were named; they were Lucy, Delia, and their children. Brown, represented by counsel, pleaded not guilty. His counsel, William P. Grace, was a well-regarded Pine Bluff lawyer.[7]

The trial took three days. The first prosecution witness was the post adjutant, whose testimony consisted simply of an account of what Brown had told him, as we have stated. Next the prosecution called a sergeant clerk of the adjutant, who had heard Brown's recital; his testimony generally repeated the adjutant's account, adding that Brown had said that the black woman (obviously referring to Lucy) had "had some children" by McAfee, and that McAfee at first had told Brown that he wanted to take her and her children away with him. Then the prosecution called a son of Brown's. He testified that McAfee had taken away Lucy, Delia, and their children; he did not know where they had gone. He also said that McAfee had a white wife, who remained at her home in Flat Bayou. (Incidentally, the 1860 census showed that McAfee and his wife had three young children.)[8]

The next witness was a white neighbor of Brown's. He testified that Brown had told him that, after the Union occupation of Pine Bluff, he had sold Negroes to McAfee, among them Lucy and her children. His impression was that the blacks had been "carried South somewhere," but he did not know that. It was his impression also that Brown had said that he had made the sale because the blacks wanted to go with

McAfee. Then Lucy's black husband testified. Brown's counsel objected to his testifying on the ground that it was not legal to receive testimony by a black against a white; the objection was overruled. He testified that he and Lucy had been married for nine years. Her two eldest children were his, one of them of about six years in age, one of four or five. She had two other children, mulattoes. He and McAfee had had an agreement to live together during the past year. He said that he had last seen Lucy and the children about six weeks before. He had left them on a Monday morning, but on his return on Tuesday evening they were gone, he did not know where, and despite his inquiries he had not found them. He also testified that he and Lucy had had a talk about her going away with McAfee; "she said she was not willing to go." He told her to stay if she could, and he never consented to the children's going with McAfee.

Next came testimony by Delia's husband, again over defense objection to a black witness. He was living in Pine Bluff, where he had gone after its Union occupation when Brown had told him he was free and could leave. Delia's children were his, the younger born after he left. When he had departed he had wanted to take Delia along but she could not go because she was sick. (She may have been on the verge of giving birth.) Although, after he left, Delia had repeatedly sent for him, he had been unable to go back for her because he had been taken sick.

Delia's husband's testimony closed the prosecution's case. In its course there had been but most minimal cross examination by defense counsel, none of it of real significance. The defense case then consisted of brief testimony by only one witness, the Brown son whom the prosecution had examined. He testified that Lucy had told him that she wanted to go with McAfee and that Delia had said that she wanted to go with Lucy wherever she went. On the prosecution's cross, the witness testified that Lucy had said that McAfee wanted to take her to Texas and that Delia had said that "she wanted to go with Lucy." The prosecution thereafter recalled Lucy's husband, whereupon he testified that Delia had told him that she did not want to go, asking that he take her away, but he told her he could not do so.

Thereafter the commission deliberated. Soon its judgment was announced: guilty on each of the two charges, and a sentence to military prison for five years.

In due course the trial transcript and the commission's judgment were submitted to the army's department headquarters at Little Rock. On March 23, General Steele, the department commander, approved the judgment and forwarded the transcript and judgment "for the action of the President of the United States."[9]

In the meantime, in February, Brown had taken the oath of loyalty to the Union and opposition to the Confederacy, prescribed pursuant to President Lincoln's amnesty proclamation of December 8. Such oaths began to be gathered in Arkansas by Union officers at least by January, and in February the gathering was going on in the Pine Bluff area; the oath, among other things, swore support for presidential proclamations "having reference to slaves." Well over two hundred such oaths were procured in the Pine Bluff area during February. There was some controversy at this time as to whether oath taking would provide amnesty for one already under arrest or convicted for rebellion. In any event, there seems no indication that it ever was contended that Brown's oath taking called for amnesty for him; his "crime" had been not simply disloyalty but a violation of the Final Emancipation Proclamation by sending freed blacks back into slavery, an offense beyond the literal terms of the amnesty proclamation.[10]

Almost at once upon Brown's conviction by the military commission sympathy for him among Arkansans began to be manifested. It seems that he had been jailed immediately upon his arrest. By early March there were thirty-two signatures on a petition for his release on bail, and on March 11 Colonel Clayton sent it on to General Steele, recommending that it be granted. On April 6 Steele approved Brown's release, pending action by the president in his case, upon his posting bond for good behavior and on condition that he was not to go beyond the lines of the army.[11]

Release on bail, however, did not satisfy Brown's supporters. Soon after General Steele's approval of the conviction, to be forwarded "for the action of the President," thirty-five signatures had been secured on a petition to the president for a pardon of Brown. On May 20 that petition was sent to the president by a new congressman-elect from the Pine Bluff district. More than that, it had been endorsed by none other than Colonel Clayton, who wrote that Brown's offense had occurred in circumstances "of an extenuating nature" and that the confinement he already had undergone "sufficiently punished" him. The congressman-elect wrote that, while he did not approve of what Brown had done, Brown had intended no wrong, that his action had occurred just after the Union occupation while all was in confusion. On May 23, the president transmitted the file to Judge Advocate General Joseph Holt, to "examine and report on this case."[12]

On the very next day, May 24, Holt reported. It is to be kept in mind that the only facts concerning the offenses that were in the file were those appearing in the trial tanscript. Holt's report was at great length, reflecting his outrage that a minister of the gospel, knowing that his slaves had been freed, should have sent them back into slavery when induced by payment of money. Holt's review accepted Lucy's husband's account that Lucy had not wanted to go with McAfee, despite Brown's son's testimony that she had told him that she wanted to go. In any case, as Holt wrote with some heat, the little children of Lucy and Delia could not be deemed to have consented to becoming enslaved. Holt recommended that Brown's sentence be confirmed.[13]

On June 2, John Hay, of the president's staff, wrote Holt that the president wanted the record of the case. No indication of the extent of the president's study of the case has been found, but it may be observed that much was demanding the president's attention at this time. In any event, on August 12 the adjutant general was notified that, on the president's order, Brown was to be confined in the military prison at Alton, Illinois; so the president had agreed with Judge Advocate General Holt's conclusion.[14]

Under date of October 11 Brown wrote the president, from the military prison in Little Rock, asserting that his sale of the Negroes had been at the request of the Negro woman (i.e., Lucy), that he then had not considered himself "within the lines of Federal jurisdiction," had been ignorant of the applicable law, and had not known that he was doing wrong. He said that he was in feeble health and that serving his sentence would cause his death; he pleaded for clemency and pardon. There also was a petition to the president, undated but obviously in October, joining in Brown's request for pardon. It stated that medical officers opined that, because of Brown's ill health, sending him to the Alton prison would result in his death. Further, it urged that his act, though criminal, had been done "unwittingly" of wrong, that he was one of the few who had taken the loyalty oath with the intention of full compliance "in letter and spirit," and that the imprisonment to this point had served the ends of justice. Supporting that petition were virtually all of the newly installed leading state officials, including the chief justice and the lieutenant governor (but not the governor), joined by the presiding elder of the Methodist church. And General Steele himself transmitted the petition with a note that, from what he had heard of Brown, he recommended "a remission of his sentence." On October 25 John Hay noted that the president had referred the petition to the secretary of war.[15]

In due course the secretary of war referred the matter to Judge Advocate General Holt, obviously including Brown's letter of October 11. On November 22 Holt wrote the secretary of war that his previous report of May 24 covered the case. But he added two points. Brown's petition, asserting ignorance that at the time he was doing wrong in selling the blacks, was a pretense; it had been proved at his trial that he previously had told his slaves that they were freed by the president's proclamation. "The prisoner's desire to escape from a just punishment now triumphs over his veracity as his cupidity then got the better of his prudence." Second, Holt said that, although in August Brown had been ordered incarcerated at Alton, he was "still at Little Rock." Holt "deplored" that "so conspicuous a criminal" should have been given thus "a lenity which is without sanction." On December 3 the secretary of war referred the matter to Chief of Staff Gen. Henry W. Halleck; on December 6 Halleck noted his agreement with Holt, saying that the order for imprisonment at Alton should be carried out immediately, with an inquiry as to why it had not been done previously. The result was that by mid-January 1865 Brown was en route to the Alton military prison. It seems that, after Brown had been released on bail in the spring, he had remained free of jail until receipt of the president's August determination that he be imprisoned at Alton, but that he then had been jailed at Little Rock on the supposition by General Steele that the pleas for clemency that were to come in October would be granted.[16]

That in January Brown was off to Alton was far from ending effort in his behalf. Even as he was departing the lieutenant colonel who had been head of the military commission that had convicted him was sending to the president his petition for Brown's pardon. That officer asserted that the commission members had understood that Brown had not intentionally done wrong and ought not to be punished, but that they had convicted and sentenced him simply to vindicate the Emancipation Proclamation and to prevent similar wrongs by the people of Arkansas. Further, the officer pointed out that although Brown had been released from jail and allowed to visit his home, and so might have escaped, he had behaved as a loyal and law-abiding citizen, so his pardon was urged. That petition was transmitted to the president with a notation by the provost marshal in Arkansas that Brown had been sent to Alton, but that he was "quite infirm" and many loyal citizens had appealed in his behalf.[17]

On February 19 President Lincoln transmitted the petition to Judge Advocate General Holt, asking whether this was "the case of the Methodist preacher who sold his slaves South to evade the emancipation proclamation." Holt responded on February 21 that it was that case and that it had been carefully considered and decided by the president; Holt commented, "In view of the atrocious character of this man's crime & of his conspicuous social position, I should regard his pardon as affording a deplorable example." That ended the matter as far as President Lincoln was concerned.[18]

But that did not end our story. In less than two months there was a new president, Andrew Johnson. Although, despite the collapse of the rebellion, President Johnson at first seemed more severe than Abraham Lincoln in his attitude toward those who had defied the Union's governing there soon was indication that he might prove conciliatory. Moreover there also was indication that the grip of the military was being loosened. One manifestation of loosening was the closing of the Alton military prison at the end of June. Some of its prisoners, including Brown, were transferred to the Missouri state prison at Jefferson City.[19]

At some time during the summer of 1865 the son-in-law of Brown, J. P. McGaughey, began another effort at pardon. Four petitions to President Johnson for Brown's pardon were gathered, dated at Little Rock from July 31 to August 18. One had 744 signatures, the others 39, 22, and 12, among them important state officials. All vouched for Brown's good character. Also prepared were nine sworn affidavits, dated in early August, by Brown's wife, two of his children, and six of Brown's former neighbors, variously stating facts concerning Brown's "sale" of the blacks to McAfee. In addition there was an undated and unsigned memorandum (presumably prepared by McGaughey), based on the affidavits, asserting that Lucy had wanted to go with McAfee to Texas with her children, one of whom was fathered by McAfee, that McAfee was a dangerous man, that he had insisted on a sale so that he would have "title" to the blacks, that Brown had tried to persuade Lucy not to go with McAfee but either to seek safety within the Union army's lines or to stay with her black husband, that Brown finally had made the "sale" only on McAfee's threat to kill him and to set fire to his property, that the payment was made in Confederate States notes that Brown knew were worthless, and that at the time Brown's residence was not within the lines occupied by the Union army. The memorandum also asserted that these facts were not brought out at Brown's trial. It might have said also, and rightly, that among all the petitions that previously had been presented for Brown's pardon there had been no such exposition of alleged facts. Finally, the memorandum asserted that all during Brown's imprisonment he had been hospitalized because of old-age feebleness, and that attending physicians stated that he would not survive the term of his imprisonment.[20]

By mid-September McGaughey was in Washington with these documents, and a letter of introduction to Attorney General James Speed, a Kentuckian, from several Louisville merchants attesting to his being well known among Louisville merchants and his high standing. Presumably the attorney general submitted the documents to President Johnson, for on September 18 the president ordered the case to be referred to Judge Advocate General Holt "for report (speedy)."[21]

Holt's report, dated September 21, stated that Brown had been tried "for the atrocious crime" of selling into slavery colored persons who, "with his full knowledge," had been freed by the Emancipation Proclamation, and that the evidence against him had been "most conclusive," indeed "substantially admitted by him." Brown's case, Holt wrote, had been fully considered previously in the reports of May 24 and November 22, 1864, on petitions similar to what now was presented and executive clemency had been refused. Holt added that, though numerous, the present petitioners did not express disapproval of Brown's act, so it was fair to conclude they sympathized with the sentiments that prompted Brown's crime.

Answering the main points in the affidavits, Holt said that Brown had resided near Union lines and had informed his slaves that they were free, so he was "well advised of the terms of the proclamation and of its full effect in his locality." Further, Holt said, Lucy's husband had testified that she went with McAfee only under compulsion; moreover the young children could not be said to have "voluntarily accepted a life of bondage"; in any case, Brown's defiance of the proclamation was illegal. Finally as to the alleged threats of violence by McAfee, if Lucy and Delia had gone with him voluntarily as now claimed it would have been absurd for him to have threatened violence to induce Brown to accept $7,000 dollars. Nor at Brown's trial was there any mention of threatened violence by McAfee. Moreover, Brown could have obtained protection from the Union forces in his neighborhood. Holt commented that the statement as to Brown's health was in an unsigned document and without a medical certificate. Also, said Holt, if Brown's friends were truly sensible of the enormity of his crime they would have taken steps to seek out "the helpless beings" who had been enslaved and to restore their liberty; until they made some such effort "no prayer of theirs can be favorably entertained." Holt concluded that, in view of Brown's position as a clergyman, his case was "one of the most atrocious ever passed on by a military court; and his sentence of imprisonment for but five years, when his victims were doomed to a bondage for life, is seen to have been by no means commensurate with the gravity of his crime."[22]

The secretary of war submitted Holt's report to the president on September 23. It is apparent that McGaughey was allowed to read it, probably by Attorney General Speed's arrangement. For on September 30 he submitted to the president a very persuasive rejoinder. He noted that the eight affidavits revealed that the blacks had gone with McAfee voluntarily, and the affiants had not been witnesses at the military trial; that Brown had refused to comply with McAfee's demands until McAfee had threatened violence; that had he sought protection from the Union army, twelve miles away, McAfee probably would have murdered him; that McAfee insisted on "a bill of sale" so that he would have "some show of title" on taking the blacks into a land of slavery under his mantle; that the Confederate notes given by McAfee were known to be valueless and Brown never received, or expected, any value from them. McGaughey emphasized the credibility of the affiants, noting, too, that some had been pro-Union all through the war. And he reemphasized Brown's old age and feeble health, his hospitalization during his imprisonment, and the doctors' opinion that he could not live out the term of his sentence. Finally, with slavery now abolished by the glorious results of the war, no one henceforth could commit the crime of which Brown was accused, so need for his further punishment was no more. So the president was urged to have mercy on Brown's seven fatherless children and restore his liberty.[23]

Despite McGaughey's plea, President Johnson, on October 5, declined to take any action in the case.[24]

Yet at least three more pleas for Brown's pardon were still to come to the president. And on December 11 a friend of Gen. Ulysses S. Grant wrote Grant urging Brown's release, asserting that he had not deserved punishment, but even if he did he had been "punished enough already." That letter was delivered by one of the Arkansas senators-elect. On December 21 Grant wrote the president, recommending Brown's release. Grant said that Brown already had been "severely punished by a Military Court and now as a rule I would generally recommend that sentences so given whilst the war was in progress be remitted." It is to be noted that Grant did not recommend pardon, but simply a release. On December 22 the president had Grant's recommendation referred to Holt. On the same day Holt responded that Brown already had been released. The next day the president determined that, in view of Brown's release, "no further action is necessary in the case."[25]

Back in November the secretary of war had sent an officer to interview prisoners confined at the Jefferson City state prison and to report "with a view to their release." The officer interviewed each of those prisoners, numbering 239, and on November 27 sent to the secretary a list of 154 whose release he recommended. Brown was on the list. In due time, on December 19, an order was issued by the War Department for the release of 15 civilian military prisoners from the Jefferson City prison, who would be furnished with transportation to their homes. Brown was number six on that list.[26]

So it was, at long last, though not pardoned, Brown was freed and soon was sent on his way home. Probably he was sent by river, down the Missouri, down the Mississippi, and up the Arkansas to Pine Bluff. But by the time of his arrival there he had been taken seriously ill. Word was sent to his wife at Flat Bayou and she hastened to Pine Bluff.

When she reached there, Fountain Brown was dead.[27]

Although Brown's case had attracted widest notice in Arkansas after his conviction, with leading officials in the newly established loyal state government heading efforts for pardon, strongly supported by the Union military in the state, and though few, if any, episodes in the enforcement of the Emancipation Proclamation received the attention given this case among highest officials in the nation's capital, it passed into limbo on his death, with hardly more than a mention in the literature of his church in later years.[28] Now, on resurrecting it, one cannot but speculate that had Brown's trial counsel tendered the evidence later assembled by son-in-law McGaughey, which had been readily at hand, there would have been no conviction at his trial, and Brown would have lived happily on in service to Methodism.

A word further: We observed, at the outset, that Brown's was the first conviction for a violation of the proclamation to be reviewed by the president. So said Judge Advocate General Holt in his May 24, 1864, report to the president. It may have been not only the first but also the last. Indeed, it may have been the only criminal case for enforcement of the Emancipation Proclamation.[29]

Notes

1. Walter N. Vernon, *Methodism in Arkansas 1816–1976* (Joint Committee for History of Arkansas Methodism, Little Rock, 1976), pp. 27–28, 54–56; *Arkansas Methodist*, July 10, 1880; *Minutes of the Annual Conference of the Methodist Episcopal Church, South, 1866* (Methodist Episcopal Church, South, Smith & Lamar, Agents, Nashville, Dallas, Richmond, 1916), Little Rock Conference section, p. 80; minutes of the Ouachita Annual Conferences for 1854–66 (unpublished, Hendrix College Library); 1860 U.S. Census, State of Arkansas, County of Jefferson, Township of Plum Bayou, Free Schedule No. 44, Slave Schedule No. 53. That there were two married children, in addition to the seven unmarried, appears in a letter to President Andrew Johnson by W. N. Farrar, cited in n. 2, below.

2. Case of Fountain Brown (citizen), Box 1012, File NN 1514, General Courts Martial 1812–1938, Office of the Judge Advocate General, RG 153, Nat. Arch. (hereafter cited as Brown File): letter to President Andrew Johnson by W. N. Farrar, Oct. 7, 1865; undated and unsigned memorandum with affidavits and petitions, July–Aug. 1865; charges against Brown for military commission trial beginning Jan. 8, 1864; trial testimony, John R. Johnson and Horton Record; Aug. 6, 1865, affidavit of C. A. S. Lindsey.

3. Edwin C. Bearss, "Marmaduke Attacks Pine Bluff," *Arkansas Historical Quarterly* 23 (Winter 1964):291–313.

4. James D. Richardson, comp., *A Compilation of the Messages and Papers of the Presidents 1789–1897*, 10 vols. (Published by the Authority of Congress, Washington, 1896–99), 6:96–98, 157–59; Holt to Stackpole, June 8, 1864, Record Books/Letter Books, Judge Advocate General's Office, No. 8, 529–30, RG 153, Nat. Arch.; Opinion of Atty. Gen. James Speed, Oct. 17, 1865, 11 *Ops. Atty. Gen.* 365–69; Final Report of American Freedmen's Inquiry Commission, U.S. War Dept., *The War of the Rebellion: A Compilation of the Offical Records of the Union and Confederate Armies*, 70 vols. in 128 pts. (1880–1901; rpt. National Historical Society, Gettysburg, 1972), ser. 3, 4:347–51, 354–55 (hereafter cited as *ORA*); *Martin v. Bartow Iron Works*, 16 Fed. Cas. 888, 891 (N.D. Ga., 1867); *Morgan, Adm'r v. Nelson, Adm'r*, 43 Ala. 586 (1869); *McElvain v. Mudd, Adm'r*, 44 Ala. 48, 63–81 (1870), Peters, J., dissent; trial testimony of John R. Johnson and Horton Record, and Aug. 6, 1865, affidavit of C. A. S. Lindsey, Brown File. After the war considerable state court litigation involved the question whether a slave in a region to which the terms of the Emancipation Proclamation applied

was freed prior to the time the region came under Union occupation; repeatedly it was held that he had not then been freed. Illustrative are *Henderlite v. Thurman*, 22 Grat. 466 (Ct. of App. of Va., 1872), and *Dorris v. Grace*, 24 Ark. 326 (1866).

5. Jonathan T. Dorris, *Pardon and Amnesty under Lincoln and Johnson* (Univ. of North Carolina Press, Chapel Hill, 1953), pp. 36–38, 67–68; Richardson, *Messages and Papers of the Presidents*, 6:188, 213–15 (exclusion of Virginia from the portion of the amnesty proclamation regarding establishment of a new state government was due to the fact that the Union was already recognizing a previously established loyalist government there); John L. Ferguson, comp. *Arkansas and the Civil War* (Arkansas Civil War Centennial Commission, Little Rock, 1965), pp. 261–71; Thomas S. Staples, *Reconstruction in Arkansas 1862–1874*, Studies in History, Economics and Public Law, Columbia Univ., vol. 109, no. 245 (1923; rpt., Peter Smith, Gloucester, 1964), pp. 23–43.

6. For this and the following account of the military commission's trial and judgment, see transcript, Brown File.

7. That Grace was well regarded, see item in Little Rock *National Democrat* (weekly), Mar. 26, 1864, p. 3.

8. The census item on McAfee immediately followed that on Brown.

9. Notation signed by Steele on back of last page of transcript of commission's proceeding.

10. Union Provost Marshal's File of Two-or-More Name Papers Relating to Citizens, M 416, Roll 29, RG 109, Nat. Arch. This roll lists loyalty oath-taking in Arkansas, seemingly beginning in Jan. 1864. The list for Pine Bluff and vicinity, in Feb., contains 237 names; Brown was no. 65 on the list, dated Feb. 9. Controversy as to whether the amnesty proclamation provided amnesty to one under arrest or convicted for disloyalty before taking the prescribed loyalty oath is revealed in Dorris, *Pardon and Amnesty*, pp. 53–55; President Lincoln to Judge Hoffman, and Holt to Dunn, *ORA*, ser. 2, 6:705, 802–3; Edward McPherson, *The Political History of the United States of America During the Great Rebellion* (1865; rpt., Da Capo Press, New York, 1972), pp. 148–49; *United States v. Greathouse*, 26 Fed. Cas. 18, 30, reporter's note at end (C.C.N.D. Calif., 1863); *In re Greathouse*, 10 Fed. Cas. 1057 (C.C.N.D. Calif., Feb. 15, 1864). To eliminate uncertainty, the president issued a supplemental proclamation on Mar. 26, 1864, stating that the amnesty proclamation did not apply to persons taking the oath while in confinement, under bond, or on parole "for offenses of any kind, either before or after conviction," Richardson, *Messages and Papers of the Presidents*, 6:218.

11. Petition to Steele to release Brown on bail after "nearly three months" confinement and endorsements, item on Fountain Brown, Union Provost Marshal's File of One-Name Papers re Citizens, M 345, Roll 37, RG 109, Nat. Arch. In Union Provost Marshal's File of Two-or-More-Name Papers Relating to Citizens, M 416, Roll 35, RG 109, Nat. Arch., items no. 9736, 9738–41, and 9761 indicate that Brown's confinement occurred on Dec. 24, 1863, and continued to May 13, 1864, release; but item no. 9736 suggests that, even during confinement, he was "Allowed the City Limits."

12. Petition to president, Apr. 15, 1864, Clayton endorsement, Apr. 18, 1864, notation by "A. Lincoln," May 23, 1864, and Congressman-elect A. A. Bogue letter to president, May 20, 1864, Brown File.

13. *ORA*, ser. 2, 7:159–62 (reproduces the Holt report of May 24 appearing in Brown File). Holt asserted that the episode occurred after Union troops' "occupation of the district including Flat Bayou."

14. Hay note to Holt, and notation on back of last page of Holt report of May 24, Brown File.

15. Brown's letter to president, Oct. 11, 1864; undated petition to president by state officials and Methodist elder, Steele transmission thereof, and Hay notation thereon, Brown File.

16. *ORA*, ser. 2, 7:1151–52 (reproduces the Holt letter of Nov. 22 appearing in Brown File); notations on back of last page of Holt letter of Nov. 22 appearing in Brown File. By December General Steele had been succeeded in Arkansas by Gen. J. J. Reynolds, Steele being transferred to Louisiana duty. In time, in response to inquiry, Steele reported that the order to send Brown to the Alton prison had not been executed because Steele was awaiting response to the petition by some of the best Union men in Arkansas on behalf of Brown, who was very old and in "very feeble health"; Steele thought it proper to await the response because Brown "in his delicate state of health might not have lived to reach" Alton. Reynolds' response to inquiry reported that, by Jan. 13, 1865, Brown was en route to Alton. A complex of pertinent documentation is in Brown File.

17. Petition to president, Jan. 13, 1865, by Lt. Col. E. B. Gray, with notation on back by Lt. Col. R. F. Patterson, provost marshal general, Department of Arkansas, Brown File.

18. Notations on back of Gray petition by the president and by Holt, Brown File.

19. Dorris, *Pardon and Amnesty*, pp. 139–42, 160–61; *ORA*, ser. 2, 8:694–95; Prison Records, Alton, Illinois, section on Register of Civilian Prisoners, Mar. 1863–June 1865 (unpaginated), the item on Fountain Brown; and section on Register of Prisoners Confined under Sentence 1863–1865, Sentenced Prisoners in the Alton Military Prison, p. 38, M 598, Roll 15, RG 109, Nat. Arch.

20. In Brown File there is an envelope entitled Brown's "Application for Remission of Sentence" containing a number of documents; hereafter such documents will be cited to Brown File; Remission Application. The four petitions, the affidavits, and the unsigned memorandum are in that envelope.

21. Brown File; Remission Application. The Louisville merchants' letter of introduction identifies McGaughey as a Brown son-in-law.

22. Brown File.

23. Endorsement on back of Holt report, Brown File; McGaughey letter, Brown File; Remission Application.

24. Executive Memorandum, Brown File; Remission Application.

25. Letters to president, by W. N. Farrar, Oct. 7, 1865, by Thomas L. [illegible], Oct. 12, 1865, and by Samuel Watson, Dec. 5, 1865, Brown File; John Y. Simon, ed., *The Papers of Ulysses S. Grant* (Southern Illinois Univ. Press, Carbondale, 1967–), 15:442–43; Executive Memorandum, Dec. 22, 1865, on case of Brown, Fountain, and notation on back thereof, Dec. 23, 1865, letter from U. S. Grant to the president, Dec. 21, 1865, letter from I. N. Morris to Grant, Dec. 11, 1865, Executive Memorandum (undated) concerning Grant recommendation, Executive Order, Dec. 23, 1865, Letters Rec'd by the Adj. Gen. Office 1861–1870, 1753B–1865, M 619, Roll 339, RG 109, Nat. Arch.

26. List of military prisoners confined at state penitentiary, Jefferson City, Missouri, Nov. 21, 1865, notation at end thereof, and transmittal to secretary of war by Maj. W. M. Hall, Nov. 27, 1865, along with list of those whose release Hall recommends, List of Names of Prisoners Received and Remaining in the Following Prisons: (various, including Jefferson City, Missouri), Military Prison Division, Office of the Adj. Gen., Box No. 4, RG 94, Nat. Arch.; General Court-Martial Order No. 654, Dec. 19, 1865, Adj. Gen. Office, Entry 44, RG 94, Nat. Arch.; *ORA*, ser. 2, 8:837.

27. Vernon, *Methodism in Arkansas*, pp. 94, 454; *Arkansas Methodist*, July 10, 1880.

28. In Vernon, *Methodism in Arkansas*, p. 94, there is a brief quoted mention, and in *Arkansas Methodist* there is a very short account, each inaccurately stating the time of Brown's release. The *Methodist* account concludes that in the "opinion of some" it "should not now be written."

29. The authoritative treatise, William Winthrop, *Military Law and Precedents*, 2d ed. (GPO, Washington, 1920), p. 840, n. 17, lists military commission cases for kidnapping blacks or for violations of the Emancipation Proclamation. For the latter there are cited only General Court Martial Order No. 250 of 1864, which was the case of Fountain Brown, and General Order No. 155, Department of North Carolina, 1865. But, as revealed in Judge Advocate General Courts Martial, 1812–1938, Box 1331, Case File No. 001423, RG 153, Nat. Arch., in the latter case, though one of the charges had been a violation of the Emancipation Proclamation, the evidence tendered related only to another charge, that of physical assault on freedmen; the proclamation charge was not pursued.

Index

Index

HOWARD C. WESTWOOD, a senior partner in the Washington, DC, law firm Covington & Burling, has distinguished himself as a scholar through the publication over nearly thirty years of his carefully documented articles on the Civil War. A member of his local Civil War Round Table, he is also a director of The Ulysses S. Grant Association.

JOHN Y. SIMON is executive director of The Ulysses S. Grant Association, editor of *The Papers of Ulysses S. Grant,* and professor of history at Southern Illinois University at Carbondale.